HEALING THE PAST GOD'S WAY

By Carol A. Jenkins

TABLE OF CONTENTS

This book is dedicated
to the person who
made it possible
my Lord Jesus Christ

May He be glorified in
its pages

ACKNOWLEDGMENTS

to Karen, Kim M., Gail and Mim
you each weathered the storm
and taught me how to laugh again

to James MacDonald
a faithful man who taught me
the truth of God's love

to Mom and Dad
I've always known how you've felt about me
and that's a great gift upon which to build a life

to Lorri and Kim S., my faithful accountability
partners and dearest friends

to Jerome, Clare, Larry, Rick and Christine
thank you for believing in me,
for holding me accountable,
for cheering me on
and for having an open door policy

to Lynnea, Kim H., Ara, Helen,
Kim T., Fran, Karin, Vrinda and Katie
my second set of eyes
and hearts of gold, thank you for your service

*and to the others, too numerous to mention
hopefully you know who you are
I have been gifted with family and friends
of deep faith, great patience, passion,
determination and just plain humor*

*no matter what else I do in my life
discovering the truth of God's love
hidden in the well of my pain will always
be the greatest adventure of them all!*

INTRODUCTION

THE JOURNEY FROM DESPAIR

$$\sim\!\!\mathcal{I}\mathbb{C}\!\!\sim$$

There are few emotions as all consuming as despair. Beyond discouragement, beyond depression, despair is *the* well bottom of emotions. It is hopelessness dressed in a maudlin package of 'forever'. Brokenness, from abuse of any kind, can be the precursor of despair, but the wounds of abuse are not enough to bring about the depth of such desperation. The damage of abuse, in order to fester into despair, must be corrupted with another ingredient - the infectious power of lies.

That's what happened in my life. I was abused at the tender age of seventeen by a man who was filled with an anger and brokenness too destructive for me to salve. I was too naive to understand that, so I placed myself in a situation that made me a target of his wrath. Because of my naiveté and my guilt over having 'allowed' such a thing to happen, I told no one.

And that was my initial step down the road of despair. The first lie I believed was that I somehow allowed the abuse. Couple that with the lie that God was absent during such a hurtful thing, pair that with lie after lie about who God really is, who I really am and how my life could / would never be the same, and I started to run down the dark path of hopelessness.

I tried all of the usual things to find relief. I stuffed my emotions for several years, pretending nothing had happened and all was just fine. That finally built into an explosion of anger and rage of my own, and more years of *punishing* God by living in willful sin. No

13

matter how I filled my time and with what I experimented, nothing brought the comfort or at least the ease I so desperately desired. Finally, I gave up and settled into a long winter season with my newest friend - despair.

Those years, almost 10 in all, were leading me to do something drastic and I probably would have, had two things not been true. One, I was a Christian. I had accepted Jesus as my Lord and Savior at the age of ten and I belonged to Him. And two, God wasn't going to let me go. With those two things true about me, my journey back from despair to God was about to become something of a miracle in my life.

It began with introductions. First, God brought a woman into my life who had known, first hand, the deep pain of abuse. After several months of conversations and growing trust, she pushed me, kicking and screaming, off to see a Christian counselor. Six months of meeting with him led to an awakening in my soul to return to the body of Christ. My soul was starving for truth while my broken heart and my ravaged mind were finally ready to go along. That was the final introduction needed. God had brought me full circle to His truth. As hard as it was to walk through those doors on Sunday morning, to not go was inconceivable. My soul had tasted the power - the healing power - of God's truth, and nothing was going to keep me from that feast!

Ten years later, and I am still on that path. I left despair in the dust so very long ago and I am now working with others to help them do the same. It is not psychology or working some man-made program that has led me to this place. It is, quite simply, the study, the nourishment, and the power of God's truth.

Remember the lies of which I spoke? Well, they had invaded my thinking and had taken up residence in my heart. Everything I did and said and believed was tainted by them. Every relationship was impacted. Even my hopes and dreams of the future stood knee deep in the pond of those deceits.

I was living lies about who I am, that is to say, my identity. I believed myself a failure. I believed myself too sinful, too fallen, too far from God for Him to bring me back. In fact, I believed myself to be a sort of second-class citizen of Heaven. One of God's kids but certainly one of the least in the Kingdom. You know, a bastard of sorts about whom everyone pointed and whispered but no one really wanted around.

I also believed lies about God. I believed He was weak, too weak to have stopped what happened to me or sometimes, when the pendulum swung the other way, I just believed He was too cruel to have cared. I had no correct understanding of His justice, His holiness, His love and His grace. I needed to be introduced to the Sovereign God, the King Eternal, Immortal, Invisible who could rescue me out of my prison of lies and deliver me into His promised peace.

And so the journey began. It started with the simplest and most powerful of God's truths - He loves me! There's really no reason for Him to do so. Not when you consider my track record and match it to His righteousness, but "He loves me" was never about me; it always was and is about Him. He loves; He created; He forgives; He promises - I am merely the fortunate vessel into whom He pours His abundance. And that includes His truth!

My life journey has been a living example of what Paul calls "putting off" and "putting on". The lies had to be put off, but, had I just remained in that place, they would have rushed back in tenfold. You see, "I am not unlovable" is true, but it's also empty. So what if "I'm not unlovable"? Who really cares about that? But I am not unlovable *and* I know because God loves me so much He sent His Son to die for me! Put off the lie - "unlovable"; put on the truth - "dearly beloved". I found relief in putting off the lie; I found joy and healing in the bountiful waters of God's truth.

That's what this book is about. It is a journey of truth-telling, of Biblical principles that will apply to every aspect of your life. It will be and is about foundation building. And we will do it brick by brick, stone by stone. You may find some parts of this book of more value or at least of greater need to your heart, mind and soul than others. That's okay. Filling in a foundation is of as great a value as building one from scratch. Both must be done well or the building that foundation supports will not last.

Many years ago, I wrote these words in my journal, "no matter what else I do in my life, discovering the truth of God's love hidden in the well of my pain will always be the greatest adventure of them all!" I believe you will discover the same thing if you will simply choose to take the next step and let God speak His truth, His love to your heart.

TIPS FOR USING THE BOOK

─⟨⊙⟩─

The first section of the book, *My Identity in Christ* is about gaining God's perspective, seeing through His eyes who we really are. It is about laying a firm foundation of truth so when this world says "You are _____", we can respond with the truth in love, "I am God's child; I am chosen; I am loved; I am forgiven; I am secure; I am sanctified and I am called." In this section, we explore God's heart for us and in it we discover His capacity for love. His passion for us, His kids, is beyond our wildest imaginations.

The second section, *God's Character*, is like the first in that it is about strengthening our foundation. We spend a good deal of time exploring what God has to say about Himself throughout Scripture, and believe me, God has a lot to say on the subject. This section is important for another reason. It is not just about learning what God has to say about Himself, but also, this time is intended to deepen your relationship with your Father, your Creator. To know God, to love Him, to trust Him all depends on laying a foundation on the truth of who He is. For example, when I understand God's passion and standard for justice, then I can trust Him to balance the books with every person who has ever wounded or crushed me. In fact, the way I face the rest of my life will depend in great measure on what I believe to be true about God. It is a faith thing and this section is intended to help deepen your faith in our great God!

The final section, *Healing the Past God's Way* takes a look at elements that are key to understanding what happened to us and why, as well as how to change key aspects of our lives. For example, we will spend time dealing with issues like anger, depression, forgiveness and fear, but we will also explore Biblical principles of change so our lives will more closely reflect the image of God's Son. The combination of those studies in truth will bring about healing in ways you cannot currently imagine. That's what makes this journey with God such an adventure!

In order to do this, we need to understand the difference between these three concepts: fact; faith; and feeling.

FACT is what God's Word says (see "Study Tips" in Appendix B for a guide on how to read Scripture with discernment). "God wrote a book" and this book is filled with what He wants us to know about Him, about us and our relationship with Him, about how to live and more. In order to move ahead in your life with God, you have to know what God has said. Studying God's Word will lay that foundation. **THIS IS STEP ONE: KNOWLEDGE.**

FAITH is about taking the FACT of God's Word, believing it and applying it to my daily life. Dr. James MacDonald, the pastor at Harvest Bible Chapel of Rolling Meadows, Illinois, once said, "I will *choose* to live my life in such a way that *if* God is not who He says He is, I will fall flat on my face." That is faith in the fact of God's Word to the furthest degree. Another saying that James has used about faith comes from Dr. Ron Allchin of the Biblical Counseling Center of Arlington Heights, Illinois and it states, "Faith is believing the Word of God and acting upon it, *no matter how I feel*, knowing that God promises a good result." **THIS IS STEP TWO: APPLICATION.**

FEELING is my emotional response to the FACT of God's Word and the FAITH in my life. Feelings should never lead nor can they always be trusted, as we will see in our study of God's Word regarding our broken past. Our feelings can be wounded and therefore, deceptive. Knowing well how I feel about what has happened to me, I need to put those feelings on the back shelf and take a look first and foremost at what God has said (FACT) and then look at how to incorporate that truth into my life (FAITH). My feelings will follow when my understanding of God's Word is strong and I have applied it to my life. Think about it this way: *Fact, Faith* and

Feeling are a train. *Fact*, as the driving force, is the engine; *Faith*, carrying the load, is the club car, able to hold whatever valuable cargo you need to carry; and *Feeling*, as the caboose, is bringing up, protecting the rear. For those of you who have had *Feeling* as your engine, you will appreciate how tenuous it is to live by emotions. Remember, faith requires obedience and that brings blessing. **THIS IS STEP THREE: ABUNDANT LIFE**

One of the mistakes I made when I was seventeen was to be ill equipped when the pain and the heartache of this world took hold. In the instant I needed it, I did not have the tools of either FACT or FAITH to sustain me. That is why this book will focus on the *disciplines* of the Christian life.

> Ephesians 6:10-17 "Finally, be strong in the Lord, and in the strength of His might. Put on the full armor of God, that you may be able to stand firm against the schemes of the devil. For our struggle is not against flesh and blood, but against the rulers, against the powers, against the world forces of this darkness, against the spiritual forces of wickedness in the heavenly places. Therefore, take up the full armor of God, that you may be able to resist in the evil day, and having done everything, to stand firm. Stand firm therefore, HAVING GIRDED YOUR LOINS WITH TRUTH, and HAVING PUT ON THE BREASTPLATE OF RIGHTEOUSNESS, and having shod YOUR FEET WITH THE PREPARA-TION OF THE GOSPEL OF PEACE; in addition to all, taking up the SHIELD OF FAITH with which you will be able to extinguish all the flaming missiles of the evil one. And take THE SWORD OF THE SPIRIT, which is the Word of God."

You may be hurt again. I can't promise you that you've suffered for the last time in this life. I can promise you God is faithful; His way is the way of life and of healing. If you entrust yourself to His hands, your past will be healed. Not eased, not comforted, not

SECTION ONE:

MY IDENTITY IN CHRIST

MY IDENTITY IN CHRIST

I was created by God for God. Period. I was created for His glory. Created in His image to have a relationship with the Almighty, the Sovereign, the Eternal, Immortal, Giver and Sustainer of Life! Guess what, you were too!

"In the beginning, God said. . .and it was so". Out of nothingness, out of the void, God created light and life and being. He formed the mountains and set the boundaries of the seas. He spoke the eagle and mouse, the lion and lamb into existence. When He was finished, He looked around and decided nothing truly reflected Him. Oh, all of it was *good*, but He wasn't done yet. He hadn't yet created us - a reflection of His image into whom He would pour His love and compassion, over whom He would rule and with whom He would have a love relationship. We would be a creation who could look at its Creator and see His glory, experience His power and might, worship Him for all of His wonder and awe. We would be a creation in His own image who could relate to Him with our emotion (heart), our intellect (mind) and our will (soul). Nothing else in all of creation can have that kind of relationship with the God of the universe!

Ever notice how God spoke everything into being (Genesis 1) yet with man, He formed him from the dust of the ground and breathed into his nostrils the breath of life (Genesis 2:7). Uniquely created to have a unique relationship with the Creator. Adam and

Eve actually walked with God in the garden, communicating with Him daily. Wouldn't you love to know what they discussed? Can you imagine the intimacy of such a time? The absurdity of the Creator strolling through the rose bushes and the azaleas, chatting with the work of His Hands, giving value to that creation by His time, His attention, His interest.

Adam could hardly have complained if God had set he and Eve up, wished them well and then abandoned them. What right would Adam or Eve have to insist that God share Himself with them? They were formerly dirt, clay if you will, in His nimble Hands, and now, that "stuff" was walking and talking with HIM, the GOD of all gods, the Creator, the Author of all things.

The pattern that God established in the garden with Adam and Eve is repeated throughout the Scriptures. Adam and Eve did not ask to be created, nor did they "meet" God half way by having a relationship with Him. They were, as we are, the recipient of God's generosity, His goodness and love. God made them for Him, to experience His glory, to know of His riches, to taste and see that the Lord is good! (Psalm 34).

That is the story of our lives in Christ. God is the One who has chased after us; we didn't chase after Him. In fact, before you or I even knew of our need for a Savior, the work of the cross to restore us to the Father was accomplished. David reminds us of that relationship in the Psalms (8:3 & 4), "When I consider Thy heavens, the work of Thy fingers, The moon and the stars, which Thou hast ordained; What is man, that Thou dost take thought of him? And the son of man that Thou dost care for Him?" Who are we that God would care so much?

And why is all of this so important? It's important because it is a matter of value. In fact, our identity is an *assignment* of value.

Your identity, whether it is formed by what you do, who you are, what you have to offer or what someone else has to say about you, is an assignment of value. For example: I'm a doctor and you're a janitor; I earned straight "A's" throughout college and now I work on Wall Street; my father was a drunk; my life has been an avalanche of dead-end jobs; I've been in and out of jail a dozen times; I'm beautiful and so on.

"Stuff" and "things", or if you rather, circumstances, events, decisions we make, proclamations from others all roll up into what we believe about ourselves or, for some of us, what we've been told. An assignment of value.

The world conspires daily to make us question our value as a human being. For some, it begins at birth. People, who have been told they are worthless, pass on that poison to their children. Sometimes, it doesn't come from what someone says but rather how they act, giving praise and position to one by robbing another of it. And if you were born into a family that believes you to be of great value, this world can't wait to knock you down countless pegs.

Then, issues like abuse heighten feelings of disconnection and worthlessness. Victimhood brings with it its own kind of shame and degradation. For those of us who have been wounded, our identity takes a couple thousand hits and it is a wonder some of us are standing.

In truth, if we decide to take our cues from those around us or from our own inner voices, our identity almost always becomes a weapon, capable of inflicting internal and external damage. If you base your identity on what you do, some day, you will fall because you will fail. No one can be 'the perfect anything' forever. If you base your identity on what has happened to you, that is to say your circumstances, you've already experienced an identity implosion. If you base your identity on what others think about you, your identity is a yo-yo and your life shifts swifter than the sands on a beach.

I don't know about you, but I need to base my identity on something more solid and sure than all of that. I need to know who I am and of what value so that when this world attacks, and it will, I will not be blown apart by the ferocity of the assault. All in favor of coming back to the value our Creator has placed on our lives? I sure am!

David, the Psalmist, catches a glimpse of God's heart for us in Psalm 139:

"O Lord, Thou hast searched me and known *me*.
Thou dost know when I sit down and when I rise up;
Thou dost understand my thoughts from afar. Thou

dost scrutinize my path and my lying down, And art intimately acquainted with all my ways. Even before there is a word on my tongue, Behold, O Lord, Thou dost know it all. Thou hast enclosed me behind and before, And laid Thy hand upon me. Such knowledge is too wonderful for me; It is too high, I cannot attain to it. Where can I go from Thy Spirit? Or where can I flee from Thy presence? If I ascend to heaven, Thou are there; If I make my bed in Sheol, behold, Thou art there. If I take the wings of the dawn, If I dwell in the remotest part of the sea, Even there Thy hand will lead me, And Thy right hand will lay hold of me. If I say, 'Surely the darkness will overwhelm me, And the light around me will be night,' Even the darkness is not dark to Thee, And the night is as bright as the day. Darkness and light are alike to Thee. For Thou didst form my inward parts; Thou didst weave me in my mother's womb. I will give thanks to Thee, for I am fearfully and wonderfully made; Wonderful are Thy works, And my soul knows it very well. My frame was not hidden from Thee, When I was made in secret, *And* skillfully wrought in the depths of the earth. Thine eyes have seen my unformed substance; And in Thy book they were all written, The days that were ordained for me, When as yet there was not one of them. How precious also are Thy thoughts to me, O God! How vast is the sum of them! If I should count them, they would outnumber the sand. When I awake, I am still with Thee."

The Creator's love for His creation. It is intimate; it is detailed; it is eternal; and it is never driven by the prevailing wind of opinion or of innuendo or of change. Do you know that if you and I had lived in the Garden of Eden before the fall, God would have been walking and talking with us each evening as He did with Adam and Eve? God didn't meet with Adam and Eve because they were so special or great or worthy. He met with them because *He is so special and great and worthy!*

Do you see that yet? Our value to God has already been established. Certainly, we've experienced it in the act of creation, but more, we are living in freedom and hope because we have experienced firsthand God's heart, God's value of us. There are a lot of verses that capture this truth, but one of my favorites is this one: "He who did not spare His own Son, but delivered Him up for us all, how will He not also with Him freely give us all things?" Romans 8:32 Do you imagine that there is a person that God could or would love more than His Son? Absolutely not! The Bible is filled with verses which declare God's love of and for His only Son. And yet, God, Himself, delivered up His Beloved Son for our sakes, to bring us back to Himself. What a stamp of value that places on your life and mine!

Here's the place where Christians must differ from the world in defining our identity. The world states that you as an individual are valuable. The Bible, however, says, you and I are not valuable in and of ourselves. In fact, Scripture goes as far as to say through Peter this very thing, "I most certainly understand *now* that God is not one to show partiality, but in every nation the man who fears Him and does what is right, is welcome to Him." Acts 10:34 & 35.

On our best days, we walk up to the throne room of God and hold out empty hands. What do I have to offer that God doesn't already have? What can you give Him that He doesn't own? We are not *valuable*, as this world states, in and of ourselves, but, we are instead *highly valued* by the King of Kings and Lord of Lords!

Let me explain the difference. A couple of years ago, there was an auction of personal items owned by JFK. One of the items sold was a pair of golf clubs that President Kennedy used on hundreds of occasions to play golf. Golf clubs, in and of themselves, are valuable. A very good set can run you several thousand dollars. This particular set of clubs, however, was sold for tens of thousands of dollars. This price tag was placed on them not because they were golf clubs, but because a legendary person used them, valued them. JFK played golf with them; that was what gave them their value.

Same thing, in essence, with God. I am one of billions of people that God has created. In and of myself, I am not valuable. I am, however, highly valued by God. I know this because He has created me, sustains me and He has provided for my salvation, paying the highest price that could be paid. And He is preparing a place for me, because some day, He will call me home. The emphasis is not on me - one of billions. It is on Him! *He* wants me; *He* loves me; *He* highly values me! That is my identity, and it is chiseled in stone.

As we stated earlier, if you've been abused, your sense of identity has been trashed. In that, we need to hear from God's heart toward those of us who've been so deeply wounded. In Isaiah 61:1 - 3 we read:

> "The Spirit of the Lord God is upon me, because the Lord has anointed me to bring good news to the afflicted; He has sent me to bind up the broken-hearted, to proclaim liberty to captives, and freedom to prisoners; to proclaim the favorable year of the Lord, and the day of vengeance of our God; to comfort all who mourn, to grant those who mourn in Zion, giving them a garland instead of ashes, the oil of gladness instead of mourning, the mantle of praise instead of a spirit of fainting. so they will be called oaks of righteousness, the planting of the Lord, that He may be glorified."

God's heart for the brokenhearted, for those of us who have been wounded and abused is a heart of compassion, a heart of love and tenderness, a heart of healing and it is a heart overflowing with a promise - our brokenness will never be more than God can fix and fill, because our brokenness will never be bigger than God.

Have you shed so many tears that you've stained your cheeks and numbed your heart? God captured every one of those tears and He is holding them for you (Psalm 56:8). He knows that you hurt. He knows what has happened to you and He knows what you've done. He knows every moment of every day, every comment ever made, every heart motivation, every sin, every evil you've endured and He is the One, the God of eternity, who will comfort and soothe and restore you, *because you are His beloved child.*

Have you surrounded yourself with a wall of brick and mortar, never again to let anyone too close, to give anyone intimate access because you don't know whom you can trust? Jesus knows what it is to be betrayed. Remember Judas? How about Peter? Jesus also knows what it is to be faithful and to keep His promises. He has made a promise to you - that your life, and all of its experiences, will be redeemed, restored so that you will "be called oaks of righteousness, The planting of the Lord, that He may be glorified" (Isaiah 61:3). He is calling you to tear down those walls and put your faith in Him because He is the Faithful One!

Have you nearly drowned in a sea of fear or of anger or of revenge, needing to protect and defend or merely destroy those who have nearly destroyed you? God, Himself, the Righteous Judge has promised a day is coming when all who have bloodied you will stand in judgment and receive their just due. Will you trust those injuries to His Righteous Hands?

Those words in Isaiah were spoken long ago. You may be tempted to think them quaint and out-dated for your life and your past, but let me tell you, they are a promise from the Holy One of Israel. They are a prophecy about the coming Messiah. They were and are the Word from the Everlasting God.

Jesus, standing in the synagogue, rolled open the scroll and recited those words from Isaiah (Luke 4:16 - 30). Then, He proclaimed in a strong voice, "Today this Scripture has been fulfilled in your hearing." (v.21). Did you hear that? Jesus proclaimed Himself the Messiah; He established His Kingdom by proclaiming Himself *the* comfort for those who mourn, *the* freedom for those held captive; *the* hope for those who've been hopeless and helpless for too long.

Jesus could have come into this world and proclaimed Himself its Ruler! He is you know. He could have laid the foundation for the establishment of His Kingdom as the Righteous Judge. Jesus could have laid a legal case for His right to be worshipped, His place of authority, His ownership over His creation. He could have called ten thousand angels and done anything.

Instead, with a handful of words, He proclaimed His mission - to comfort, to free, to heal, to ease, to serve. . .to save. He stated in those words His love for all of us who have been lost, broken, captive and enslaved by the evil of this world. He stated, without mincing words, His passion for us and His desire to restore us to a relationship with our Father. In those words, we learn that we are Jesus' passion, His priority, His purpose for setting aside His Divine rights and coming as a babe, born to die - for us! (Philippians 2)

CHAPTER ONE

I AM GOD'S CHILD

—◁※◎▷—

We were orphans in this world until we came into a relationship with the Father through Jesus Christ's death and resurrection. Imagine that. Orphans. We were without a place in God's universe until we chose to accept what the living God had *literally* died to make available to us. And then, because of Jesus' death and resurrection, we have become God's children! Taken off the streets, dressed in His heavenly robes, given the seal (the Holy Spirit indwelling us) of our relationship with Him. You are His child! I am His child! Take a moment to speak that truth to your heart.

This world will tell you there are groups and classifications of people. Scripture agrees up to this point: there are, according to Scripture, two kinds of people - orphans (those hostile to God) and children of God (1 John 5:11 & 12, John 5:24). Two kinds of people in the whole world and it has nothing to do with color or race or gender or socio-economic status. It is not an external trait, such as the world embraces, but an internal one. It is the mark placed on us by our heavenly Father that sets us apart from all others. And even that has nothing to do with us, but with Him! (If at this point you don't know if you are a child of the King, please stop and go to *Appendix A*. There, I will show you how to become a child of God.)

There is a story in the Gospel that has always fascinated me in relation to our status as children of the King. It is in Luke 15:11 - 32, *The Prodigal Son*.

31

Now the story, as some of you may recall, is about a father and his two sons. The oldest son was a steady lad, working for his father, faithful to his commitments, toiling for a purpose. The younger son, on the other hand, had a wild streak, self-involved and determined to take what was his and live on his own terms. One day, the younger son came up to his dad and said, in essence, "I want what you *owe* me for being your son". He wanted his inheritance, but he wanted it before his father had died. The amazing thing is this - even though it was a terrific insult for the boy to ask, his dad gave it to him. The younger son split, off to live a life of decadence abroad - sort of like a tour throughout Europe at 18 without your parents - lots to try, too many temptations, no accountability. Jesus, when telling the parable, did not fill in the details, but where the money went was understood.

And go it did! The money was soon exhausted and so was the young man. To add to his dilemma, there was a famine in the land. So, this young guy did the only thing he could think of to survive - he accepted a job sloppin' hogs. He went from wealthy landowner to fieldhand in a matter of minutes and even then, his problems weren't over. He found himself hungry and in need of food. He even found himself envying the hogs for the meals they would get. It got so bad he finally decided to make a drastic choice. He would humble himself, go back to his dad and beg for mercy.

Here's where the story amazes me. As the young son was on his way home, practicing his speech of repentance, he turned down the road that led to his home. The passage reads like this, "And he got up and came to his father. But while he was still a long way out, his father saw him, and felt compassion for him, and *ran* and embraced him, and kissed him (v. 20)." *(Italics added)*

What a "coincidence" the father would happen to look down the road at that moment and spy his youngest son limping home. Or do you think, instead, for the months, maybe even years his son was gone, the father always had one eye down that road? And what of the distance? The Bible makes it clear this boy was "still a long way out". How intimate, how personal that the father, no matter how far away, knew his son's carriage and cadence and stature and demeanor. How utterly miraculous that the father, knowing his son's walk, wanting his son home - ran! He ran with all of his hope and expectation, his mercy and forgiveness, his joy and his tears leading the way.

And then, as the boy was laying out his sins and asking for forgiveness, the father interrupts him and says to his slaves, "Quickly bring out the best robe and put it on him, and put a ring on his hand and sandals on his feet". The young man was happy to become a slave of his father's, knowing he did not deserve even that. The father, however, *demanded* he be dressed as an heir, with robe and ring and sandals to communicate to anyone who saw him that he was a son of the father.

This story sweeps over me! It is the waiting gaze of the Father that speaks to *this* child's heart. The certainty of His heart that He knows me in a way no one else can. The hopefulness of our reunion. The unmerited, undeserved grace, mercy, love and forgiveness of my sinful, pride-filled ways. The willingness of the Father, before all of creation, to place on me His seal, His sign of my place in His kingdom. I am a child of the King!

Fanny Crosby captured the sentiment in this classic hymn:

Blessed assurance, Jesus is mine!
Oh, what a fore-taste of glory divine!
Heir of salvation, purchase of God,
Born of His Spirit, washed in His blood.
Perfect submission, perfect delight,
Visions of rapture now burst on my sight;
Angels descending, bring from above,
Echoes of mercy, whispers of love.
Perfect submission, all is at rest,
I in my Savior am happy and blest;
Watching and waiting, looking above,
Filled with His goodness, lost in His love.

Another indescribable truth about being God's child is this - we belong to Him. Because I am God's child by His choosing; I am His child for eternity. Do you see the connection? God did not pay the highest price, His Beloved Son, for a relationship with the creation of His hand that would dissolve over time. God was never interested in "for now" or "someday"; God is all about NOW AND FOREVER; WE SHALL NEVER AGAIN BE SEPARATED! Jesus refers to this in John 10:14 & 15 and 27 - 29 "I am the good shepherd; and I know My own, and My own know Me, even as the Father knows Me and I know the Father; and I lay down My life for the sheep. . .My sheep hear My voice, and I know them, and they follow Me; and I give eternal life to them, and they shall never perish; and no one shall snatch them out of My hand. My Father, who has given them to Me, is greater than all; and no one is able to snatch them out of the Father's hand."

Now, if you are tempted to test God in this arena, let me tell you - He is not kidding. No one is able to snatch you out of God's hands if you are His child, not even you. I know this by Scripture, but also first hand. I told you earlier that I had stepped away from God for a period of about ten years. And during that time, I experienced not a moment of peace, not a smattering of hope, contentment, not rest. Throughout, God hounded me. Sometimes with whispers to my heart of His love, sometimes with consequences for the sins I was embracing, always in a proactive and purposeful way. God chased and hounded, out-maneuvered, out-witted and out-waited me until I found myself bone weary and ready to come back home. God did all this because as my Father, He knew what was best for me - HIM!

We belong to God for eternity *and* we are identified with Him. 1 John reminds us of the separation between us and this world. 1 John 3:1 states "See how great a love the Father has bestowed upon us, that we should be called children of God; and such we are. For this reason the world does not know us, because it did not know Him." We carry a mark that sets us apart from this world. It is not about salvation, though we certainly are headed to a different place than those who refuse God, but rather it is about Lordship. If I am God's child, that means that my life is a reflection (or should be) of His passions, His priority, His purposes. And every time, God's passions, priorities and purposes are at odds with this world. If I belong to God, then I am, by definition, an enemy of this world. There is no neutrality between good and evil; there is only an intractable divide.

Our relationship to our heavenly Father, through Jesus Christ, is seen so beautifully in I Peter 1:3 - 9: "Blessed be the God and Father of our Lord Jesus Christ, who according to His great mercy has caused us to be born again to a living hope through the resurrection of Jesus Christ from the dead, to obtain an inheritance which is imperishable and undefiled and will not fade away, reserved in heaven for you, who are protected by the power of God through faith for a salvation ready to be revealed in the last time. In this you greatly rejoice, even though now for a little while, if necessary, you have been distressed by various trials, that the reproof of your faith, being more precious than gold which is perishable, even though tested by fire, may be found to result in praise and glory and honor at the revelation of Jesus Christ; and though you have not seen Him, you love Him, and though you do not see Him now, but believe in Him, you greatly rejoice with joy inexpressible and full of glory, obtaining as the outcome of your faith the salvation of your souls."

Being a child of God is not a small matter. It is a matter of life and death, certainly, but more, it is a matter of direction, of place and of power! Being a child of God is about privilege; the position of honor as the King's children; the promise of hope in an eternity spent in paradise; and the power of the Holy Spirit to help us overcome the suffering of this present time. But, it is also about responsibility.

You and I belong, in every way, to our Creator, our Sustainer, our Father and Lord. We have given Him our hearts, our minds, our bodies and our wills (Galatians 2:20). We have yielded ourselves to Him because we have learned there is no other in whom we will find safety, ease, healing, love and more, in measures beyond our small imaginations, beyond our tiny need. Now, we need to begin to address how all of that goodness and mercy impact our daily lives. As God's children, we are now disciples of His Son, Jesus Christ. That means that we owe Him our very lives. We are to follow His commands to love, to serve, to be spent for the Kingdom of God on a daily basis. We have a responsibility to mature, growing in our faith and understanding so that we can lead others into a greater knowledge and faith in Jesus. This is a life style and a calling that we will explore deeply in the following chapters.

In addition to being God's child, by definition, God is our

Father and we will learn from His Word, that He is the perfect Father. There is a temptation, when you hear the word 'Father' to assign to it a meaning from your own experience. If your dad was a bad dad, you think of God, as Father, in a similar light. If your dad was decent or at least harmless, you think of God as benevolent and innocuous as well. It is a shame that we cannot create an alternative word for God as our Father, one that hasn't been wasted on human history and human experience. Perhaps, God intended for us to approach a word like Father with some hesitation. At least when we approach with uncertainty, we may approach with more thought. And God wants us to "think through" the *vast* differences between our earthly, fallible dads and our perfect heavenly Father.

First, our heavenly Father disciplines for the right and necessary reasons. Hebrews 12:7-8; 11 - 13 states, "It is for discipline that you endure; God deals with you as with sons; for what son is there whom *his* father does not discipline? But if you are without discipline, of which all have become partakers, then you are illegitimate children and not sons. . .All discipline for the moment seems not to be joyful, but sorrowful; yet to those who have been trained by it, afterwards it yields the peaceful fruit of righteousness. Therefore, strengthen the hands that are weak and the knees that are feeble, and make straight paths for your feet, so that the limb which is lame may not be put out of joint, but rather be healed."

God, our Father, who created us and knows us better than we know ourselves will discipline, reprove, correct and train us so that we will not only look more and more like His Son, but that we will live in peace. Dr. James MacDonald is fond of saying, "Choose to sin; choose to suffer." God does not want us to suffer and so He will stand firm with us and love us enough to interrupt our lives, disturb our broken plans, interfere and invade and insert Himself so that we will have an obvious choice to make. Our perfect Father is a God who disciplines. It is an element of His love that patiently endures with *this* stubborn child. Without it, I would be destroyed.

Secondly, He is a Father who provides. In Matthew 6, Jesus reminds us God knows of our every need and He promises to supply according to His great riches. Sometimes, our argument with God is that it is not what we want, when we want it, but God, our good Father, knows what we need and when we need it. Notice the difference. There has *never* been a time in my life when my plans to satisfy my wants came to greater fruition than God's plans to satisfy my needs. I don't always appreciate that at the time, but I always see it more clearly down the road. God's ways *far* exceed my silly, little designs.

God has given it *all* in the Person of His Son. Anything else that you require from your heavenly Father is a small matter indeed. Not to you, but for Him to accomplish. Do you need hope? He pours out in abundance to those who believe in Him. Do you need faith or patience or healing? He grows those in us by experience, by study of His Word and over time. Do you need to hear from someone that you matter, that you are loved, that you belong - He is speaking to your heart every moment of every day! The God of Creation, The Alpha and the Omega, the Beginning and the End died to give you life eternal. He has conquered death; He has conquered sin and despair and pain and He has promised salvation from your past, healing in your present and hope for your future. That's what it means to be a child of the King!

In his book, "In The Grip of Grace", Max Lucado reminds us of the story of Mephibosheth who was the son of Jonathan, son of Saul, Israel's first king. (Read 1 Samuel 31 - 2 Samuel 9) When Saul and Jonathan were both slain on the battlefield, the rest of the king's household fled, fearing they too would be destroyed. Mephibosheth was an infant and when his nurse retreated in haste, she dropped the young boy. He was horribly crippled from the fall. He would never again walk right nor would he enjoy the privileges of his royal birth because of his grandfather and father's defeat.

King David, the victor, had made a promise to Jonathan, however and it was a promise that, though delayed twenty years, he kept. David took Mephibosheth into the royal household and took care of him. Though Mephibosheth was born of another household, one hostile to David, (Saul had spent the last part of his life trying to hunt David down and kill him), Mephibosheth had been brought, by grace, back into the royal kingdom.

Lucado writes: "Pause and envision the scene in the royal dining room. May I turn my pen over to Charles Swindoll to assist you?

The dinner bell rings through the king's palace and David comes to the head of the table and sits down. In a few moments Amnon - clever, crafty, Amnon - sits to the left of David. Lovely and gracious Tamar, a charming and beautiful young woman, arrives and sits beside Amnon. And then across the way, Solomon walks slowly from his study; precocious, brilliant, preoccupied Solomon. The heir apparent slowly sits down. And then Absalom - handsome, winsome Absalom with beautiful flowing hair, black as a raven, down to his shoulders - sits down. That particular evening Joab, the courageous warrior and David's commander of the troops, has been invited to dinner. Muscular, bronzed Joab is seated near the king. Afterward they wait. They hear the shuffling of feet, the clump, clump, clump of the crutches as Mephibosheth rather awkwardly finds his place at the table and slips into his seat. . .and the tablecloth covers his feet. I ask you: Did Mephibosheth understand grace?

. . .Children of royalty, crippled by the fall, permanently marred by sin. Living parenthetical lives in the chronicles of earth only to be remembered by the king. Driven not by our beauty but by his promise, he calls us to himself and invites us to take a permanent place at his table. Though we often limp more than we walk, we take our place next to the other sinners-made-saints and we share in God's glory."

Lucado gets it. It isn't about our worthiness to be God's children. It's about His faithfulness to His promises. He takes us in because of who He is for He can do nothing else. Mephibosheth could have refused David's offer. He did not. We can refuse God's offer by refusing to accept Jesus as our personal Lord and Savior, but once we have accepted Christ as that, we have accepted God's offer into His kingdom!

It doesn't matter if you are lame just as it didn't matter that I was broken and battered and bruised beyond recognition. What mattered in my life was that THE KING had taken me in.

When I was a kid, my mother had a rather unique CB handle. She called herself the 'King's Kid!' I've always loved that. It was as if she was standing tall and proclaiming her place in God's kingdom. She knew to whom she belonged and He belonged to her. She was and is His kid; He is her Father. That's the first truth that you need to know. You are a child of the King!

I AM CHOSEN

In I Corinthians 4:1, believers are called "servants of Christ, and stewards of the mysteries of God". Two remarkable titles. The latter, a steward is defined as a person charged with the keep of something valuable, a ward or an individual entrusted with responsibility. You and I, as God's children, are called to be good stewards of our lives, of our resources and finances, of our time and talent. And here, in this passage, we are called to be "stewards of the mysteries of God".

There are more "mysteries of God" than you or I could ever comprehend. God's beginning is a mystery for He has none. God the Father's relationship with God the Son and God the Holy Spirit, the Three in One, is a mystery; we can not hope to define it. To be first, one must be last. To live, one must die. All mysteries of God. Here is another mystery - God chose us in Him before the foundation of the world (Ephesians 1:4) *and* we have free will to choose God (Revelation 3:20).

Predestination or election is how we define God's choosing. It is found throughout Scripture. "But we should always give thanks to God for you, brethren, beloved by the Lord, because God has chosen you from the beginning for salvation through sanctification by the Spirit and faith in the truth." (2 Thessalonians 2:13) And in Romans 8:29 - 30, we read, "For whom He foreknew, He also predestined to become conformed to the image of His Son, that He might be the firstborn among many brethren; and whom He predestined, these He also called; and whom He called, these He also justified; and whom He justified, these He also glorified." And finally, in Isaiah 43:3 & 4 it says, "For I am the Lord your God, the Holy One of Israel, your Savior; I have given Egypt as your ransom,

Cush and Seba in your place. Since you are precious in My sight, Since you are honored and I love you, I will give other men in your place and other peoples in exchange for your life". We are chosen by God.

In addition, man's free will to choose God is also throughout Scripture. ". . .that if you confess with your mouth Jesus as Lord, and believe in your heart that God raised Him from the dead, you shall be saved" (Romans 10:9). And in John 3:18 we read, "He who believes in Him is not judged; he who does not believe has been judged already, because he has not believed in the name of the only begotten Son of God." We have a will to choose to accept or reject what God has freely made available to us.

So how do these two seemingly incompatible truths meet? In the mysteries and in the mind of God. There are truths of God and His ways that are so far beyond our understanding we can not reconcile them in our minds, but that has no bearing on their veracity. God's Word gives us both doctrines as true and compatible in God's mind; *therefore*, God chose us in Him before the foundation of the world *and* we choose to accept what God freely offered.

If you are struggling with how "fair or just" it is to acknowledge that some have been chosen for salvation and therefore, others have been chosen for destruction, let me remind you that we are the creation; He is the Creator. God is our Maker and He has every right to determine what is just and fair in His creation. In Isaiah 45:9 it says, "Woe to the one who quarrels with his Maker - An earthenware vessel among the vessels of earth! Will the clay say to the potter, 'what are you doing?' or the thing you are making say, 'He has no hands?'".

If you disagree with God's right of rule over His creation, then when you create your own universe, you can set the rules, but until then, we are living in God's universe. As a writer of fiction, I appreciate that. I have control over what I have created, limited though my powers are. God, with His unlimited powers, has control over what He has created. That's not the remarkable thing, however. The remarkable thing is not that God chose us (though that is miraculous in its own right); the remarkable thing is that God, *somehow*, allows us to choose Him or reject Him. The God who set the stars in place, who knit me in my mother's womb allows me the freedom to embrace Him or to reject Him and walk away. It is, in full color, the essence of our love relationship. God chose me; then I chose Him.

In addition, while we don't have the mind of God, we also don't have the vision of God. We can not see what He sees; we can not know what He knows. God is so far beyond us, to put on Him our views of fair play or justice is to mock His perfect standards of justice. When we spend more time on His character, this may be an easier truth for you to grasp. For now, as an element of my identity in Christ, we are going to focus on His choosing us. We need to appreciate our unworthiness to be chosen (no need to reiterate our track records here), and address God's choosing us as His own.

So, how should we react to God's choosing us? Certainly, it is a gift and a reason to praise God!

> "*In love* He predestined us to adoption as sons
> through Jesus Christ to Himself,
> *according to the kind intention of His will*,
> to the praise of the glory of His grace,
> *which He freely bestowed on us in the Beloved*."
> Ephesians 1:4b-6 (italics added)

"*In love*" God chose us. Think on that phrase, "in love". God, the Alpha and the Omega, the Beginning and the End, created us in His image, put us (Adam and Eve) in the garden with the tree of knowledge of good and evil. Do you imagine for a moment God did not know what would happen? Of course not. God allowed Adam and Eve the freedom to choose. They chose "freedom" and found bondage and death in their sin. But, God wasn't finished with them. In Ephesians 1:4, we are reminded God "chose us in Him before the foundation of the world". That means, before God spoke anything into being, He knew we would choose our own way, our own sins over Him. God knew He would have to provide a way for us to get back to Him. He planned for our salvation before He set one star in place. "In love", God chose us.

Imagine if you will, giving birth to a child whose entire life story you knew in advance. Now imagine that that child was destined to bring you *nothing* but heartache and pain. You would never hear one word of gratitude or love from this child but would instead have to watch this child destroy himself and everyone around him, including you. Now imagine you have the choice to bring this life into the world or to terminate this life, a life that is going to decimate everything and everyone you love. What would you do?

Now think about God and His choice. Billions and billions of beings created in His image with a chance to rejoice in His glory and to bask in His love. Instead our focus is self and sin and death and destruction. Do you think we have the slightest vision in our minds of what God has had to withstand in order for you and I to be born into this fallen, sinful world, be found by Him and choose a love relationship with Him? Do you imagine the love for us, His creation, that it takes for God to *endure* for a time so that we could be chosen; we could be saved? "In love", God chose us.

"According to the kind intention of His will", God chose us. Let me ask you this: Have you experienced the kind intention of God's will today? You woke up and had air in your lungs; that's the kind intention of His will. You most likely had food and clothes and a job; that's the kind intention of His will.

Sometimes, I am guilty of thinking that somehow, I earned what I have or I deserve or have a right to the "stuff" God has given me. I don't! Remember what we said earlier - Adam and Eve had no *right* to insist God share Himself with them. We have no right to demand God clothe and feed us, provide for us, save us or do any of the millions of things He does over the course of our lives. *That's* "the kind intention of His will".

But maybe you're someone who feels as if you've not experienced *the kind intention of His will*, having endured hardships and pain for the bulk of your life. Well, let me ask you this question: can you list all of the things *from which* God has spared you? You can't; no one can. You and I don't have a clue of the trials and evil and hardship and pain *from which* God has protected us. You and I can not possibly know or see what God knows and sees. Even in your pain and hardship, you and I have experienced *the kind intention of His will. "In love. . .according to the kind intention of His will"*, God chose us.

"Which He freely bestowed on us in the Beloved", in grace, God chose us. One of the things I love about Paul's writing is his word choice. Freely bestowed is a powerful description of abundance that overflows need. God lavished upon us all we needed; He withheld nothing! The grace we needed but didn't deserve; the mercy required to spare us the judgment due; the Beloved (Jesus) who paid with His life for the creation of His hands. *"In love. . .according to the kind intention of His will. . .which He freely bestowed on us in the Beloved"*, God chose us.

Being chosen is a gift from God and I should never cease to praise His name for it day and night. It is not a choosing in merit because I earned it; it is not a choosing in potential because someday I would be worthy of it; it is a choosing in love! You and I are chosen; how many billions of reasons do you and I have to praise our gracious Father indeed!

How else should we respond to His choosing? It is a reason to give ourselves over to Him in service and submission.

God saved me! From death, from judgment, from eternal heartache and despair, from my need, from my sins, from my hopelessness, from every powerful evil and sin, God has delivered me in His choosing. Therefore, my life and yours (if you are a child of God's) are no longer ours; our lives belong to Him. One of the verses to which we shall often refer is Galatians 2:20 "I have been crucified with Christ; and it is no longer I who live but Christ lives in me; and the life which I now live in the flesh I live by faith in the Son of God, who loved me, and delivered Himself up for me." God chose us; we belong to Him.

"I am chosen" is not a reflection of my worthiness but rather a statement of God's goodness, grace and mercy. Because you are chosen (as am I), our life perspective regarding our purpose and plan must change. We have been singled out, not just in our inheritance and lineage but in our life direction. Working for money, living for pleasure, holding onto things that won't last are no longer our priorities. Our priority, as an expression of gratitude and of indebtedness, is God and His Kingdom! (Colossians 3:12)

You have lived through circumstances in your life that are at best, difficult and at worst, horrific. No one knows what that was like, not with clarity, not even you. But to understand the truth of being chosen by God, it's important to lay down what has happened to you and what you have done (sins you have committed) and focus on one thing - God's grace.

Life isn't about the circumstances of our life; it is about our attitude and our faith. Whether you have suffered at another's hand or you have forced another to suffer, being chosen of God means leaving the shame and guilt of that past behind. It means we all, abuser and abused, as children of God, are living in the shadow of grace.

There is a story of a man who exemplifies what it is to live in the shadow of the Almighty. John Newton was a ship's captain for the better part of his early life. He traded in human flesh; he was a slave trader. One day on a voyage, his ship was almost lost in a savage sea. It was during that moment John Newton picked up "Imitation of Christ" by Thomas a´ Kempis and soon after experienced personal conviction and then conversion as he accepted Jesus Christ as his Lord and Savior. He wrote two things about himself that speak to God's choosing of us by His grace.

> For his tombstone he wrote: "John Newton, clerk, once an infidel and Libertine, a servant of slavers in Africa, was, by the rich mercy of our Lord and Savior Jesus Christ, preserved, restored, pardoned, and appointed to preach the Faith he had long labored to destroy."

And then he wrote this hymn:

> Amazing grace, how sweet the sound,
> that saved a wretch like me!
> I once was lost but now am found,
> was blind but now I see.
> 'Twas grace that taught my heart to fear,
> and grace my fears relieved;
> how precious did that grace appear
> the hour I first believed!

Thru many dangers, toils and snares
I have already come;
'Tis grace hath brought me safe thus far,
and grace will lead me home.
When we've been there ten thousand years,
bright shining as the sun,
we've no less days to sing God's praise
then when we'd first begun.

CHAPTER 1: I AM GOD'S CHILD; I AM CHOSEN

GOING DEEPER: QUESTIONS FOR STUDY

1. How do you know that you belong to God?

2. What responsibilities do you have as God's child? Colossians 3

3. Express in your own words how you've experienced "the kind intention of God's will" (Ephesians 1:4 - 6)

GETTING TO THE HEART OF THE MATTER: APPLICATION

Write out in your journal how you came to be a child of God - thank God for rescuing you from a life as an orphan, that is to say from a life hostile to God!

LAYING THE FOUNDATION: QUIET TIME

DAY ONE: John 10:1 - 18
   To whom do you belong?

DAY TWO: Philippians 2:1 - 18; Colossians 1:13 - 23
   What right does Jesus have to lay claim to you?

DAY THREE: Hebrews 12:1 - 13
   List some ways that God has disciplined you - have you been trained by that discipline?

DAY FOUR: Ephesians 5:1 - 21
   What does it mean to "walk as children of the light"?

DAY FIVE: Romans 5:6 - 11 Our choosing is a measure of God's grace and mercy. How does Paul describe God's grace and mercy in this passage?

CHAPTER TWO

I AM LOVED

The word "love" has come to mean so many things that it truly means almost nothing today. We are told in commercials we are to love toothpaste and deodorant. We hear about people hopping into bed with everyone and their neighbor and "making love". We see marriages begin with promise and end with "we just fell out of love". And even our most enduring relationships are crippled by self-love, self-involvement and selfish love. When seen through the world's eyes, love is not a many splendored thing. It is hobbled and weak, sinful and destructive. It is all emotion and no commitment; it is all talk and no show; it is antithetical to God's definition of love.

In God's Word, the word love is defined by God. "Beloved, let us love one another, for love is from God; and everyone who loves is born of God and knows God. The one who does not love does not know God, for God is love." (I John 4:7 & 8) *God is love*. He is the perfect expression of love. When He creates, it is love. When He disciplines, it is love. When He answers prayer, provides for our needs, when He purchased us with the blood of His Son, it is love. God's every action, even His perfect standard of righteousness, is grounded in love, for He is love's very definition, its only foundation.

Notice too, how the world will say, "I love you" and then show you, if it can, and even then, words rarely match action. God instead shows us His love through action, long before He ever tells us about it. John 3:16 is a verse with which the world seems acquainted in passing, but have you ever considered its message? "For God so loved the world, that He *sent* His only Begotten Son, that whosoever believes in Him should not perish, but have eternal life." God loved; God sent. Because He loved, He needed to act. His love directed His action, even the most painful, horrific action of all time in the universe - the Perfect Lamb would be sent to die for a sinner such as I.

You and I did not encourage God to love us because of who we were or are - we are sinners, unholy and unworthy. "But God demonstrates His own love toward us, in that while we were yet sinners, Christ died for us." (Romans 5:8). It is in God's love we have the ability to choose a love relationship with the God of the universe! He loved us so we *could* love Him.

God's love is perfect; it is plentiful; and it is even primary. In 1 John 4:19, we see that God's love is the starting point of our own ability to love, "We love, because He first loved us." Through God's love, we now have the ability to learn to love as He does - with another's spiritual condition of primary concern. God's love draws us to Him. Our love of others should then point them to God, for that is their greatest good. God is love's beginning, bidding us to come, and love's end teaching us to draw others to love's source.

By definition then, God's love completes us because of Christ Jesus. His Son is the final picture in a masterpiece created by the Master. God's *love* turned darkness into light, void into space, a word into flesh. God's *love* pulled a thread woven throughout history with redemption its design. God's *love* sent His Beloved born a helpless babe, stripped of His splendor to walk among us. God's *love* endured insult and betrayal, temptation and injustice, agony and bloodshed. God's *love* saw His Son hanging on a tree, sacrificed for the object of His love. God's *love* hunted us down in our darkest hour; God's *love* delivered us, sustains us and daily renews and remakes us.

Throughout Scripture, God paints many pictures of His love for us. Each communicates a central truth. One of my favorite pictures is that of Hosea and Gomer and the central truth of God's faithful love.

Hosea was a prophet around 700 BC in the Northern Kingdom of Israel. His message, as a prophet, was to warn the children of Israel of an impending exile due to their determination to prostitute themselves before other gods. The children of Israel's Northern Kingdom had chosen to worship idols and gods such as Baal. Hosea was sent to tell them that God was going to punish them for their sinful ways. Hosea's message was also one of restoration. He promised that although the people would suffer the consequences of their sin, God would not abandon them and He would one day bring them back from exile. Then Hosea went on to promise an extraordinary thing, even while in exile, God would not turn His back on them; He would still be their God.

To show them a picture of His faithful love for His people, God commanded Hosea to marry a prostitute named Gomer. Hosea married her and they had several kids together. After a number of years, however, Gomer returned to her prostituting ways. Hosea sought the Lord on what to do about his wife who had been unfaithful to him and had left him for her old bondage. God responded, "love a woman who is loved by her husband, yet an adulteress, even as the Lord loves the sons of Israel, though they turn to other gods. . ." (Hosea 3:1b-2a). God was using this marriage as a symbol to illustrate how unfaithful Israel had been to God AND how unchanging, faithful and perfect God's love was for Israel and is for us!

So, Hosea had to actually go and buy back his wife out of her prostitution. He had to redeem her from her sin, literally purchase his wife out of her chosen slavery, as God has had to redeem us, purchase us from ours.

I wonder what Gomer was thinking as Hosea showed up to bring her back home. I wonder how she felt. I imagine there was shame and guilt and a sense of feeling unlovable, unworthy that could be seen in her eyes, in her carriage, in her walk. I also imagine those feelings may have been what led her back to her old bondage, her old ways. *Feeling* as though she didn't belong with a righteous man like Hosea, that she didn't deserve his love and affection, she went to the one place where she believed her shame became shapeless and less defined, the darkened shadows of sin. What she missed is that in the light of God's love our shame is not exposed; it is destroyed.

What a picture of our relationship with God! We are Gomer over and over again in our lives. We run, with abandon, into the arms of so many lovers - money, power, pleasure, pain and others - and our God comes faithfully back to redeem us from the bondage those lovers afford. It is God who is faithful in His love of us because it is God who is faithful to Himself. He can *be*, He can *do* nothing else.

This story screams out about God's faithful love. No matter what Israel, His chosen people did, God loved them and He redeemed them through the promise and fulfillment of His Son's death and resurrection. But this story also reminds us of another foundational truth about God's love. It is not dependent on us or on what we do.

Shame is a powerful emotion. It was one that held great position in my life for years. I would *never* have told you that you could earn your salvation; I understood grace. But I lived my life as if I could earn God's love. I believed if I could be the perfect Christian, the tireless servant, the matchless emissary of God, then God would reward my effort with an equal measure of love. When I failed miserably, I lost hope of embracing God's love in my life. Truth is, *if* I could earn God's love, *then* I could lose God's love.

But this story of Hosea and Gomer and others throughout the Scripture tell us as plain as day we can not earn God's love, therefore, we can not lose God's love. God does not love us because of who we are or what we do; God loves us because of who He is.

> Romans 8:26-39 (v.37-39) "But in all these things we overwhelmingly conquer through Him who loved us. For I am convinced that neither death, nor life, nor angels, nor principalities, nor things present, nor things to come, nor powers, nor height, nor depth, nor any other created thing, shall be able to separate us from the love of God, which is in Christ Jesus our Lord."

The case that Paul is making for love in this classic passage of

Scripture is that God's love is as sure and unchanging as He is. Numbers 23:19 reminds us "God is not a man, that He should lie, Nor a son of man, that He should repent; Has He said, and will He not do it? Or has He spoken, and will He not make it good?" Paul in the Romans passage is stating clearly that God's love is more powerful than every circumstance or force, person or power that would come against it. God's love is eternally secure, almighty and unyielding with infinite capacity and fortitude. No one can weaken or diminish or lessen God's love for you - not even you.

Do you say that you can't *feel* God's love? Tough! It's there. God's love is not dependent on your feelings. God does not demonstrate His love of you when you agree with Him you are somehow lovable. God's love is independent of your feelings, your whims, your emotional droughts and floods. God loves you! Learn to live with it.

Is that a load off of your shoulders, to know you are not responsible in any way for God loving you? It sure was for me. When I finally learned this lesson, that God loves me because of who He is, then I finally realized I am eternally safe in His arms. What sin, past, present or future, will rob me of God's love and affection? None! What failure, what shame, what cascade of emotions will convince me my Father's love wavers and wanes with circumstance or event? None!

"I am loved" is a measure of God's character; therefore it is more sure than the rising of the sun! Indeed, it will last longer, burn brighter and warm my soul for eternity. "There is no fear in love; but perfect love casts out fear, because fear involves punishment, and the one who fears is not perfected in love. We love, because He first loved us." I John 4:18 & 19

I AM FORGIVEN

I owe God. It is a debt I can not escape. I am a sinner by birth (Romans 5:12), by nature (Romans 7:14 & 15) and by choice (Romans 6:12 - 19). I have violated God's holy law, His perfect standard and now, I owe a debt that must be paid.

Not only do I owe a debt that must be paid, but if my sin is not covered by Jesus' death and resurrection, then a relationship with the Father and Creator, for which I was created, is impossible. "But your iniquities have made a separation between you and your God. And your sins have hidden His face from you, so that He does not hear." (Isaiah 59:2) Recognizing then, I am a sinner, inescapably so, I am in desperate need of a way to pay that debt in order to escape death and enter into life, repay God what I most certainly owe, and enjoy a relationship with my Creator.

Here's the problem: it is a debt I can never satisfy. "Now we know that whatever the Law says, it speaks to those who are under the Law, that every mouth may be closed, and all the world may become accountable to God; because by the works of the Law no flesh will be justified in His sight; for through the Law comes the knowledge of sin." Romans 3:19 - 20 We can not be saved by the Law for the Law's purpose is to condemn. It is God's perfect, holy standard and as we've seen, we are without hope when we stand before it.

Here's the good news, the great news - when I accepted Jesus Christ as my Lord and Savior, I acknowledged my sin and my need to be saved. I also acknowledged I can not be saved by my own strength and that Jesus had to come as the perfect Lamb to die for my sins. When you and I entered into the family of God, we entered into a place where our debt has been eternally stamped *"paid in full"*. Jesus, the only one who could have satisfied our debt, did just that on the cross. It was *the* sacrifice required and it was the ONLY sacrifice required.

That sacrifice was once and for all. For every sin you've committed, are committing or will commit. Jesus carried on the cross every evil, every sin of all time - the debt has been paid! I can not stress this point enough, for sadly, the evil one has convinced far too many of God's kids that their particular brand of sin is far too evil, too large, too grotesque to be covered by such a Perfect Sacrifice.

I was fooled by that lie for a time. The lie that somehow what I had done was too much for the cross. That's like saying, 'nice try God with the cross and all but it wasn't enough; Jesus' death and resurrection may cover everyone else's sin, but it can't cover mine'. I don't know about you, but I don't want to be the one saying to

God that His Son's agony, His Sacrifice, His death wasn't enough. Our Father delivered up His Beloved Son on our behalf and the work that was accomplished on the cross was enough, completely enough, eternally enough to pay the debt you and I owed and to bring us back into a relationship with God.

If you are living in shame for the sins you've committed, the things you've done, then you are living a lie. Jesus Christ carried that sin, every sin on Calvary's tree and the moment you repent, it is forgiven and forgotten by God. To believe yourself too sinful, too bad, too dirty for God is to live in pride that somehow, your badness is more and better than anyone else's in the history of man. If you live as if you believe you have sinned so greatly or deeply it is literally beyond God's measure to forgive, what you are saying is that Jesus Christ's death and resurrection were not enough. You are saying something more is required in order for you to be redeemed. Nothing can be further from the truth of God's Word and His heart than that! God's Beloved Son willingly gave Himself up as *the* sacrifice for your sin, for my sin, for all sin for all time! And I can promise you two things: one, God is bigger than anything you've done in that His Son's sacrifice is more than enough; and two, pride will only bring more heartache. Whatever you may be holding onto, let it go. Say it with me - I am forgiven of ALL my sins; thank you God!

Now, in understanding "we are forgiven" is an aspect of our identity, let's make some distinctions right now. If you were abused or broken in any way by a spouse or family member, friend or stranger, you (and I) are not responsible for the abuse. That is their sin and they will have to deal with their sin before God. The person abused or broken is not responsible for the abuse and the wounding. But as Christians, here is where we part ways with the world's philosophy. The world says, if you've been abused or hurt in any way, then you are not responsible for how your react, what you become or what you do as a result of such a painful experience. It is called victimhood and it is, literally, a license to sin. It will only lead to more brokenness and greater heartache. Some of you know personally what I mean.

God's Word, as we will see in future lessons, makes it clear - we *are* responsible for our own lives, our own choices, our own thoughts, words and deeds. You and I can not stand before God and claim amnesty on actions taken as a result of being broken. God will forgive, but He will not excuse. I am not responsible for what happened to me (abuse, violence, rape, incest, etc.); I *am* responsible for every moment after it happened. What I said, did, didn't do - *I* am responsible for *my* actions and *my* thoughts and *my* words. Some of those actions, thoughts and words were sin and because of that, I need to understand the truth about forgiveness.

Before we go further, it is important to understand why some of our reactions have been sinful. Remember that we've already said, as children of God, you and I have a purpose on this earth. That purpose is really captured in two commandments: "And He (Jesus) said to him, "'YOU SHALL LOVE THE LORD YOUR GOD WITH ALL YOUR HEART, AND WITH ALL YOUR SOUL, AND WITH ALL YOUR MIND.' This is the great and foremost commandment. The second is like it, 'YOU SHALL LOVE YOUR NEIGHBOR AS YOURSELF.' On these two commandments depend the whole Law and the Prophets." (Matthew 22:37-40).

You and I are commanded by Jesus to spend our lives loving God with every fiber of our being, purposefully and without reservation. So, if I am living in anger or depression over the abuse that I've suffered, I am not capable of loving God with the proper intensity and abandon. If I am focused on revenge, do you believe God has the appropriate place in my life? If I am completely independent and self-reliant, how can I surrender my heart to my God, loving Him with all my being?

If you were abused as a child by a trusted adult, that betrayal may have taught you to build up barriers to your heart in order to protect it from further damage. Those barriers became impenetrable and now, you are using them to keep your husband and kids from getting too close and worse, you are keeping God at arm's length. The Bible, as we said, tells us we are to love the Lord our God with all our heart, soul, mind and body but with your walls, that's impossible. What started out to be a protection has become a hardened shell of separation and continuing to live within those walls is sin.

Or maybe every moment from the time you were abused, you

have been plotting the demise of your assailant, but here's the thing, hate and murder and revenge are sin. They separate us from God and more; they deny God's sovereignty and His character of justice.

Self-sufficiency, self-reliance, self-protection, unholy fear, unrighteous anger, depression (anger turned inward over a period of time), shame - these are all sins. And this list is not exhaustive. Can you picture a character trait or a pattern that you can now see as sin in light of Jesus' commandment to love?

For almost 10 years, I lived in fear because of the rape. Almost every night, during the years when I lived alone, I would wake up around 2 or 3 AM and check the door and window locks. I was choosing to live in fear; I was choosing to live in sin.

Since then, two things have happened, God has taught me about Himself, that He is Sovereign and Almighty and has an eternal plan for me (things we are going to learn in subsequent chapters). The second thing is this; I came to realize by living in fear, I was choosing to deny God's character. My fear (a form of self-protection) was a sin. I have since repented and in God's truth and a growing faith, I have been freed from the bondage of the sin of physical fear. It has completely disappeared from my life. Now my sleep is unhindered because I rest in God. *That* is freedom from the bondage of sin.

God doesn't want you or me to be living in bondage to the sin of self-reliance or of self-protection or any other sin; He wants us to be living in abundance under the shadow of His wings. To do the latter, we will spend some time learning about this Almighty One of Israel. But first, you will have to acknowledge that if you are *choosing* one or more of those "arrows of protection and reaction" to the wounding that you've received, you are living in sin. You need to ask God for forgiveness in order to move into healing. Remember, "faith is believing the Word of God, and acting upon it, no matter how I feel, because God promises a good result".

We've said no one is without sin, except the Son of God. We all have sins that need His forgiveness. The question to ask is this, do you want to hold onto the sin or experience the healing salve of God's forgiveness?

Daily we all desperately need to hear God's heart about forgiveness:

Isaiah 1:18 "Come now, and let us reason together," says the Lord, "Though your sins are as scarlet, They will be white as snow; Though they are red like crimson, They will be like wool."

I John 1:9 "If we confess our sins, He is faithful and righteous to forgive us our sins and to cleanse us from all unrighteousness."

Ephesians 1:7, 8a "In Him we have redemption through His blood, the forgiveness of our trespasses, according to the riches of His grace, which He lavished upon us."

Romans 5:10 "For if while we were enemies, we were reconciled to God through the death of His Son, much more, having been reconciled, we shall be saved by His life."

God's heart is this: I am forgiven. My sins are as far from Him as the east is from the west (Psalm 103:12). And when God looks at us, He sees the blood of His beloved Son, covering us so that we are forgiven indeed! Romans 8:1 promises us that, "There is therefore now no condemnation for those who are in Christ Jesus."

"I am forgiven" has always been a pivotal element of my relationship with God. When I have struggled, it has almost always been because of my sin. Sometimes, we think of sin only as some 'pleasurable' excursion into diversion and then, when we suffer the consequences of those 'feel-good' moments that yield only bondage, we repent and move on. But sin is so much bigger than that. Sin is denying God's character in the face of trials. Sin is believing the lies that God does not care or is weak. Sin is thinking that somehow no one can be trusted with the core of who you are and feeling the need to barricade yourself off from the world. Sin is whatever separates us from the love relationship that God yearns for, desires and has created us to have with Him. "I am forgiven" is a proclamation of God's undying love and provision, for nothing, not even me, can keep us apart!

Isaac Watts wrote a hymn that captures the essence and the simplicity of forgiveness. It is entitled, "When I Survey the Wondrous Cross"

> When I survey the wondrous cross,
> On which the Prince of glory died,
> My richest gain I count but loss,
> And pour contempt on all my pride.
> Forbid it, Lord! that I should boast,
> Save in the death of Christ, my God;
> All the vain things that charm me most
> I sacrifice them to His blood.
> See, from His head, His hands, His feet,
> Sorrow and love flow mingled down;
> Did e'er such love and sorrow meet,
> Or thorns compose so rich a crown?
> His dying crimson, like a robe,
> Spreads o'er His body on the tree;
> Then I am dead to all the globe,
> And all the globe is dead to me.
> Were the whole realm of nature mine,
> That were a present far too small;
> Love so amazing, so divine,
> Demands my soul, my life, my all.

Isaac Watts had tasted God's forgiveness and in gratitude, he proclaimed himself forever in His Savior's debt!

CHAPTER 2: I AM LOVED; I AM FORGIVEN
GOING DEEPER: QUESTIONS FOR STUDY

1. What is the manifestation (evidence) of God's love in your life?

2. Knowing that God loves us because of who He is, how does His love provide you with security?

3. Understanding that you are not responsible for the abuse that happened **to** you, *but* that you are responsible for your actions, thoughts, words - what are some ways in which you may have sinned in response to the abuse?

GETTING TO THE HEART OF THE MATTER:
APPLICATION

Understanding that the Bible is God's *love letter* to us; write a *love letter* back to God.

LAYING THE FOUNDATION: QUIET TIME

DAY ONE: Philippians 2:1 - 13
    What did Christ leave behind for you? Describe sacrificial love using concrete examples.

DAY TWO: Psalm 31
    Understanding that godly love is about actions, describe the ways in which God has loved you through the hard times in your life.

DAY THREE: I John 4:1 - 21; John 10:27-29
    Has your understanding of love, as defined by God, changed? How?

DAY FOUR: Psalm 51 & 103

Ask God to reveal any sinfulness with which you need to deal. Spend some time on your knees with the Lord. Be honest with Him.

DAY FIVE: 2 Timothy 1:12; Ephesians 1: 13, 14

In response to God's love, what have you entrusted to God?

CHAPTER THREE

I AM SANCTIFIED

—⟨☞⟩—

"And such were some of you. . ." Paul, who wrote a good deal of the New Testament, wrote often about the process of sanctification which happens in a believer's life. It is a process of being formerly alienated or hostile to the things of God and now becoming "holy, pure, set apart" because of Jesus Christ. Notice the word *becoming*. It is not about arriving, at least not yet, it is rather about the journey. Sanctification is about change, about transformation. It is a process and in that process, we work, in cooperation and agreement with the God of the universe!

Sanctification is the process of being re-made into the image of Jesus Christ. It sets us apart from this world in two ways: first, we have a different set of morals, values, priorities and purpose; and second, we have as our model the perfect Son of the most Holy God. The latter gives us a different appearance from the rest of the world. We look differently and behave differently because we embrace God's truth and not the world's lies.

Sadly, some Christians take this process as an invitation to express their moral superiority to the world. To stand up and say 'we are holy and favored; you are not'! Being "set apart" or sanctified is not about being sanctimonious or "religious" or filled with pride, it is about reflecting the Servant King as light in a darkened world. It is about standing up in love to those who would denounce Christ. It is about serving those who would take advantage of your service. It is about tending to the sick and the dying with humility and love as our Teacher did. It is about being transformed from my old, self-centered nature into a new creation.

Sanctification, at conversion and throughout our Christian lives, is about grace. "For by grace you have been saved through faith; and that not of yourselves, it is the gift of God; not as a result of works, that no one should boast." (Ephesians 2:8 & 9). If you can wrap this verse, this teaching around your heart, that "by grace you have been saved through faith", then you will, by God's goodness, live in humility. And humility is at the heart of change.

Sanctification *began* at conversion. 1 Corinthians 6:11 reads "And such were some of you; but you were washed, but you were sanctified, but you were justified in the name of the Lord Jesus Christ, and in the Spirit of our God." Colossians 1:21, 22 is very specific when it states, "And although you were formerly alienated and hostile in mind, engaged in evil deeds, yet He has now reconciled you in His fleshly body through death, in order to present you before Him holy and blameless and beyond reproach." An amazing start it is.

There is nothing like "the hour I first believed" to quote Newton. That process of being washed, cleansed, having a new appreciation and deeper knowledge of one's sin and then, covered by grace, to come into a new and even deeper appreciation and knowledge of one's Creator and Father, Savior and King! Add to that the indwelling of the Spirit and those first few hours, few days, few weeks and months are unlike any other time in a believer's life.

In those first days, I cried myself to sleep most nights, not in sadness but overwhelmed in joy. Feeling for the first time as if I could reach up and touch the sky and capture the wind. For the first time in my life, I felt safe and loved in a way I hadn't before. And it wasn't because I wasn't safe or loved by my family, I was. It was just that I had discovered the puzzle piece which had been missing in my young life and I couldn't find the words to express my gratitude. I knew the Bible stories, but now, when I read those words, I could see His hand and purpose behind them. I'd heard the songs, the hymns, but now, the voices around me couldn't drown me out for I had such reason to sing. I went for long walks and talks with

Him and I found myself drawn to others who knew my Lord.

I was in love for the first time in my life. It wasn't a childlike or childish love, even though I was only ten years old. It was a love that flowed from a part of me I had never before known. I found I wasn't as flip or casual with my mouth and my attitudes. I had a different appreciation for people. I wanted to give, to serve, to do for others and I didn't understand from where it came, but I felt such an abiding gratitude to Jesus I could not find enough ways to express myself to Him.

What a ride, but it didn't last. It couldn't. It was more feelings than faith, more fun than focus. I'll never forget that "first love" though. That change, the spiritual, emotional, relational, mental and even physical changes that take place at conversion are unique and uniquely timed. For me, there has been no other time like it. That's the first aspect of sanctification.

Sanctification *continues* throughout our Christian lives. It doesn't end with our conversion. Sanctification is a process that continues throughout our Christian life on earth because it is an agreement and a cooperation with God in the work of being renewed, a submission and obedience to being re-made in Christ's image and it will require *work*.

Notice what Colossians 1:21 & 22 states, "hostile in mind, engaged in evil deeds". You see, orphans (those living apart from God's Kingdom) are not benign souls, lost and weary. They (and we, for a time) are actively working against God and His throne. At one time, you and I were warriors fighting for satan's kingdom. Remember, there are only two sides in this conflict and we don't rate even a footnote in the annals of history when it comes to this battle. Two sides: God and satan; good and evil; life and death. If you're not on one side, you're on the other.

Paul makes that pretty clear in his writings to the early Church. In Romans 6:11 & 14 he states, "Even so consider yourselves to be dead to sin, but alive to God in Christ Jesus. . .For sin shall not be master over you, for you are not under law, but under grace." And in verses 17 - 18, he continues, "But thanks be to God that though you were slaves of sin, you became obedient from the heart to that form of teaching to which you were committed, and having been freed from sin, you became slaves of righteousness." And finally, in the second letter to the Corinthian church (3:18), "But we all, with unveiled face beholding as in a mirror the glory of the Lord, are being transformed into the same image from glory to glory, just as from the Lord, the Spirit."

Transformed, changed into what God intends us to be. When I accepted Jesus as my Savior, the saving work of the cross was accomplished at that moment. When I accepted Him as my Lord, He and I began a journey together, one in which He is the Master and I am His servant. Loving the Savior is trusting His eternal promises, but loving the Lord is living in the palm of His hand, yielding myself to His will, humbly coming to the foot of the cross daily.

There is a maturity that *should* come with time in Christ. Sadly, time does not always equal maturity in the Church. There are immature and stunted 80 year old Christians who accepted Jesus in their teens and wonderfully mature Christian teens who have known the Lord for only a few years.

Sanctification, unlike security or forgiveness or love, requires *effort* on my part. It is not about wearing a label or acknowledging a privilege of one's inheritance, but rather, it is about living in agreement with God that I am not perfect, but rather, sinful, and that I need to be changed at my core. It is about knowing God's Word and desiring to put that truth into effect in my life. It is about having family and friends look at me today and see me differently tomorrow as a reflection of God's work in my life.

Recently, I've had people come up to me and tell me I am much more patient today than I use to be (though there is a way to go in this area). That change is sanctification. It is God working in my life to bring about a fundamental transformation so that my spirit reflects His image.

This is the part of understanding my identity in Christ where I am to put those words and beliefs into actions of obedience. This is the place, apart from feelings, where God's truth intersects with my life and I CHOOSE (my will) to submit to His perfect plan for my life.

Think of sanctification as being an aspect of your identity in Christ like discipline is an aspect of a soldier's identity. If I were to introduce you to a 20 year veteran of the Marine Corps, you would, most likely, greet him with a degree of expectation. You would, not knowing anything else about him, assume that he was a man of great discipline. That is because discipline is an indispensable aspect of being a soldier. No man or woman could serve in the Marine Corps and be undisciplined. If he or she was, they would be "drummed out of the Corps". Discipline, is not only what a soldier does, it is who he fundamentally is. You cannot remove one from the other.

Sanctification and children of God are similarly yoked. The change that happens at second birth is undeniable and essential. By definition, once we accept Jesus as our Lord and Savior, we are forever changed. The sanctification that happens after conversion is an element of our identity in Christ. It is a continuous thread of purification and transformation throughout our lives in Him. Jesus, in Matthew 7:17 - 20, when describing the difference between those who have a personal, saving relationship with Him and those who don't, proclaimed we could tell by the work of sanctification in their lives. "Even so, every good tree bears good fruit; but the bad tree bears bad fruit. A good tree cannot produce bad fruit, nor can a bad tree produce good fruit. Every tree that does not bear good fruit is cut down and thrown into the fire. So then, you will know them by their fruits."

Faith in Jesus would produce change just like fire produces heat. It is an elemental aspect of the relationship.

However, continual sanctification is not guaranteed. You and I have to choose to participate. God will always love us and forgive us because those two elements of our identity rely on His character and His promises. He will not, however, force us to yield to Him in relation to change. We have to submit. Do you see the difference here? Saving faith brings about change, but it is not an automatic. Sanctification is like a chart in our lives on which we can graph our growth. That chart will show great spurts of change or steady climbs followed, potentially, by some downward trends and some zero growth seasons. Now do you see how interwoven grace has to be with sanctification?

Understand, in yielding to God in this process of sanctification, that *God is the primary force of change in our lives*. I can, for example, give over to God my self-pity for not having everything in this life that I wanted, but only God can give me a new perspective, His eyes, to learn to see what is really important and of value. If my issue is pride, I can agree with God that that needs to change, but only God can humble the proud and bring about eternal change in my heart, replacing pride with humility. If I struggle with an issue like addiction, I can agree with my need for change, but God is the One who will replace my brokenness and lies with His truth. This will happen when I am engaged in study, prayer, fellowship and accountability.

We are all at different places in this process of sanctification. God is the One who will direct what needs to change in your life. Sometimes, He is loud and obvious, screaming it from the mountaintop. More often, though, God works in simpler ways.

For example, *repetition*, that is to say, numerous people and Scripture passages bringing the same issue up over and over again. *Consequences of sin*, allowing us to reap a difficult harvest for sin, so that we will be spared a more painful harvest later in life. *Encouragement*, brothers and sisters who notice a change in you and comment on it over and over again, giving praise to God for how He is impacting your life and giving you hope in continuing to submit to God in that area of your life.

Our God is so creative. He will, when affecting a needed change in our lives, work in so many different and exciting ways. Our part is so small in relation to God's part, but God cannot and will not do His part if we will not yield ourselves to Him.

Now, let's go back to the example of a disciplined Marine. Where and how do you imagine that he learned the art of discipline? The moment he stepped off the bus at boot camp? Of course not. When he stepped off the bus at boot camp, that Marine recruit was, most likely, as undisciplined as you or I. No, it took weeks and months and years for him to learn the art of discipline. He had to make a *choice* that the hard work and effort and even punishment of being disciplined was worth the reward. He had to decide that advancement as a Marine, service of country, protection of fellow Marines, a life of order and simplicity that are the harvest of the seeds of discipline, a life spent in pursuit of purpose, and so on are worth the effort.

You and I were sanctified at conversion. You and I can now choose to cooperate in the process of sanctification in the rest of our Christian lives. To do so, however, you may want to step back and determine the rewards of choosing the hard and necessary work of sanctification.

First, remember that God chose you. What an act of gratitude and of love for you to submit to Him in every aspect of your life. What gift would be more precious to Him?

Second, the more and more time you spend in obedience to your Creator, the better you will get to know Him, living in the shadow of the Almighty's wings. What else in our lives has greater value?

Third, you will reflect God's glory and light in a darkened world. What a privilege to do for others what someone, maybe even God Himself, has done for you.

Fourth, you will be blessed by obedience. What ease in yielding to God's abundance.

Fifth, you will have the opportunity to draw other's to Christ. What a promise that those faithful with little will be given much.

Sixth, you will be spared the consequences of sinful choices. What a relief to finally cease in being my own worst enemy.

Seventh, you will come to the end of your life on this earth having spent the time well, invested wisely and will find yourself amply rewarded in heaven. What a portent of joy to come.

Eighth, you will be a blessing to your Father, a willing instrument in His hands. What an honor to be a small part of God's redemptive story. Ninth, tenth, eleventh and so on and so on. So many reasons to yield. . .

There is abundance in choosing to yield to God's sanctifying work in me. "All discipline for the moment seems not to be joyful, but sorrowful; yet to those who have been trained by it, afterwards it yields the peaceful fruit of righteousness." (Hebrews 12:11) *There is suffering in choosing to stand on my own two feet.* "Therefore, strengthen the hands that are weak and the knees that are feeble, and make straight paths for your feet, so that the limb which is lame may not be put out of joint, but rather be healed. Pursue peace with all men and the sanctification without which no one will see the Lord. See to it that no one comes short of the grace of God; that no root of bitterness springing up causes trouble, and by it many be defiled; that there be no immoral or godless person like Esau, who sold his own birthright for a single meal. For you know that even afterwards, when he desired to inherit the blessing, he was rejected, for he found no place for repentance, though he sought for it with tears." (Hebrews 12:12 - 17)

Before we move on, I want to talk about one more aspect of being sanctified. It is this: there is joy in the journey. As we walk this path of sanctification, we will endure many trials. Some will be the consequence of our sin; some will be circumstances beyond our control. All will enable us to make choices in how we will react. Remember, we are not victims; we are sons and daughters of the most High. Every necessary change, every bump in the road of our lives is an opportunity to meet Jesus in a new, deeper and more personal way. If your life focus is ease and comfort, you will be disappointed and angry most days. If your life focus is growing in Christ, every opportunity afforded will bring contentment and joy.

I learn more about my Lord in the valleys of my life than in the mountaintop retreats. I need the mountaintops for rest and restoration, but I need the valleys for maturity. The author of James understood that when he penned, (1:2 -4), "Consider it all joy, my brethren, when you encounter various trials, knowing that the testing of your faith produces endurance. And let endurance have its perfect result, that you may be perfect and complete, lacking in nothing."

I AM CALLED

We are *called* by God is certainly an element of His choosing us *in Him before the foundation of the world.* But, *I am called,* is also another element of our identity in Christ because God has placed a *call* on our lives for His purposes.

There is a reason that God, the moment that we first believed, did not yank us up out of this decaying world and take us home to Him. If He had wanted to do that, He could have. But, because we are still here, for a time, we need to understand that we are here for a purpose as well.

Paul clearly understood that God had a job for him to do when he penned the letter to the Philippians (1:21 - 24) "For to me, to live is Christ, and to die is gain. But if *I am* to live *on* in the flesh, this *will* mean fruitful labor for me; and I do not know which to choose. But I am hard-pressed from both *directions*; having the desire to depart and be with Christ, for *that* is very much better; yet to remain on in the flesh is more necessary for your sake."

Every moment of every day, we belong to God. In a celebration of that truth, we can *daily* bring God glory by pointing others to Jesus, reflecting our Lord, by serving at His command, by teaching and preaching and carrying the good news to the ends of the earth as we were commanded to do in Matthew 28:19 & 20. This passage, classically referred to as the great commission, says "Go therefore and make disciples of all the nations, baptizing them in the name of the Father and the Son and the Holy Spirit, teaching them to observe all that I commanded you; and lo, I am with you always, even to the end of the age."

The need is all around us. Widows and orphans living in poverty and illness. Abuse and evil perversions of all kinds devouring souls. Empty and devious sins like *lust* and *greed* and *self* controlling minds and hearts and appetites. People who need to hear about Jesus. People who need to be touched by His healing power. Men and women and children living in hopelessness, driven by need out into the streets, seeking that which promises freedom and only produces bondage.

The hospitals are full of people on the fast track to meet their Creator. They need to meet Him here and now; there is very little time. Prisoners locked in cells with metal bars and locked in their hearts by shame and guilt and anger who need to be freed from their spiritual prisons. The wealthy who live by mottoes of mammon (god of money), poverty-struck in the ways of God. Masses and masses of billions around the globe who are step-marching into oblivion unless they are drawn to the God who died for them.

"And such were some of you" is a phrase that perfectly captures the reason to answer the call. Most of us came to Christ because someone else has been obedient to the call that God placed on his or her life. Most, if not all of us, have grown in understanding and knowledge of Scripture because of faithful followers of Christ.

Most, if not all of us, have survived painful circumstances that would have crushed us apart from God's gift of encouragement and fellowship through prayer warriors and willing hands that eased the pain. Most, if not all of us, have been blessed by encouragers, nurtured by mature Christians and overwhelmed by those with the gift of *helps*, of *hospitality* and of *faith*.

In Romans, Paul incites us to action by this challenge (10:14 - 15), "How then shall they call upon Him in whom they have not believed? And how shall they believe in Him whom they have not heard? And how shall they hear without a preacher? And how shall they preach unless they are sent? Just as it is written, 'How beautiful are the feet of those who bring glad tidings of good things!'" And Peter, in 1 Peter 3:15 exhorts us "but sanctify Christ as Lord in your hearts, always being ready to make a defense to everyone who asks you to give an account for the hope that is in you, yet with gentleness and reverence". In Christ, we have the cure for this dying planet. How can we stay silent and sit still as so many shuffle off this "mortal coil" into eternal damnation and death?

Certainly, there is work to be done. Much work, too much work for us on our own. But here's the thing, God doesn't tell me that I have to meet every need - I can't. God doesn't expect for me to fix what is broken - I can't. God only wants me to follow His leading, using the gifts and talents that He has given me to address the needs that He places before me – this I can do. Remember, He alone is God. I am His child. I only have to do what the Father commands. I receive my marching orders from the King!

To understand that there is a great need in this world and that God has left me here for a purpose is to also accept that God has a unique plan or call on my life. There is a job to do for which God has equipped me.

First, let's understand what we mean by "equipping". To equip is to train, to provide every tool or ability necessary to accomplish a task. Doctors require 8 years of school and internship in order to be equipped with the knowledge, experience and ability to treat the sick. As Christians, God has provided the training (His Word), the tools (talents and gifts unique to us) and the ability (time, desire, need) to adequately meet the needs of those God places in our path.

Paul, writing to young Timothy in order to encourage him in the work that God had for him, spoke of this process (2 Timothy 3:16 & 17). "All Scripture is inspired by God and profitable for teaching, for reproof, for correction, for training in righteousness; that the man of God may be adequate, equipped for every good work."

Notice that answering God's call on our lives is completely dependent on God. First of all, He chooses us, draws us to Himself and sanctifies us in the process of being saved and now, transformed. God then equips us to accomplish the purpose for which we have been created and finally, God supplies the needs to be met. My part is simple. I am to be equipped, that is, prepared to answer the call. And I am to be available, willing to be used.

Several years ago, I heard two stories that truly blessed me. One was about a husband and wife, children of God, who opened their home to single women who were pregnant and without a place to stay. The women would stay, rent-free in a safe environment until they had the child, then this couple, in conjunction with their local church would attend to whatever needs they had to get them on their feet, either as new young moms or as single women who had given up their children for adoption. Sometimes, education was involved, often financial help. Always, spiritual and emotional issues needed tending. Whatever it was, this couple would serve. How many lives these two saved will never be known except by God. How answering the call blessed this couple will never be known except by God.

I also knew of a woman who kept her ears open in the small community in which God had placed her and her husband. Whenever she heard, in passing, of a family that had lost their source of income or had a special need, she would quietly slip into action - delivering groceries to back porches or sending money anonymously - meeting spiritual and emotional needs by meeting physical and financial needs first. I can't tell you of the thousands spent, nor can I give you a picture of how those needs were completely met. I do know that there were entire families and neighborhoods touched deeply by this woman's quiet generosity. In each case, she included a verse or two of encouragement, pointing a finger upward that God would get the glory and the individual would be directed to the source of "every good and perfect gift".

There are two stories in the billions that could be told. God has been using His children for centuries to meet needs, to bring light into a darkened world, to be salt in a world that's lost its taste, to be salve to open wounds and to beat back the enemy with the most powerful weapon of all - God's love.

So, let me ask you, have you seen the bigger picture of God's call upon your life? Do you know what it is that He has for you to do? Or are you one of God's kids who believes that God doesn't really "need" you and so you choose not to answer the call.

Paul, a man with a gift for analogy, refers to our giftedness as the body. In 1 Corinthians 12, he explores this issue by stating that "even as the body is one and yet has many members, and all the members of the body, though they are many, are one body, so also is Christ". And he goes on to say, "For the body is not one member, but many. If the foot should say, 'Because I am not a hand, I am not a part of body,' it is not for this reason any the less a part of the body. . .if the whole body were an eye, where would the hearing be? If the whole were hearing, where would the sense of smell be? But now God has placed the members, each one of them, in the body, just as He desired."

You and I are members of that body, uniquely equipped and personally called for service. What a powerful stamp of identity on our lives - we are instruments in the hands of the Master.

God called us to serve, therefore, our identity in Christ is as that of a servant. But, we are to serve out of the *overflow* from our lives. That overflow is our relationship with God through Jesus Christ. That relationship is made up of the following: It is prayer, daily and in desperation, knowing that we cannot possibly get through the day on our own merit or steam. It is study of God's Words and application of His truth that brings blessing and protection and greater desire for obedience. It is fellowship with God's people and accountability with the same, living in agreement that the children of God, like gold, must be refined in the fire. It is quiet time, along a mountain stream (or any place of peace and solitude), alone with my Father, my Shepherd, my Lord, being restored and renewed. It is victory in the battles, knowing that the source of that victory is the Lord Most High! That overflow is a filling in my heart, my life of God's faithfulness, His love and His power, a monument to His covenants and fulfilled promises. That overflow is a seal of our future, knowing that God, Himself, has promised to provide all of our needs in abundance.

It is a physical impossibility, however, to continuously overflow a broken or cracked jar no matter how much is poured into it. God has to mend the broken jar. Remember, He is the potter and we are the clay. Mending the jar or the brokenness of our lives is not difficult for God; it is, however, vital for us. He will mend the jar for His glory, for our sanctification and for His purpose, His plan to be fulfilled in our lives!

So, understand that our need for healing (mending of the jar) is an element of our equipping and preparation to answer the call. We need to focus, for a time, on God's healing work in our lives. Do you see that powerful connection? Stepping forward and proclaiming our need to be fixed is an act of obedience because it is in that action that we are committing ourselves to be used as God intends when we are finally, fully prepared to serve.

That is not to say that you can not serve where you currently are. Certainly you can. In fact, what you are doing, in small measure, to serve an Almighty God, will bring swifter healing and an overflow of blessing to you and to others. When you serve, your focus is not on your need, but on the needs of another, trusting God to meet your needs Himself. Pretty cool trade-off, don't you think? I focus on another and God focuses on me.

"I am called" is a daily opportunity to walk with Jesus. He uses His calling on our lives to deepen our faith and to grow our expectation of His promises. This calling is not easy, nor is it intended to be. Jesus never said, "Follow Me and I will give you comfort". Instead, He commanded us to take up our cross and follow Him, knowing that, in answering the call, we would find the very peace our wounded hearts so desperately need.

Dietrich Bonhoeffer in "The Cost of Discipleship" talks about the urgency of responding to the call by using as an example, Jesus' calling of Matthew, the Levi and Peter, the fisherman. Here is what he wrote:

"Until that day, everything had been different. They could remain in obscurity, pursuing their work as the quiet in the land, observing the law and waiting for the coming of the Messiah. But now he has come, and his call goes forth. Faith can no longer mean sitting still and waiting - they must rise and follow Him. The call frees them from all earthly ties, and binds them to Jesus Christ alone. They must burn their boats and plunge into absolute insecurity in order to learn the demand and the gift of Christ. Had Levi (Matthew) stayed at the post, Jesus might have been his present help in trouble, but not the Lord of his whole life. In other words, Levi would never have learnt to believe. The new situation must be created, in which it is possible to believe on Jesus as God incarnate; that is the impossible situation in which everything is staked solely on the word of Jesus. Peter had to leave the ship and risk his life on the sea, in order to learn both his own weaknesses and the almighty power of his Lord. . .The road to faith passes through obedience to the call of Jesus."

CHAPTER 3: I AM SANCTIFIED; I AM CALLED
GOING DEEPER: QUESTIONS FOR STUDY

1 What area(s) is God working on with you in the process of sanctification?

2. Understanding that we are called to serve, have you seen the bigger picture of God's call on your life? Do you know what it is that He has for you to do?

GETTING TO THE HEART OF THE MATTER:
APPLICATION

We've made it abundantly clear that identity by sanctification is yours by birthright (salvation) and by choice, consider these three scriptures, Galatians 5:22-23 Peter 1:5 - 7; and Colossians 3:12 - 13. As you do, pray for God to reveal what area(s) in your life need change. Ask God for the wisdom, courage and power to change it. Thank God for what He will accomplish in your life.

LAYING THE FOUNDATION: QUIET TIME

DAY ONE: Colossians 1:21 & 22, 2 Corinthians 3:18
List some ways that God is changing you, "to present you before Him holy and blameless and beyond reproach".

DAY TWO: Philippians 2:1-8
What needs to change for you to model Jesus?

DAY THREE: Galatians 5:13-26
Write out the fruits of the Spirit. How are you living them out in your life?

DAY FOUR: 1 Corinthians 12
Explain how the analogy of the body works in comparison to

the use of spiritual gifts. How vital is each part? How vital are you?

DAY FIVE:
Spend time in prayer, asking God to use you to serve Him.

CONCLUSION

There is a woman who has heard from her parents every day of her life for more than fifty years that she is a loser, a waste of space and the source of her family's difficulties. Recently, she has begun to hear another voice in her ears and that voice has been saying:

> Beloved, you are God's child!
> You are chosen; you are loved; you are forgiven;
> You are sanctified and you are called!

Each day since she has first heard it, she has chosen to listen to the new voice in her head and she is turning down the volume of her parents lies. Today, she walks around with a smile on her lips and a lightness in her step.

Here's the thing. Early in our study, I reminded this daughter of the Most High, that it took fifty years to build a belief system based on lies; therefore, I encouraged her that it might take a bit of time to tear down and re-pour her foundation on God's Truth. Remember, we are not going for a patchwork of feelings, but rather a firm foundation of faith based on fact.

So, every morning, I encouraged her to speak that truth outloud to herself, beginning her day with great promises. When her parents began their tirades, I encouraged her to speak the truth, in love, over their lies. I told her to write those truths and Scriptures down and put them all over her walls and office, reminding her throughout the day that she is God's beloved daughter. Finally, I encouraged her to spread those truths, those promises to all who would listen, knowing that freedom for one was hope for so many!

SECTION TWO:

GOD'S CHARACTER

INTRODUCTION

THE CHARACTER OF GOD

I met God when I was a young child. He was only as big as my child's mind and my child's eyes saw Him to be. Many of us approach God as adults the way we did as kids. We live as if He is limited by our understanding or our emotions and we don't take that *essential* step to see Him as He truly is.

The approach of limiting God, whether intentional or not, is crippling to one's faith, especially when the tides of pain or heartache rise. It is like building a mansion on the white pristine sands of a tropical seashore. It looks perfect and solid and beautiful on the outside, but because the sands are no foundation, not one brick will be left on another in the wake of a mighty hurricane. Rest assured, if it hasn't already, the hurricane *is* coming.

Most likely, you've already experienced a hurricane or two in your life. You've known the heartache and despair of loss or abuse or pain in a way that has defined your life. If you are like me, when that pain came crashing down, your understanding of God's character was built on your emotional well-being and on your limited understanding of Scripture, making the pain doubly sharp because you found a God so weak or cruel that He only added to the weight of your burden. Your past overwhelmed and buried you in the lies of God's cruelty and you limped along convinced that *if* God exists, He is a fearsome beast at best and a sorry, pathetic God at worst. And you spent your time trying to rationalize your faith in a God who is completely unknown to you.

Or perhaps, it has not been in the center of crisis, but in the disappointments of daily life that your relationship with God is less than desired. You try to live your life a certain way, hoping to discover the love, goodness and faithfulness of God that others seem to enjoy. You believe that if you can "do enough" service or prayer or deeds, that you will gain His notice and pleasure and then life will be less painful. And when the pain does come, you believe that you did not love or serve God enough to stop it.

At either end, God is either a bully or a wimp. We allow the circumstances of our life to define Him or create Him as a mere shadow of Himself. Sadly, we are comfortable with this shadow god until something big and ugly invades our lives, and then, in anger, we turn on our own creation and rail against the sky.

All in favor of adding some truth to your life? Here it is - *God is who He says He is, not who you and I believe Him to be.* That's huge!

C.S. Lewis, a former atheist, had said once when giving his testimony that J. R. R. Tolkien had challenged him to read the Bible cover-to-cover before making his decision about God. When Lewis finished, he declared that there *must* be a God because man could *never* create the God of the Bible. That God was far too holy, too righteous, too loving and merciful and forgiving than mankind could or would ever be. In essence, he said that man cannot create beyond himself and so God must exist separate from man because God, in all of His glory, so far exceeded man as to be absolutely distinct from His own creation. In other words, God is God and we are not!

I had believed God to be weak in relation to the power of this world's evil, but that did not make God so. God, in His Word, declares Himself sovereign, almighty and eternal. Hardly the trappings of a "weak god". Then, not only did God declare those things to be true of Himself, but He went on to show us His character in the miracles and stories of the Bible and in the majesty of His creation.

Here's the thing. If I continue to believe that God is weak, despite the teachings in the Bible, then the god I follow is not the Father God, the Creator God, but rather an idol of my own creation. Do you see how that works? If God declares Himself "just" (as He has), *the* absolute standard of justice, and in that character trait is an eternal promise that some day, all who have violated God's standard will pay, then if I decide that the God of love would never punish anyone because of sin, I have just created a false god. God has said that He is just, righteous and holy. If I choose to not believe that about Him, in word or deed, then I am not believing in the One, True God!

Let's say it again, *God is who He says He is, not who we believe Him to be.* Now, if God declares Himself holy and you and I believe that He is holy and we respond to Him in reverence and awe, then we are on solid ground, not only in our faith, but also in our trials.

God gave us His Word for many reasons. It is the good news of salvation to all who believe. It is the manual for how we, as Christians, should live. But more than that, it is our introduction to God. The Bible has a great deal to say about who God is. It is both loud and clear on His character, His attributes, His purpose and plan for this universe and our lives. And it is there for us to study. If God is who He says He is and nothing else, than we had better know what God has had to say about Himself.

As I've told you before, it was *in* the truth of God's Word that the healing process finally took root in my life. When I undertook the task of addressing the brokenness in my life, it became imperative that a firm and unshakable foundation be laid. To do that, two issues had to be addressed: my *Identity in Christ*; and *God's Character.*

I had to grasp the truth of how God views me *and* how I view God. In the former, I learned: I am chosen, loved, forgiven, sanctified and called. In short, I am God's child. No matter how I feel or struggle with the depths of God's love for me, I can not change it or lose it or even earn it. God loves me because of who He is; this is an immutable fact.

How I viewed God was another matter. In the past, I had taken my child-like understanding, beliefs and life experiences and measured God by them. He came up horribly short! In light of my wounds from this world and the shallow grasp I had of God's character, how could He have measured any other way?

Since then, however, I have learned that it is absolutely *essential* that I take my understanding of God's character and measure it against the only perfect and sure yardstick - God's Word. And when my understanding or what I believed about who God is did not

CHAPTER FOUR

GOD IS ALMIGHTY

"Oh, the depth of the riches
both of the wisdom and knowledge of God!
How unsearchable are His judgments
and unfathomable His ways!
For WHO HAS KNOWN THE MIND OF THE LORD,
OR WHO BECAME HIS COUNSELOR?
Or WHO HAS FIRST GIVEN TO HIM
THAT IT MIGHT BE PAID BACK TO HIM AGAIN?
For from Him and through Him and to Him are all things.
To Him *be* the glory forever. Amen."
Romans 11:33 - 36

When Paul wrote those words, the "oh" at the beginning of those verses wasn't a simple "oh". It was a gut-wrenching, lung-exploding "OHHHHHHHH!" that escaped his lips and oozed down his pen. Paul was trying to capture in truth that which can not be measured by words. God is God; there is no other.

Who is like God? Paul's answer mirrors all of creation and that of the rest of Scripture - NO ONE! The book of Job (11:7-9) puts it like this: "Can you discover the depths of God? Can you discover the limits of the Almighty? They are high as the heavens, what can you do? Deeper than Sheol, what can you know? Its measure is longer than the earth, and broader than the sea." The question, "can you?" would require us to become like God so that we can view Him as He really is, in all of His glory. The writer of the question appreciates the absurdity of the request. I can not even be god-like in my ability to glean knowledge in order to grow my understanding and truly appreciate how majestic and awesome and almighty is this God.

So, what does "almighty" mean? It means ALL. Not some, not a part or even a significant measure. It means *all* power and *all* might are His! Therefore, by definition, because God is ALL-MIGHTY, than, by reason, there is NO OTHER LIKE GOD.

GOD is **OMNIPOTENT**; that is to say, *all* powerful.

When I was a kid, I loved to hear about the stories in the Bible. Joshua and the battle of Jericho or in battle when the sun stood still. Meshach, Shadrach and Abed-nego in the fiery furnace. Moses and the Exodus of Israel followed by the parting of the Red Sea. God's ability to do anything at any time simply amazed me. But as a child, I never truly grasped the re-occurring themes in all of those miracles; they required the supernatural suspension of the "laws" of nature.

Fire burns, consumes and finally destroys that which gets in its way. But Meshach, Shadrach and Abed-nego escaped without even smelling like smoke though they stood in the center of a furnace that had been heated so hot that the soldiers who cast them in had been killed by the intensity of the flame.

And what of Moses and the Israelites being chased by the entire Egyptian army with Israel's only escape route cut-off by the Red Sea? Their escape, indeed, their salvation from destruction would require a miracle of epic proportion. The estimate of the exodus includes between 1 and 2 million people who crossed the bed of the Red Sea at night on dry land. In order to get that many people across, it's been estimated that it would take a 3 mile wide gap in the Red Sea so that the Israelites could walk 5,000 abreast allowing them to cross in one night. Cecil B. deMille in "The Ten Commandments" couldn't help but downplay the miracle; it was too big, too grand for any theater screen or television to capture. And what of feeding and providing water, wood and the like for 1 and 2 million people (not counting the women and children), DAILY, for forty years as they wandered a desert?

Each miracle, including the prophesied birth, death and resurrection of the promised Messiah in the person of Jesus Christ, is a mockery of natural law. Water doesn't part; the sun (really, our orbit) doesn't just stop; fire never refuses to incinerate; hungry lions don't just choose to fast; virgins don't have babies; two fish and five loaves don't feed five thousand. In those and so many other acts, we learn the truth about our God. The One who created *all* by spoken Word, controls *all* by the force of His will. God set the world in motion; does it really surprise us when He chooses to stop it on its axis for a day? The very definition of *all* powerful means that He controls His creation. No one else can.

And if the stories of the Bible don't convince you, look around and spy our natural world: the mountains; the oceans; and the vastness of our universe. Remember that our God did not even break into a sweat hanging the stars in their place. In a prayer, Jeremiah prays (Jeremiah 32:17) "Ah Lord God! Behold, Thou hast made the heavens and the earth by Thy great power and Thine outstretched arm! Nothing is too difficult for Thee". And the Lord responded (Jeremiah 32:27) "Behold, I am the Lord, the God of all flesh; is anything too difficult for Me?"

In Genesis 18, we read that Abraham was visited by the Angel of the Lord who told Abraham that he and his wife, Sarah, both near 100 years of age, would have a child. Upon hearing the news, Sarah simply laughed. The Angel of the Lord responded by saying in verse 14a, "Is anything too difficult for the Lord?"

The angel Gabriel proclaimed in Luke 1:37 "For nothing will be impossible with God" as he was telling Mary that even though she was a virgin, she would bear a child who would be the Son of God. Mary's response was: "Behold, the bondslave of the Lord; be it done to me according to your word."

Our Almighty God is *all* powerful. Can anything in your life be too much for Him to handle? Is there any need He can not meet? The resounding answer is one that we can *now* truly know for certain - "NO!".

GOD is also **OMNIPRESENCE**; that is to say, *all* present, everywhere.

At this very moment, there are some six billion, that's billion with a "b", people currently alive on the face of the earth and Psalm 91:1 reminds us that "He who dwells in the shelter of the Most High will abide in the shadow of the Almighty." There is no corner or end of the earth, or heaven, for that matter, where God is not. In fact, the only place that has or will experience the absence of God is hell because by definition, the absence of God is hell.

So, God is everywhere at all times. Nothing and no one is beyond His reach or His view. Again, in Jeremiah 23:23-24 we are reminded, "Am I a God who is near," declares the Lord, "And not a God far off? Can a man hide himself in hiding places, so I do not see him?" declares the Lord. "Do I not fill the heavens and the earth?" declares the Lord.

And no one place can hold God. Isaiah 66:1 "Thus says the Lord, 'Heaven is My throne, and the earth is My footstool. Where then is a house you could build for Me? And where is a place that I may rest?'"

As an element of His character but also as a reminder of our position in relation to God, His omnipresence sets us off from God in desperate and definable ways. I have forever been limited by the hands on a clock and the curve of the earth. I can not hope to ever grasp what it is to be in two places at once, let alone throughout this vast universe and beyond. God created the boundaries of this earth, including the limitations of time and of space. But as God, He continues to rule over both time and space without limitation.

David, a shepherd boy who studied the stars turned a King who ruled a nation, understood this when he penned in Psalm 139:7-9 "Where can I go from Thy Spirit? Or where can I flee from Thy presence? If I ascend to heaven, Thou art there; if I make my bed in Sheol, behold, Thou art there. If I take the wings of the dawn, if I dwell in the remotest part of the sea, even there Thy hand will lead me, and Thy right hand will lay hold of me."

Notice what David is saying. He asks, where can you go to hide from God? Not up (heaven), not down (Sheol), not East or West. Not even deep (the sea). NO WHERE!

David found comfort in *living* the daily presence of God. So many of us, however, find shame in that same place. We've been taught to view God's continuous presence only as the Righteous

Judge who watches and knows and never leaves. And while God does see all, know all and exist everywhere at all times, we need to learn to embrace this aspect of His character as David did, as a comfort. "I will say to the Lord, 'My refuge and my fortress, My God, in whom I trust!'" (Psalm 91:2)

I am *never* alone because God will *never* leave (there is nowhere for Him to go). In fact, Jesus used this truth to comfort His disciples who were about to experience the loss of His physical presence after having spent an intensive 3 1/2 years with Him. After giving them the great commission, having prepared them for their work and having completed His own, He said, "and lo, I am with you *always*, even to the end of the age." (Matthew 28:20)

God is present in all places and at the same time. It is an aspect of His eternal being (time is not His captor) and an element of His nature. By comparison, we live in buildings and travel through time. God is eternal and is everywhere at all times. We can not even comprehend His might.

Finally, God is **OMNISCIENT** which means, He is *all* knowing.

A pastor at my church once said, "Because God knows everything, we can tell Him anything." For days and weeks and months after that, I continued to ponder those words. The truth that I can hide nothing from God has actually brought a great deal of comfort to me of late. Think about it. How much time and energy do you and I spend in trying to "appear" or "be" what we are not? How much focus is there in our lives in hiding those dirty secrets and horrible lies and ugly sins? And now, how much relief is there in realizing that God knows everything there is to know about me, even more than I know myself, *and* He loves me anyway? 1 John 3:20b reminds us "for God is greater than our heart, and knows all things."

David in Psalm 139:1-6 whispered this to an all-knowing God, "O Lord, Thou hast searched me and known me. Thou dost know when I sit down and when I rise up; Thou dost understand my thought from afar. Thou dost scrutinize my path and my lying down, And art intimately acquainted with all my ways. Even before there is a word on my tongue, Behold, O Lord, Thou dost know it all. Thou hast enclosed me behind and before, And laid Thy hand upon me. Such knowledge is too wonderful for me; It is too high, I cannot attain to it."

What a weight is taken off my shoulders when I finally realize that God is God and I am not. I know nothing and understand even less in comparison with Him. God, on the other hand, is the definition of wisdom, of thought, of knowledge and of understanding. Nothing escapes Him and nothing is too complicated for Him to understand. The mind of God, referred to often in Scripture, is beyond our measure or our comprehension.

We are at the beginning of a course of study that will never end. You and I can spend an eternity learning about the character, the nature, the very heart of our Creator God and we will never reach His end. In fact, we will never be able to complete our study because we are utterly incapable of gleaning and then embracing God in His totality. Glimpses, that's all we get because in essence, it's all that we can handle.

God is too, too, too great and grand and beyond description. And that is where we need to begin to lay our firm foundation. We need to cull the differences between God and ourselves because apart from an appreciation of those differences, we will never have a right relationship with God.

I have no power over life and death, over natural law, even over my own destiny. I can't promise you that I'll be here in two months, let alone two weeks or two days. In addition, I am completely limited by time (the hands of the clock and the changing of the season) and by space. Finally, I don't know enough of anything to proclaim an expertise, let alone a firm grasp. I'm not even familiar enough with my own heart to accurately predict every motivation and every emotion. Chances are better than even, the same can be said about you.

God, in essence and by definition, is limitless in power, in presence and in understanding. And the curious thing is, as I learn that truth about God's nature, it doesn't make me feel insignificant. It only makes me grateful. You see, I *know* who I am in Christ. I know that I am God's beloved child; I am chosen, loved, forgiven, sanctified and called. And I am all of those things to a Creator, Sustainer, Father God who is without measure or equal. I am an object of His devotion, proven so by His willingness to sacrifice His most prized and Beloved Son to redeem, restore and reclaim me as His own. That is the big picture of a limitless and amazing Almighty God.

The universe was created by Him and for Him and to Him as we are told in both Romans 12 and Colossians 1. That, then, is the definition of almighty. In our frailty, we can trust His power. In our need, we can trust His presence. In our ignorance, we can trust His wisdom. And, therefore, in our brokenness, we can trust His purposes.

It is easy to struggle with the concept of God's omniscience, omnipotence and omnipresence when you have been abused. The question, "Why didn't God stop it" is a legitimate question. And I promise, we will address that in the chapters to come. Right now, our concern is to understand the depth and the height and the width of God's character, of His Being.

It is like painting a picture. First, we want to define the image with broad, purposeful strokes. Any artist will tell you that it is in the broad stroke that the image has its definition and in the detail that it has its value. We will get to the detail of God's character, of His purpose and of His plan. But first, we need to understand as best we can what an awesome and powerful God He is. He is bigger than our circumstance. He is stronger than our pain. He is of greater value than anything on the face of this earth! So with these strokes of the brush, we will frame the study of God's character.

GOD IS SOVEREIGN

Jesus, the perfect picture of the unseen God.
Maker of things we cannot comprehend.
Wisdom, the earth displays Your strength and beauty.
Sovereign, yes every throne knows you are God.
Every inch of the universe belongs to You, O Christ.
For through You and for You it was made.
Your creation endures by the order of Your hand.
So You must have in all things the first place.

Written by Matthew Westerholm (1999)* Used by permission

Sovereignty is the right of rule. A king is sovereign over his kingdom. He has the final authority to choose, to bless and to punish and there is no one in that kingdom who has the right to question that rule. God's sovereignty, though similar in theory, is vastly different in this one way - God's sovereignty is absolute because His authority stems from His unique position in this universe. He made it; He owns it; everything and everyone belong to Him. His right of sovereignty has nothing to do with birthright or even battle. It is His by force of creation.

God's sovereignty, then, is the ability and the exercise of that ability to act over His creation. Those who are in power are there because God has allowed them to be. "Let every person be in subjection to the governing authorities. For there is no authority except from God, and those which exist are established by God." Romans 13:1

What, then, about evil governments led by evil men? An appropriate question if our eyes were on the power of those evil men, but remember, we are studying about a limitless God. God's sovereignty, and the living out of that truth, are based on a powerful principle. This creation will never outsmart or confuse or even challenge its Creator. God's sovereignty is absolute and His purposes, His plans, even His passions are about Him and His glory. In that certainty, can God use an evil government to accomplish His will? Of course He can and He does - again and again and again!

If our lives were about ease and comfort, we could challenge God on His choices for some of our circumstances. But our lives are about something more fundamental than we can imagine. Our lives are about our one purpose for living - Him! We are here for Him - "Let Us make man in Our image, according to Our likeness; and let them rule over the fish of the sea and over the birds of the sky and over cattle and over all the earth, and over every creeping thing that creeps on the earth." Genesis 1:26

Remember what we said before, we are uniquely created to have a unique relationship with the Creator. God's attentions are never focused by our pathetic attempts to define our lives, our surroundings or even our futures. His devotion is to His glory, to His Son and then to His children. Even His creation of this heaven and this earth, we are told in Revelation, won't last. So, in God's eternal exercise of His sovereignty, He will accomplish His plans for our present and our future as He, the King Immortal, determines.

Over the course of my life, I've talked with many people about God. Scores of those individuals have reached an interesting conclusion that to this day amazes me. They believe that God does not have the right to impose Himself on His creation. His standards are too high; His holiness too stringent and His requirement for salvation (though free and available to all) is too brazen.

This thinking is a little like having a four year old question his parents' rights to set his bedtime or to make him eat his vegetables. By nature of their position, their parenting, their wisdom, age and knowledge, they have every right. But we, as pride-filled human beings, question God's authority in a way more absurd than a four-year-old questioning his parents. God is sovereign; the Bible is clear on that. He answers to no one and He is ruled by no one.

It is important to note, however, that sovereignty is not incompatible with the Biblical teachings on man's free will. If anything, God's sovereignty is underscored by free will. God has allowed us the opportunity to choose to accept or deny the saving work of Jesus Christ on the cross and His Lordship in our lives. God's rule or authority is not lessened by our denial nor is it enhanced by our acceptance. God is sovereign apart from our acknowledgment but that acceptance or denial is not possible apart from God being the absolute authority in this universe. The Creator of all the universe has given His creation the opportunity to deny its Creator. Only a sovereign God would have that authority and that power. We are free to choose (responsibility and will) because He is sovereign ("the supreme ruler, independent of any authority outside of Himself").

When Job questioned God about his predicament, namely having lost his family, his wealth and his health in short order and having endured the long-standing accusations of three friends, God responded in a remarkable way. He didn't defend His actions; He didn't explain Himself; He didn't even acknowledge Job's right to ask the question. God simply said (Job 40:6-14): "Then the Lord answered Job out of the storm and said, "Now gird up your loins like a man; I will ask you, and you instruct Me. Will you really annul My judgment? Will you condemn Me that you may be justi-fied? Or do you have an arm like God, And can you thunder with a voice like His? Adorn yourself with eminence and dignity, and clothe yourself with honor and majesty. Pour out the overflowings of your anger, and look on everyone who is proud, and make him low. Look on everyone who is proud, and humble him. And tread down the wicked where they stand. Hide them in the dust together; Bind them in the hidden place. Then I will also confess to you, That your own right hand can save you."

What was God asking? He wanted to know - who are you, Job, to question Me?

We are inundated with conversations and lessons about our rights as citizens, as human beings. We have, afterall, "inalienable rights" to quote several prominent statesman. And among those rights are that of "life, liberty and the pursuit of happiness. . .". And we are fond of quoting those rights and we even like to add to them. But here is the thing, when I stand before God, I have no rights. I have no authority to demand that He act or behave in any manner that is contrary to His own.

God doesn't answer to me. I learned that as a child when my life wasn't going as I desired and I demanded He pay closer attention to my requirements. Things got a little quiet for a while. They even got hard for a while. And then, after God had my full attention, He reminded me that it's His Word, His world, His way, His will and I am His child. God owes me nothing! I, on the other hand, owe Him everything!

Jesus taught that very lesson to His disciples in the parable of the vineyard laborers (Matthew 20:1-15). In the parable, a landowner goes out early in the morning and hires some workers for his field, promising to pay them a denarius for their day's work. The landowner went out again in the third hour, the sixth hour, the ninth hour and the eleventh hour, each time hiring the workers who stood on the street corner and promising to pay them a fair wage for the work they would do. At the end of the day, the landowner had the workers line up beginning with those who had been hired last to those who had been hired first. Those who had worked for only an hour each received a denarius. When those who had worked from early morning saw that, they were sure that they would be paid much more because they had worked a great deal longer. But when they stepped up to receive their pay, they each received a denarius. They grumbled against the landowner saying that they had borne the heat and burden of the day and surely deserved more than those who had worked only an hour.

The landowner responded, "But he answered and said to one of them, 'Friend, I am doing you no wrong; did you not agree with me for a denarius? Take what is yours and go, but I wish to give to this last man the same as to you. Is it not lawful for me to do what I wish with what is my own? Or is your eye envious because I am generous?'" (verses 13-15).

As a child, I was told that if I refused to acknowledge and accept the sovereignty of God, then my life was certain to be full of deep pain and continuous heartache. Refusal to embrace this truth usually stems from one of two places. Either we do not adequately appreciate God's right and might (that is to say, His almighty rule over His creation) and we place ourselves in some god-like position of questioning Him (which did not work well for Job). Or, we do not grasp that God's purposes flow from His position as an omniscient and omnipotent King and we lose the comfort of taking refuge in Him. Either way, we are immersed in pride and setting ourselves up for a fall.

God does not need a nod from me to exercise His rule. I, however, need to acknowledge His rule in order to find peace. Paul puts it like this (Romans 9:20-21): "On the contrary, who are you, O man, who answers back to God? The thing molded will not say to the molder, 'Why did you make me like this,' will it? Or does not the potter have a right over the clay, to make from the same lump one vessel for honorable use and another for common use?"

Embracing in word and in deed, God's ownership over all the earth, including me, brings me to a place of balance in my relationship with God. God owns; I use that which He lends to me (time, talent, resources, relationships, etc.). God plans; I live out those plans in circumstances, in consequences for my sin, in His eternal design. God acts and gives and allows and chooses and when I understand His sovereignty, I stop swimming up stream and work with Him to accomplish His good purposes.

God's almighty nature and His sovereignty speak to the very definition of who God is. He could not be God and at the same time answer to anyone else. And we see by what we've learned already that that power is absolute and His rule is supreme. There are, however, some things that God can not do. His is limited by His nature in several ways.

In his book, *Systematic Theology*, Wayne Grudem touches on those limitations: "However, there are some things that God cannot do. God cannot will or do anything that would deny his own character. . .For example, God cannot lie. In Titus 1:2 He is called (literally) "the unlying God" or the "God who never lies.". . .II Timothy 2:13 says of Christ, "He cannot deny Himself." Furthermore, James says, "God cannot be tempted with evil and He Himself tempts no one" (James 1:13). Thus, God cannot lie, sin, deny Himself, or be tempted with evil. He cannot cease to exist, or cease to be God, or act in a way inconsistent with any of His attributes."

The aspect of God's limitations that *always* brings me joy is this, God is faithful to Himself; therefore, He is faithful to me. If He says it, He will do it. If He promises; He will deliver. If He reveals; it will never change. How safe and secure and knowable is that? God is God; I am not. Neither of those two things will *ever* change. Trust builds on these two things – *knowability* and *consistency*. God's Word is our window into who God is. The more we know Him, the more we learn to trust Him. The more we learn to trust Him, the deeper our faith grows and the more intimate our relationship becomes. It is a cycle that leads to indescribable joy because when I trust God, my eyes gaze not upon my life's circumstances but rather upon Him who holds those circumstances, indeed, that life in the palm of His hand.

CHAPTER 4: GOD IS ALMIGHTY; GOD IS SOVEREIGN
GOING DEEPER: QUESTIONS FOR STUDY

1. In what ways have you attempted, in the past, to get to know God? What are some of the best ways to deepen that relationship?

2. How have you experienced God's almighty power? Give an example of a time of great joy and a time of desperate need.

3. Why is it important to understand that God has limits? (i.e. - Can not lie, can not deny Himself, etc.)

GETTING TO THE HEART OF THE MATTER:
APPLICATION

Read Job 38:12-39:30 and list all of the things that God, in His might and power, has accomplished. How does that impact your life?

LAYING THE FOUNDATION: QUIET TIME

DAY ONE: Genesis 18:1 - 14 & 21:1 - 8
How did God display His power to Abraham?

DAY TWO: Jeremiah 23:23 - 24 and Psalm 103
Have you ever tried to hide from God? Is it possible to do so?

DAY THREE: Romans 9:20-24
Do you yield to God as Ruler of your life?

DAY FOUR AND FIVE: Psalm 56 or 97 or 105 (pick two)
What are some proclamations about God's sovereignty?

CHAPTER FIVE

GOD IS ETERNAL

W e don't understand eternal. It is not in our nature to grasp
something that exceeds our capacity to experience it firsthand. In that we are all created beings, we can not know what it is
like to never have begun, rather to always have existed.

Curious, isn't it, that the first book, indeed the first chapter of the
Bible records time. "In the beginning". . .the beginning of what? Us,
our world, not of God. He comes before and certainly during and
especially after (the end of our world) and in that non-existent timeline is the essence of eternal. God the Father, God the Son and God
the Holy Spirit forever present, without beginning and without end.

"And God called the light day, and the darkness He called night.
And there was evening and there was morning, one day." Genesis
1:5 The chapter goes on to record 6 more days, our favorites usually
are the sixth day (us) and the seventh day (rest). In the center of His
creation, God established time and space, the essence of order on a
newly formed world. And God, being eternal and limitless, continued to exist apart from the limitation of His new creation.

God created time to bring order to chaos. Our lives are seasoned
by the spinning of the earth on its axis and the bending of one year
into another. Even our understanding of eternity begins with the
simple thought of one moment blending into the next until the
moments move forward forever. But God did not need to create
time to define Himself. The opposite is true. God is timeless.

The bridge between God and us is vast, especially in light of eternity. We have a beginning and even though death is not our end, it is an exit. Either way, we live our lives on a timeline of dates. The first date, our birthday, and the last date, our farewell from this world, merely bookends to all the dates in-between. God, however, does not need events to chronicle His existence.

So what does eternal look like in relation to God? It has several dimensions worth exploring. To begin, God and His Son, Jesus Christ are a *continually present existence*.

When God was sending Moses to Pharaoh to speak on behalf of His people, Moses asked (Exodus 3:13 and 14), "Behold, I am going to the sons of Israel, and I shall say to them, 'The God of your fathers has sent me to you.' Now they may say to me, 'What is His name?' What shall I say to them?" God's answer is more telling about His eternal nature than you or I could imagine. "And God said to Moses, 'I AM WHO I AM'; and He said, 'Thus you shall say to the sons of Israel, 'I AM has sent me to you.'"

God could have used any of His other names or attributes to describe Himself. The people of Israel were about to be tested by God in their faith as Pharaoh would intensify his abusive grip over the children of Israel before the ten plagues would convince him that he was no match for the Almighty God of Israel. In that testing, God wanted to remind them of His authentic self, I AM. I AM who? Exactly. I AM what? Yes, the One and Only. I AM HE about whom you've heard all of your life and I AM THE ONE who will now free you, lead you and redeem you from captivity. Pharaoh would learn firsthand of the powers of I AM. But, so would these children of Israel who heard the stories but now, needed to see and experience Him for themselves.

But God is not the only One who has used that name to identify Himself. In John 8:58, Jesus used it when speaking to a crowd of Jews, "Jesus said to them, "Truly, truly I say to you, before Abraham was born, I AM."

Both God and Jesus are not tied to a time frame or a timeline but rather exist apart from and independent of time. Even Jesus, who was born in a manger and died on a cross (two specific dates in time), told us that "before Abraham was born, I AM." Not "I was" - that is to say, pre-existed Abraham, but "I AM" - that is to say, a continually present existence. God has no beginning and no end; He is the eternal I AM.

It also means that God is present at all times at the same time. He has no past tense and no future tense. All of time is now for God. Because it is impossible for us to divorce ourselves from a point in time, this aspect of God's continually present existence can only be understood in light of His Name, "I AM".

In addition, God is *the uncaused cause*. That is to say, God is the Originator, the Creator and the Architect behind all that was or is created. But no one and no thing created God. He was the first and He is the last. He created all things. Colossians 1:16 "For by Him all things were created, both in the heavens and on the earth, visible and invisible; whether thrones or dominions or rulers or authorities - all things have been created by Him and for Him."

I love reason. I adore arguments based on logic. I am amused, however, at the arguments of the evolution crowd. As I understand it, in order for evolution to work, at least in theory, two 'some-things' came together and collided, creating the initial building blocks of evolution. So what created the first two 'somethings'? How does *nothing* turn into 'something' so that it can randomly collide and orchestrate itself into organized matter that eventually evolves? Sorry, I have to stop and chuckle at that.

At some point, something has to exist in order for something else to exist. If you believe in evolution, even the building blocks have to come from somewhere. And if you believe in creation, Someone has to be there in order to do the creating. And that Someone can not have been *caused* by anything. He has to be the *uncaused cause*, literally, the beginning of all that followed.

The Scriptures continually bring us back to the Creator God. Why? I believe that it is because we have to be grounded in Who did the creating and the purpose for which we were created. Throughout the Word of God, Old Testament and New, we see the threads of God's salvation plans, the fingerprints of His purposes. And in those blueprints, if you will, we can glean a number of things. One, we can glean comfort that nothing happens apart from His purposes. You and I are not hostages to the random evils of this world nor pawns in some bizarre game. We belong to the One who controls all things (sovereignty) and created all things (the Uncaused Cause). Therefore, even if I don't understand the "whys", I am comforted in knowing the One who has made me for Himself. Two, there is a reason for our very existence. I am no mistake. There is Someone for whom I live and breathe and have my being. Three, someday, the *Uncaused Cause* will usher us into the next phase of His eternal plan. This world is not my home. I am a passerby and someday, my Creator will bring me home.

Celebrate the FACT that you were not an accident or freak of nature but rather a careful and deliberate piece of artwork. You were *caused* by Him who is *uncaused*. What blessed meaning and reason and joy in knowing that we are part of God's eternal plan. Imagine the stamp of value that He has placed on your life!

Three, God is *the beginning and the end,* that is to say, *everlasting to everlasting.* "I AM the Alpha and the Omega," says the Lord God, "Who is and who was and who is to come, the Almighty." (Revelations 1:8) And in 1 Timothy 1:17 we are reminded who God is, "Now to the King Eternal, immortal, invisible, the *only* God, be honor and glory forever and ever. Amen."

We've already hit this point in several ways, but it is fundamental in establishing a right relationship with God, so it bears repeating. God is limitless; I am not.

Geologists and scientists of all kinds can use this physical world to define and expand our knowledge and understanding of it. They can measure time, eras, entire civilizations by empirical data. But how, using those same prescribed methods, can we measure God? The answer is, we can't. That truth is not meant to discourage but to encourage. God is bigger than my imagination, bigger than my capacity to glean empirical data and certainly bigger than my most reasoned intellect. Job wrote (36:26), "Behold, God is exalted, and we do not know Him; the number of His years is unsearchable." And the Psalmist proclaimed (90:1-2), "Lord, Thou hast been our dwelling place in all generations. Before the mountains were born, or Thou didst give birth to the earth and the world, even from everlasting to everlasting, Thou art God."

The prophet Isaiah had an incredible grasp of God's limitlessness when he penned (40:28), "Do you not know? Have you not heard? The Everlasting God, the Lord, the Creator of the ends of the earth does not become weary or tired. His understanding is inscrutable."

Saying that God is eternal then is like saying that the sun is hot. Eternal defines not just a characteristic of God but more, it defines God. If God were not eternal, He would no longer be God because He would then be subject to time as you and I are. In the same way, the sun is the sun because it is hot. Heat defines what we understand the sun to be. Eternal is fundamental both to who God is and how He operates.

Four, God *sees events in time and acts in time at specific moments and for specific reasons.* In other words, God, who operates outside of the limits of time, still uses those boundaries to accomplish His purposes. See what Paul says in Galatians 4:4-5 "But when the fullness of time came, God sent forth His Son, born of a woman, born under the Law, in order that He might redeem those who are under the Law, that we might receive the adoption as sons."

That phrase has always given me pause, "when the fullness of time came". Precision is the word that comes to mind when I read that, even the events of Jesus' birth, death and resurrection where timed perfectly. Every prophesy, every character's Old Testament story, the entire thrust of the history of the children of Israel all planned to lead up to one exact moment in history when God, through His Beloved Son, would make it possible for you and I to be restored in relationship to Him. The *fullness of time*, the fulfilled promise of God's almighty and sovereign Hand at work, centuries before I would know of my need for restoration and redemption. What a God we serve!

One of the great lies of satan is that God has somehow lost touch with His creation and that things are spinning out of control on this earth. It is easy to look around and feel as if evil has a free hand and that we are simply at its mercy. The lie of that denies, certainly, God's sovereignty, but more, it denies all of the work that God has done up to this point to accomplish His will. Isaiah 46:9-10 says "Remember the former things long past, for I am God, and there is no other; I AM GOD, and there is no other like Me. Declaring the end from the beginning and from ancient times things which have not been done, saying, 'My purpose will be established, and I will accomplish all My good pleasure.'"

One of the books that had a great impact on me when I was a child was *"The Hiding Place"* by Corrie ten Boom. She and her sister were two Christian women, in mid-life who were thrown into a Nazi prison camp for smuggling Jews out of Holland during the occupation. Reading the book, it's not hard to be overwhelmed by the horror of the Nazis and their talent for degrading and robbing their prisoners of all dignity and humanity. Reading the book, it's also easy to wonder why God would allow this family who loved Him and trusted Him to suffer such a violent and horrific end. And then, it's spelled out right there in the pages. The light of two of His children shining in such a dark and hopeless place. Jewish women, some of whom were about to be murdered, hearing the gospel of Jesus Christ and choosing to trust Him for their eternity. The frail and broken hands of His two daughters used to minister and bring hope to those who had no hope. One of those sisters would never again, on this earth, breathe free air. The other, Corrie, would survive to testify to God's power and peace in the center of great affliction. God's purposes accomplished just as He promised.

And then, the end of this age. The greatest example of a time-less God working at a specific point in human history to accomplish His purposes. Matthew 24:36 tells us "But of that day and hour no one knows, not even the angels of heaven, nor the Son, but the Father alone." No one knows when it is coming, not even Jesus, but rest assured, it is coming and God will bring to pass everything that He has promised. And just like the flood in the time of Noah, no one can hide, no one will escape from the judgment seat of Christ. We will all stand before Him and give account, some of us for the work we've done for the Kingdom, others for their sin. The latter will learn that an eternal God who has no beginning and no end is indeed "the King Eternal, immortal, invisible, the *only* God".

And finally, God's *view is eternal.* That's a simple way of saying, God's got the bigger picture in mind, even when it comes to the details and daily struggles of my life. And I've got news for you; God does not work on our timeline nor honor our agenda. He is zealous, however, about guarding and accomplishing His own timeline and agenda.

Because God does not view, engage or even deal with time as we do, with second hands ticking away, His perspective encompasses a much broader scope. Psalm 90:4 tells us that "For a thousand years in Thy sight are like yesterday when it passes by, or as a watch in the night." We are reminded that God is without obligation to the sun when it rises or sets and therefore not impressed with our vantage-point of "now". Therefore, He will do what He will do and when He will do it. That includes answering prayer, opening or closing doors in our lives and even changing our life's circumstances.

We've learned in earlier chapters that God is focused on our sanctification. Certainly, He can use that maturity and growth in our lives to bring Him glory and to bless ourselves and others in this current time. But, that sanctification is also a staging platform for the life to come. Philippians 1:6 reminds us of that when it says, "For I am confident of this very thing, that He who began a good work in you will perfect it until the day of Christ Jesus."

Remember, God knows what comes next before it comes next. He knows every moment of every day of my life before He created me to live even one of those days (Psalm 139). That gives Him a definite advantage over my infinitesimally limited vantagepoint, captive as I am to the second hand of any watch. In addition, because God is eternal and He has in His plans eternal things, God's focus for my life is for a future I can not comprehend. God is not interested in my comfort but rather in my transformation. God is my comfort.

In defiance of this characteristic of God, I've heard more than a few people argue with God about His timing, long and short term, (amazingly, one of those voices sounded remarkably like my own) an experience that is likely common to the majority of us. In fact, let's take a moment to consider 2 Peter 3:8-9 "But do not let this one fact escape your notice, beloved, that with the Lord one day is as a thousand years, and a thousand years as one day. The Lord is not slow about His promise, as some count slowness, but is patient toward you, not wishing for any to perish but for all to come to repentance."

Certainly, there is not one person who has endured the evil of this world who hasn't wondered why God doesn't just put an end to it. Afterall, we know it is His plan for the future. Why not end all suffering and pain and sorrow much earlier so that the young and the old alike will finally be free of this sinful and evil world?

Well, let me ask you one question. What if God had put an end to this world just before you realized your need for a Savior? What if you missed the deadline for salvation by one month, or by one day or even by one hour? Missed is missed. Aren't you glad that God "is patient toward you, not wishing for any to perish but for all to come to repentance." I sure am. Isn't it worth enduring the pain and trials of this world until all who've been chosen by God come to Him?

Hebrews 12:2 reminds us that Jesus "for the joy set before Him endured the cross". He did it for us. For the joy set before us, namely living with our God for all eternity, will we endure for a time, knowing that all of those trials and sufferings and sorrows have a purpose? They will some day end, and they may even be the light that points another to Christ.

Our God is eternal. He is timeless. He is limitless. And He is the Master over every tick of the clock, every turn of the season. Nothing happens apart from His will or separate from His perfect timing.

Genesis is all about the beginning. Revelation is also about a beginning, *the* beginning of life eternal with Him. "And there shall no longer be any curse; and the throne of God and of the Lamb shall be in it, and His bondservants shall serve Him; and they shall see His face, and His name *shall be* on their foreheads. And there shall no longer be *any* night; and they shall not have need of the light of a lamp nor the light of the sun, because the Lord God shall illumine them; and they shall reign forever and ever." Revelations 22:3-5

CHAPTER 5: GOD IS ETERNAL
GOING DEEPER: QUESTIONS FOR STUDY

~bc we are not.

1. Why is it important to understand that God, in the Trinity, is the *uncaused cause*, the only eternal Being to exist? How does that affect my understanding of my existence and of creation?

2. From what you know of God's Word, what are some of God's purposes and plans as described in His Word? How is He accomplishing them?

3. Understanding God's eternal view of your life, how does that change your perspective of your current circumstances?

GETTING TO THE HEART OF THE MATTER: APPLICATION

Read over the scripture passages in the book and select one that reveals an aspect of **eternal** that you did not know. How has this changed for you the statement, "God is eternal"? Praise God by praying the verse back to Him, declaring the truth about who He is.

LAYING THE FOUNDATION: QUIET TIME

DAY 1: Exodus 3:14 and John 8:58
Choose one and memorize it.

DAY 2: Colossians 1:13-18
According to these verses, why do you and I exist?

DAY 3: Revelations 1:8 or 1 Timothy 1:17 Rewrite one of these verses in your own words - focus on God's eternal nature.

DAY 4: Psalm 90:1-2; Isaiah 40:28-31
How have you experienced *the* Everlasting God?

DAY 5: Isaiah 46:9 - 10; 2 Peter 3:8 - 9
How have you been blessed by God's eternal view?

CHAPTER SIX

GOD IS IMMUTABLE (UNCHANGING)

"For I, the Lord, do not change; therefore you, O sons of Jacob, are not consumed." Malachi 3:6 There are times in my life, when I frustrate myself to the point that I can *imagine* everyone, including God, finally and completely giving up on me. Sinful patterns, bursts of selfish indulgence, pride and arrogance overflowing with no substance or reason, so full of myself that I become exhausted by those thoughts and feelings and actions. If *ever* God were to change His mind or His method of operation, I imagine it will be because I've worn Him out.

But that's just it. I can not wear Him out; I can not force Him to rethink or retool or simply adopt a new way of dealing with me, no matter how thickheaded and sinful I am. Paul said as much in Romans 6 when talking about God's grace. But it's more than God's grace that endures with me, it is the underlying truth that God can not, will not, is incapable of changing. In fact, He is the unchanging God. We see it in His proclamations, but more, in His practice. "I, the Lord, do not change; therefore you, O Carol, are not consumed. . .condemned. . .cut-off. . ."

God's promises, purposes, practices, perfections and being do not, can not change. What God says, He will accomplish. What God promises, He will do. Who God says He is, He is. What great truths! We can trust God because He is our rock, our fortress, and our safe harbor in the stormy seas of this life.

The Dutch theologian, Herman Bavinck captures it like this, "The doctrine of God's immutability is of the highest significance for religion. The contrast between *being* and *becoming* marks the difference between the Creator and the creature. Every creature is continually becoming. It is changeable, constantly striving, seeks rest and satisfaction, and finds this rest in God, in Him alone, for He is pure being and no becoming. Hence, in Scripture God is often called the Rock."

What a great distinction between our Immutable God and ourselves. We are in the process of becoming! God is *always* in a state of being. He does not need to change or grow or mature - God is perfect in all His ways!

And it's not just God's perfections that teach us and comfort us in embracing His unchanging nature, it is in His unchanging nature that we find true rest in God's promises. Imagine if this could be true: standing before the throne of Christ on judgment day and finding out that God has decided it's not just by faith in Christ that we are saved but that we had to perform a certain number of pious acts to make the grade. How devastating it would be for our eternal future to hang on the whim of a God who changes His mind. Or what about living through a period of physical and emotional drought only to learn that God's promise of provision has been revoked. And not just His promises, but His character. What if His standard of justice or His mercy suddenly increased or lessened? What hope would we have then?

God's immutable nature is the launching pad for all of His other attributes and promises because without an unchanging, consistent God, His other attributes would have no leg upon which to stand. He would be like us, captive to whim and fancy. And for our part, without the assurance that God never changes, we could never abide in peace or contentment or even joy. Our hope would be hopeless because we could not grow our faith in a God who changes day by day.

Grasping what is a simple truth "God does not change", we lay our foundation on the Rock of our salvation! "God is not a man, that He should lie, Nor a son of man, that He should repent; Has He said, and will He not do it? Or has He spoken, and will He not make it good?" (Numbers 23:19) "Every good thing bestowed and every perfect gift is from above, coming down from the Father of lights, with whom there is no variation, or shifting shadow." (James 1:17)

We live in a world of shifting shadow. Those who appear to be so rock solid over and over again disappoint us in their variations. In fact, consistency and trustworthiness are in such short supply, we are actually surprised when someone keeps their word or adheres to their proclaimed code of ethics. It's no wonder, then, that this attribute of God is difficult for us to grasp.

We assume that God, like many others in our lives, is going to fail us. Perhaps our fathers have betrayed us and so God, as our heavenly Father is measured by the same stick of disappointment that we've come to expect. The same could be said for most human relationships. At some point, everyone will disappoint us, or worse. But, as Numbers says, God is not a man. He is steadfast and immutable. God will not change with the seasons or fall with the tides. God is the only One who can claim this truth. God is immovable by nature when it comes to His character. What a cornerstone upon which to build our lives!

GOD IS FAITHFUL

Faithfulness means that God will do what He has said He will do and He will accomplish what He has promised to accomplish. We can completely trust in Him because He will never disappoint or fail us. He will not prove unfaithful to anyone who puts his or her faith in Him. Remember the great definition of our relationship with God? "And without faith it is impossible to please Him, for he who comes to God must believe that He is, and that He is a rewarder of those who seek Him." (Hebrews 11:6)

The emphasis, indeed, the essence of faithfulness to God is held by two unbreakable cords. One, it is *the* defining measure of His character. And two, it is *the* defining measure of our relationship with Him. C. S. Lewis helped explain this when he described faith like a rope. He argued that the rope would be trusted in one way if it was merely used to bind together a box and that it would be an entirely different matter should that same rope be used to hold one's body weight while dangling off of a cliff. The latter rope would be tested in a way that would be unlikely in the former situation. In other words, do you believe what you say you believe, or is it just talk? God is faithful to Himself; are you faithful to Him as well?

Paul describes the relationship of faithfulness, One to the other like this, (2 Timothy 2:11 - 13) "It is a trustworthy statement: For if we died with Him, we shall also live with Him; If we endure, we shall also reign with Him; If we deny Him, He also will deny us; If we are faithless, He remains faithful; for He cannot deny Himself."

What a perfect picture of God's faithful nature. As in our experience of God's love, He is faithful because of who He is. It is not dependent on our nature, on our beliefs or even on our actions. God's faithfulness is independent of us and completely dependent on Him. To deny Himself is to implode the universe. In one nanosecond, all would be lost.

And because of that certainty, God's faithfulness to Himself, to His promises, to His children is more certain than the dawn. The reality of these words are a comfort, a refuge, a place of utter security for those of us who live in restored relationship to our Father. In fact, Proverbs 30:5 promises us that "Every word of God is tested; He is a shield to those who take refuge in Him." However, the faithfulness of God must also be a warning to all.

In the next chapter, we will be learning about God's justice and His holiness. As we study them, we will learn that God is the absolute standard of justice. He has one and only one prescribed path to reconciliation and redemption for the debt of our sin - abiding faith in Jesus Christ as our Lord and Savior, trusting His death and His blood as the payment for our sin. If a person refuses to yield himself (or herself) to that plan of salvation, he or she will stand in judgment for that debt. No matter the mountain of good deeds or the massive amounts of regret for evil deeds that one may feel, apart from God's plan for salvation, that individual is condemned.

You see, God is faithful to Himself. He is faithful to His plan of salvation and faithful to His standard of judgment, of justice and of payment for sin. The promise of hell is very real. We know it because God promises it to those who deny the saving work of His

Son. But we also know it because God is faithful. He has said it and He will do it. There is no negotiating with God for a reduced sentence. You are either on the side of His redeemed or on the side of destruction. No credit here for half way because our God is faithful to the fullness of His justice and His holiness.

God's faithfulness is both promise and fulfillment. And even though He is a mystery in so many ways, He is clear on those things that He wants us to know and to grasp. God is clear about our future; we have only to choose. God is clear about His plans; we have only to obey. God is clear about His character; we have only to abide in Him. "So then, my beloved, just as you have always obeyed, not as in my presence only, but now much more in my absence, work out your salvation with fear and trembling; for it is God who is at work in you, both to will and to work for His good pleasure." (Philippians 2:12 - 13)

God is God; therefore, I can learn to wait on Him. Waiting on God is one the most difficult things we are asked to do in this life. When we can't see or understand God's intentions or purposes, we must obey, putting our faith in the promise of His Word, the promise of who He is! That is the nature of walking by faith. It is not by sight; it is by trust. As we said before, "trust builds on these two things – *knowability* and *consistency*". God has offered Himself up to be known by us. In fact, He promises in Jeremiah 29:11 - 14 that if we seek Him with all our heart; we will find Him. Consistency, however, speaks to His character of faithfulness. There is a great old hymn that *celebrates* God's consistency; it's call "Great is Thy faithfulness".

> Great is Thy faithfulness, O God my Father,
> There is no shadow of turning with Thee;
> Thou changest not, Thy compassions they fail not;
> As Thou Hast been Thou forever wilt be.
>
> Great is Thy faithfulness! Great is Thy faithfulness!
> Morning by morning new mercies I see;
> All I have needed Thy hand hath provided -
> Great is Thy faithfulness, Lord, unto me!

Summer and winter, and springtime and harvest,
sun, moon and stars in their courses above
Join with all nature in manifold witness
To Thy great faithfulness, mercy and love.

Great is Thy faithfulness! Great is Thy faithfulness!
Morning by morning new mercies I see;
All I have needed Thy hand hath provided -
Great is Thy faithfulness, Lord, unto me!

Pardon for sin and a peace that endureth,
Thy own dear presence to cheer and to guide,
Strength for today and bright hope for tomorrow,
Blessing all mine, with ten thousand beside!

In that growing trust, is a deepening of our relationship with God. It is not about us; it is about Him. Taking a look at the years of your commitment to God through Jesus Christ, I wonder what your hymn of God's faithfulness would celebrate. Is it His provisions, His control, His love, His justice or His mercy that rings through your heart? Or have you not yet learned to celebrate God's faithfulness? If not, let me remind you about our lesson on God's eternal purpose for our lives - it is not our comfort or ease that concerns God, but rather our changed hearts and lives.

God will allow circumstance (what happens to us) and consequence (the result of our sin) to interrupt our lives. We have two choices when that happens: one, we can submit to God's process in our lives and learn what He wants to teach us; or two, we can refuse to submit and refuse to relinquish control over that area or aspect of our lives. The former brings about change and God's good pleasure in our lives (rewarded either here or in heaven as God promises) and the latter brings about more trouble and pain and usually more sin. God requires us to have faith not just in the peace of a calm ocean but in the high, dangerous waves of a stormy sea.

Remember, He keeps His promises: "Come, let us return to the Lord, for He has torn us, but He will heal us; He has wounded us, but He will bandage us. He will revive us after two days; He will raise us up on the third day that we may live before Him. So let us know, let us press on to know the Lord. His going forth is as certain as the dawn; and He will come to us like the rain, like the spring rain watering the earth." Hosea 6:1 - 3 *unchanging — mutation - change*

CHAPTER 6: GOD IS IMMUTABLE; GOD IS FAITHFUL
GOING DEEPER: QUESTIONS FOR STUDY

1. How are you and I impacted by God's immutability? How does it change your perspective or deepen your faith?

   God will never disappoint. He is the one constant.

2. If God can not be unfaithful to Himself, what promises has He made to us that we know He must keep?

GETTING TO THE HEART OF THE MATTER: APPLICATION

How has God been faithful to you in your life? Choose one of the following: write your own hymn celebrating God's faithfulness or keep a gratitude journal for a week of everything that God provides, gives and bestows on you. Do you see the pattern of His faithfulness? Do you believe that God has provided and cared for you even in situations when you may not have been aware of it? Spend some time thanking Him for His faithfulness!

LAYING THE FOUNDATION: QUIET TIME

DAY 1: Hebrews 6:9 - 20
   What is our hope?

DAY 2: Jeremiah 29:11 - 14
   What is God's promise?

Day 3: Psalm 19
   Who is your Rock?

DAY 4: Psalm 34
   How is God faithful?

DAY 5: Proverbs 30:5
   How do you / have you taken refuge in God?

CHAPTER SEVEN

GOD IS JUST

—⌘—

There is a *standard* of right and of wrong. This world, however, believes that right and wrong are negotiable. It believes that an individual can determine what is right or wrong for him or herself. That LIE denies two things: one, that God is the ultimate judge, the standard of righteousness (God as the Sovereign ruler of everything is the only one with the RIGHT to set that standard); and two, we are unrighteous by nature and therefore not able to define any standard. It would be like asking a child to determine which of his/her behaviors is acceptable and right and which is unacceptable and *deserving* punishment. What child would acknowledge and accept punishment if he or she could redefine his or her behavior and avoid all punishment?

If there is a standard for right, there is a definition of wrong. It is necessary for God to punish sin because it deserves punishment. Christ's death and resurrection are the payment for the penalty of our sin, our unrighteousness. Just as God defines the standard, He provides a way, the only way, for us to meet that standard outside of ourselves.

We understand justice, then, as a moral imperative imposed from outside of ourselves, but in defining God's character, we must now focus our attention on the very source of that standard. A. W. Tozer captures that truth perfectly when he stated, "God, being perfect, is incapable of either loss or gain. He is incapable of getting

117

larger or being smaller. He's incapable of knowing more or knowing less. God is simply God. And God acts justly from within, not in obedience to some imaginary law; He is the Author of all laws, and acts like Himself all the time."

By definition then, justice flows from God. He created by His righteousness a standard, a Law that is impossible for us, as unrighteous individuals, to keep. R. C. Sproul, in "The Character of God" put it this way: "In Biblical terms, true justice is always 'according to righteousness.' Justice is not determined merely by an abstract legal code nor even by the collective decisions of the law courts. Justice is weighed by the standard of righteousness, which in turn is measured by the standard of God's character." God imposes a standard and by His righteous character, we are condemned.

Paul did not mince words when he penned Romans 3:9-20: "What then? Are we better than they? Not at all; for we have already charged both Jews and Greeks are all under sin; as it is written, "THERE IS NONE RIGHTEOUS, NOT EVEN ONE; THERE IS NONE WHO UNDERSTANDS, THERE IS NONE WHO SEEKS FOR GOD; ALL HAVE TURNED ASIDE, TOGETHER THEY HAVE BECOME USELESS; THERE IS NONE WHO DOES GOOD, THERE IS NOT EVEN ONE. THEIR THROAT IS AN OPEN GRAVE, WITH THEIR TONGUES THEY KEEP DECEIVING, THE POISON OF ASPS IS UNDER THEIR LIPS; WHOSE MOUTH IS FULL OF CURSING AND BITTERNESS; THEIR FEET ARE SWIFT TO SHED BLOOD, DESTRUCTION AND MISERY ARE IN THEIR PATHS, AND THE PATH OF PEACE HAVE THEY NOT KNOWN. THERE IS NO FEAR OF GOD BEFORE THEIR EYES." Now we know that whatever the Law says, it speaks to those who are under the Law, that every mouth be closed, and all the world may become accountable to God; because by the works of the Law no flesh will be justified in His sight; for through the Law *comes* the knowledge of sin."

The Law, to the Pharisees (teachers of the Law), was something to be kept. Strict adherence, they believed, would lead them to God. In fact, they were so taken by the "rule book", if you will, that they added hundreds of laws or rules to help them keep God's laws.

For example, the Bible says to honor the Sabbath and keep it holy. That meant no work could be done on the Sabbath. Walking a far distance on the Sabbath was work; therefore, they reasoned, no one could walk more than a mile from one's home on the Sabbath. But, what if you wanted on the Sabbath to visit your relatives who lived two miles away. The clever Pharisees came up with a "provision" in the law to allow you to accomplish that without breaking the law. The day before the Sabbath, you simply set out and walked one mile in the direction you needed to head and placed there a personal item, like a hairbrush. You could then claim that brush as an extension of your home, walk the mile to that brush on the Sabbath and a mile past it without breaking the "law" of no excessive walking and thereby working on the Sabbath. Whew!

The point of the Law that the Pharisees and so many of us miss is this, it's purpose is not to redeem; it is, as Paul states, to condemn. In other words, you and I can never be "good enough" to satisfy that Law. By God's standard, then, none of us are safe. That is what makes God's grace and His love so incredible and powerful indeed! By His own standard of justice, we deserve death. Because of His love, He sent His Son to meet that standard and to restore us in relationship to Him. One cannot embrace and be stunned by His love if he or she does not appreciate the depth and the measure of the debt that love covers. Redemption, for us wayward souls, is not a small thing.

Throughout the years, I've spoken to a number of people who wrap themselves up in "the God of love". His grace and mercy make the cut when they embrace the character of God. But it is God's justice, His righteousness and His holiness that almost always sets that crowd on edge. A benevolent God, yes. A Creator God, sure. A Father God, okay. But, a just God? A God of absolutes and standards so rigid that no one is safe? Absolutely not!

But, to ignore God's standards, to turn a blind eye to His justice is to deny His character, but more, it is to negate the fortitude and the magnitude of His abiding love. It is exactly what Jesus in Luke 7:41 - 43 meant when He said, "A money lender had two debtors; one owed five hundred denarii, and the other fifty. When they were unable to repay, he graciously forgave them both. So which of them will love him more?" Simon answered and said, "I suppose the one whom he forgave more." And He said to him, "You have judged correctly."

You see, we make two mistakes in dealing with God's standard of justice. One, we either believe that we are the ones who owe *only* the "fifty" or two, we believe that it is absurd for the money lender to expect payment in the first place.

Truth is, we *all* owe God the "five hundred denarii" (we are all accomplished sinners to be certain) AND He has every right to expect payment when the debt is called (at the end of our lives). Sin is debt, pure and simple. It is a violation of God's standards and so it must be paid to the God of unyielding standards. Sometimes, I believe that we pay lip service to the price Jesus paid, but we don't appreciate the depth of His sacrifice. Sin, every shape and measure and size of it, is grievous and filthy to our God. In truth, by God's righteous standard, we will all be brought to our knees by the weightiness of the debt and the purity of the One to whom we owe that debt. For some of us, it will happen here on earth as we bow our knee and acknowledge our need of a Savior. For everyone else, it will happen before the Judgment Seat of Christ on the final day when every knee will bow and those who have ignored God's standards of justice will be made to bear the weight of the punishment those standards demand.

There is, however, another side of God's justice we need to know. I like to call this side of God's justice, the "God's-got-your-back" plan. It was a promise first to His chosen people and now it is a promise to us, His children. In Exodus 14:14 we read, "The Lord will fight for you while you keep silent." Moses told that to the Israelites as they stood hemmed in by the Red Sea with the Egyptian army bearing down on them. And Paul picks up on that promise in Romans 12:19, "Never take your own revenge, beloved, but leave room for the wrath of God, for it is written, "Vengeance is Mine; I will repay," says the Lord."

In other words, it is God's standard that is violated when there is an injustice and it is God's right and place to seek what is due from that wrong. I don't have to worry about the injustices (sin) I've endured at the hands of another. I don't have to keep track and contemplate revenge. I am not to plot and plan the ways to seek retribution. I am to leave all of that in God's capable Hands and to His much more demanding standards. Psalm 19:7–9 promises, "The law of the Lord is perfect, restoring the soul; The testimony of the Lord is sure, making wise the simple. The precepts of the Lord are right, rejoicing the heart; The command of the Lord is pure, enlightening the eyes. The fear of the Lord is clean, enduring forever; The judgments of the Lord are true; they are righteous altogether." In other words, it is in God's unyielding standards that I find protection, vindication and eventually, through Jesus, absolution.

One of two things is true about all people. Either an individual acknowledges his or her need for a Savior and accepts Jesus as Savior and Lord or an individual will stand before a holy God on Judgment Day and receive ALL that he or she is due. As God's standard of justice is more demanding than mine, so is His plan to balance the scales. Those who have hurt me will pay later for their crime or yield now to the God of grace. Either way, God's got my back and I can trust all of it to Him. In Romans 12:17 - 18; 20 -21, Paul gives us the marching orders to follow when we've been wronged, "Never pay back evil for evil to anyone. Respect what is right in the sight of all men. If possible, so far as it depends on you, be at peace with all men. . .But if your enemy is hungry, feed him, and if he is thirsty, give him a drink; for in so doing, you will heap burning coals upon his head. Do not be overcome by evil, but overcome evil with good."

God's justice is the Rock! As Deuteronomy 32:4 tells us, "The Rock! His work is perfect, for all His ways are just; A God of faithfulness and without injustice, Righteous and upright is He." We can trust Him to be the Judge because He is true to Himself and will demand more of and from those who wronged us than we could ever demand ourselves.

The more we understand the punishment that lies ahead for those who reject Christ, the greater a heart of compassion we will cultivate for all men and women, including those who have caused us great suffering. This isn't an overnight thing, so don't worry if you are not there yet. But, as you grow in your understanding of God's justice and holiness and righteousness, your gratitude for Christ's death and resurrection will deepen and grow. In that gratitude, grace and mercy and forgiveness find fertile ground. Remember, we want to begin to see through God's eyes, to glean His perspective.

As Psalm 19:7 - 9 promises us, God's standards are liberating to those of us who are in Christ Jesus. They are a spring rain to souls ravaged by the injustice of this current world. Even in His highest measure, holiness, righteousness and justice, God's immutability gives us a solid ground upon which to walk. I am a sinner, certainly, but much more, I am a sinner saved by grace! Romans 3:25b - 27 "This was to demonstrate His righteousness, because in the forbearance of God He passed over the sins previously committed; for the demonstration, I say, of His righteousness at the present time, that He might be just and the justifier of the one who has faith in Jesus. Where then is boasting? It is excluded. By what kind of law? Of works? No, but by a law of faith."

GOD IS HOLY

The holiness of God is a subject too grand and too majestic for the keystrokes of my computer or the print of a book. His manifest presence throughout Scripture is always pictured as bright and blinding, grand and glorious, fearful and frightening; certainly, it is something that changes all who glimpse the very edge of the edge of the edge of His glory. He is holy and it is evident on His face, "Then the Lord said, "Behold, there is a place by Me, and you (Moses) shall stand *there* on the rock; and it will come about, while My glory is passing by, that I will put you in the cleft of the rock and cover you with My hand until I have passed by. Then I will take My hand away and you shall see My back, but My face shall not be seen". . . "Moses did not know that the skin of his face shone because of his speaking with Him (God). So when Aaron and all of the sons of Israel saw Moses, behold, the skin of his face shone, and they were afraid to come near him." Exodus 33:21 -23; 34:29b - 30 The holiness of God encountered in His manifest presence.

The holiness of God is defined as both a complete separation from sin and evil (absolute purity) and a dedication of God to His honor and glory (His manifest presence and plan). And as we see in Scripture, God's holiness impacts everyone and everything that comes into contact with Him. Each individual who saw even the edge or passing of His glory was physically and spiritually changed - Moses at the burning bush and on Mount Sinai; Paul on the road to Damascus; and even the "tongues of fire" that descended on the believers at Pentecost thoroughly changed every man and woman who experienced it.

Throughout Scripture, the prophets and the poets grasped as best they could the holiness of God. Isaiah captured a fragment of God's holiness and of God's separation from sin in the sixth chapter of his book (1b- 5): "I saw the Lord sitting on a throne, lofty and exalted, with the train of His robe filling the temple. Seraphim stood above Him, each having six wings; with two he covered his face, and with two he covered his feet, and with two he flew. And one called out to another and said, "Holy, Holy, Holy, is the Lord of Hosts, The whole earth is full of His glory." And the foundations of the thresholds trembled at the voice of him who called out, while the temple was filled with smoke. Then I said, "Woe is me, for I am ruined! Because I am a man of unclean lips, And I live among a people of unclean lips; For my eyes have seen the King, the Lord of hosts."

We are told in Revelation even the stones will cry out in praise when Jesus comes again and the angels are constantly singing God's praises, hovering in His presence, unable to gaze upon Him. In Exodus, after God parted the Red Sea and delivered the Israelites once again, Moses sang out: "Who is like Thee among the gods, O Lord? Who is like Thee, majestic in holiness, Awesome in praise, working wonders?" Exodus 15:11.

In his book, "The Attributes of God", A. W. Tozer tries to capture the essence of God's holiness in comparison to our sinfulness:

> "I suppose the hardest thing about God to comprehend intellectually is His infinitude. But you can talk about the infinitude of God and not feel yourself a worm. But when you talk about the holiness of God, you have not only the problem of an intellectual grasp, but also a sense of personal vileness, which is almost too much to bear.
>
> The reason for this is that we are fallen beings –

spiritually, morally, mentally and physically. We are
fallen in all the ways that man can fall. Each one of
us is born into a tainted world, and we learn impurity
from our cradles. We nurse it in with our mother's
milk; we breathe it in the very air. Our education
deepens it and our experience confirms it – evil
impurities everywhere. Everything is dirty; even our
whitest white is dingy gray."

In Isaiah, we are reminded that all of our "righteousness is as
filthy rags" and we can not truly comprehend the holiness of God
except to react to His holiness with an acknowledgment of our sin.
Apart from the saving work of Jesus Christ on the cross, we are
undone by the *holiness* of God.

In the Old Testament, we read the High Priest would go into the
holy of holies once a year on the Day of Atonement. It took four
other priests to pull back the veil so an individual priest could pass
through. His sin covered by the blood of the innocent lamb, the
priest ventured into the presence of God with a rope tied around his
waist so if he fell, he could be retrieved as no one else could go near
the Shekinah (glory) of God and live. God's holiness was/is nothing about which to trifle.

Many have paid the price for ignoring God's holiness. In 1
Chronicles 13:9, a man named Uzza was struck down for reaching
out his hand to steady the Ark of the Covenant, the most holy
symbol of God's covenant relationship to His people, when the Ark
appeared unsteady and ready to fall. And God warned the Israelites
that they were to stay off of Mount Sinai when He talked with
Moses, telling them that even a wayward foot on the base of the
mountain was punishable by death. Finally, everything and everyone who was to come near God's presence in the Tabernacle and
then the Temple was to consecrate themselves in preparation. The
holiness of God is a serious matter, indeed.

In fact, it is the holiness of God that mocks our litany of "good
works". For most individuals, their plan of salvation lays in the
confidence that they have in their ability to astound God with their
wealth of gestures and activities all designed to offset their bad

works and deeds. Regular attendance at church. Money given to the poor. A kind word said to an individual to whom it is difficult to be kind. Hospital and prison visits. A lifetime of trying to be decent and kind, good-natured and fair.

The problem is this, those good deeds, when laid before a holy God will be like a sheet of toilet paper standing toe-to-toe with a laser guided missile. You and I don't even need to see the battle; it won't be close.

God's goodness, as we will study, along with His love, His grace and His mercy tempt an individual to believe that they stand a chance at the throne of God as long as their goodness outweighs their badness. God's holiness, however, completely destroys that thought process. God's holiness is the whitest white, the brightest bright, the absolute essence of purity and might. When we grasp, as Isaiah did, a vision of the edge of the fringe of the train of His robe, we will finally understand our desperate and frantic need of Someone to stand in front of us when that day comes. "being justified as a gift by His grace through the redemption which is in Christ Jesus; who God displayed publicly as a propitiation in His blood through faith." (Romans 3:24 - 25a) God's holiness doesn't just prove to us that we need a Savior, it forces us to our knees in gratitude and thanksgiving that we don't have to face the majesty of that glory in our own strength and purity.

For the masses, then, who are convinced they can stand before a holy God and justify themselves on merit, the truth boils down to this - they just haven't grasped yet a vision of the edge of the fringe of the train of His robe which is overflowing His throne room. If they had, they would do anything to not stand before Him alone.

For those of us who are, hopefully, maturing in our faith, God changes our attitudes and our perspectives to match His. We learn to love and to pray for our enemies, understanding while we were orphans, we lived as hostile enemies of God. We learn to forgive, grasping that God's justice has set the final and only necessary standard for the debt of sin. We learn to serve, having been served by the Master, Jesus Himself. And we learn to grasp the truth of our nature; we are wicked and desperately sinful, especially in comparison to our holy God. The more we grow up in our faith, the more we find ourselves in agreement with Isaiah, "Woe is me, for I am ruined! Because I am a man of unclean lips."

We serve and love a holy God. His holiness is an aspect of His character that should and must rightfully bring us to our knees in fear and trembling. As C. S. Lewis noted, God is far too holy in the pages of His Word to ever be a creation of man's imagination. We would have made Him more like us, fallible, dingy and impure. The God we meet in the pages of the Bible is nothing like us. He is holy, absolutely pure and without compromise.

And yet, though God is nothing like us, fallible and unrighteous, He calls us to be like Him - HOLY. "As obedient children, do not be conformed to the former lusts *which were yours* in your ignorance, but like the Holy One who called you, be holy yourselves also in all *your* behavior; because it is written, 'YOU SHALL BE HOLY, FOR I AM HOLY.'" I Peter 1:14-16 (Leviticus 19:2)

Be holy. God does not call us to be almighty, eternal or sovereign; it would be impossible for us to be any of those things. But, God calls us, you and me, to be holy as He is holy. What does that mean?

To be holy is to be set apart. It is to be in conflict with the things of this world and to be in harmony with the things of God. It is to be concerned about the things that have God's attention, to have His priorities, His passions and His plans firmly in ones grasp. To be holy is to be set apart *from* the world and set apart *to* God. It is important as we try to grasp the holiness of God to note that we are called to holiness, that is, a separation from sin and a devotion to God's glory.

In the Old Testament, people and objects were set apart for holy use. Hannah, in her prayer for a child, promised God if He opened her womb (she had been barren for many, many years), she would set aside that child for service to God (1 Samuel 1). God gave her a son, Samuel and she gave him back to God as she had promised. Samuel, who became a great spokesman for God, was set aside as holy unto God and God blessed both he and Hannah. One of my favorite verses is, "And the Lord visited Hannah; and she conceived and gave birth to three sons and two daughters. And the boy Samuel grew before the Lord," I Samuel 2:21 How God blesses our obedience!

Here's the thing, if God calls us to be holy, then it is possible to be holy. This means in the activity of choosing to lead holy lives, we will be an example, obvious and apparent to anyone who watches that we are truly different. Notice again, what Peter said, "As obedient children, do not be conformed to the former lusts. . ." To be holy involves obedience. It involves making a purposeful and daily choice to be surrendered to God in every area of our lives. And it has nothing to do with what is easy or quick, instead it is a choice to obey that flows from our God through us, resulting in changed lives.

To be honest, I confess as God is changing me I am catching a glimpse of this issue of holiness. In that, I've noticed a few things. I've noticed I'm less casual about my entertainment. Not in some pious and self-flagellant way, but rather I find myself uncomfortable with television shows and movies that years ago never would have bothered me. I'm also more vigilant about stewardship issues, about people who have influence in my life and about how I spend my free time. None of which are perfect, but certainly they are changing. As I study God's Word and He is faithful to reveal to me areas in need of work, I am finding myself eager to see Him accomplish the change. I can tell you there are problem areas ahead, but here's the thing I'm learning; to be holy, I have to make the *choice* to obey God. That is where holiness begins and ends - with Him.

Most often we fail in the call to be holy because we fail in our appreciation and understanding of God's holiness. We do not fear and respect what an Awful (awe-filled) Being He is. Tozer goes on to write: "It was a common thing in other days, when God was the center of human worship, to kneel at an altar and shake, tremble, weep and perspire in an agony of conviction. They expected it in that day. We don't see it now because the God we preach is not the everlasting, awful (awe-filled) God, "mine Holy One," who is "of purer eyes than to behold evil, and canst not look on iniquity. . . If we came to God dirty, but trembling and shocked and awestruck in His presence, if we knelt at His feet and cried with Isaiah, "I am undone; because I am a man of unclean lips" (Isaiah 6:5) then I could understand. But we skip (wander) into His awful presence. "

There are two things that will lead us away from a holy God.

One, a focus on self. And two, a false belief that God's holiness is more hype (i.e. Old Testament) and less relevant (today).

The former is an issue of pride. And it will never be resolved by looking inward to resolve it. The only way to change our self-focus is to gaze upon Him in all of His manifest glory. Read the Word. Dwell in the majesty of His creation. Serve with diligence. Work yourself unto "death" and then sleep as a child, without thought or care. Worship and pray and be willing to submit to this God. All of those will lead you into His presence and in His presence, you will meet a holy God.

The false belief will change by study of God's Word, dwelling in His Creation, worshipping and praying. However, a false belief usually comes weighted down with a need for that belief to be true. We need that belief to be true when we want to control this God and make Him more like us.

In order for us to "re-create" this God and make Him manageable, He needs to be less holy. As we said before, we can manage a God of infinite love. But a God of absolute holiness will not be tamed. In His holiness resides the fire and brimstone of eternity and in that power, no impurity will ever survive. By definition, we are, apart from Christ, the definition of impurity. And as Lucifer discovered, God will not share His throne with anyone, least of all an unholy, pride-filled vessel of His creation.

As we've said all along, the holiness of God is an awesome and fearful thing. A. W. Tozer agreed with the Psalmist that God is holy and His Holiness will not be denied. *It is in the truth of His Awesome Presence that we are complete.* Tozer concludes: "I tell you this: I want God to be what God is: the impeccably holy, unapproachable Holy Thing, the All-Holy One. I want Him to be and remain THE HOLY. I want His heaven to be holy and His throne to be holy. I don't want Him to change or modify His requirements. Even if it shuts me out, I want something holy left in the universe."

What a thought - even if I am doomed by God's holiness, let His standard be the unbreachable barrier! No words can capture my gratitude for the love of Jesus that bridged the gap of my sin to bring me back into relationship with the "impeccably holy, unapproachable Holy Thing, the All-Holy One"! There is a God and I am not Him. What relief! What joy! What reason to celebrate! I am the work of His Hands. He is the Master of my world and He is holy. Proverbs 9:10 "The fear of the Lord is the *beginning* of wisdom, And the knowledge of the Holy One is understanding." We must live our lives with the truth of this chorus on our lips: "and I am changed, in the presence of a Holy God. . ."

CHAPTER 7: GOD IS JUST; GOD IS HOLY
GOING DEEPER: QUESTIONS FOR STUDY

1. Why is it important that there is a standard of justice? If God alone is just, how do I view myself? How do I view the people who have wronged me?

2. Describe holiness. How are we suppose to live because of God's holiness?

3. Imagine that you and Jesus are sitting down for a cup of coffee at the local coffeehouse. The conversation begins to turn toward the choices you are making in your life regarding such things as priorities and time management, entertainment, relationships, job, financial issues and work for the Kingdom. What do you think He would point out in your life that **needs** to be changed and set apart? What would you choose to change? How?

GETTING TO THE HEART OF THE MATTER:
APPLICATION

As I acknowledge God's standard of righteousness, I understand that God will exact a payment for the penalty of sin. If the person(s) who abused me does not come to a saving faith in Jesus Christ, what is his/her ultimate future?

Spend some time each day this week praying for that individual. Ask God to teach you compassion.

LAYING THE FOUNDATION: QUIET TIME

DAY 1: Romans 3:9-20
   Growing closer to God, do you feel less / more worthy?

DAY 2: Psalm 19:7–9

How do you use God's Word for living a just & holy life?

Day 3: Deuteronomy 32:4

Write out this verse and put it where you can see it daily.

DAY 4: Matthew 26:57 - 27:56

Thank Jesus for bearing the ultimate injustice.

DAY 5: Ephesians 5:1 - 15; 1 Peter 2:4 - 12

How are you walking? As one who is choosing to be "holy" and set apart or as one of the crowd? To whom do you belong?

CHAPTER EIGHT

GOD IS GOOD

A. W. Tozer, a man who spent a lifetime studying God, once stated the goodness of God was the only reason life was worth living. In his book, "The Attributes of God", Tozer stated: "When I say that God is good, that God has a kind-heart, I mean that He has a heart infinitely kind and that there is no boundary to it. When I say that God is good-natured, good and kindly of nature, I mean that He is infinitely so."

One of the truths I've come across in the past few years of study is this, there are things God has to be to be God. For example, He has to be *almighty*. He can not be God and have anyone or anything more powerful than He. God must be *sovereign*, the ruler over all that exists. And God must be *eternal*, that is, the *uncaused cause* who is *everlasting*. But, God does not have to be "good" to be God. It is not one of His attributes essential to His performance as God. However, *that* He is good, is both our abundance and our salvation.

Tozer continues "The goodness of God means He cannot feel indifferent about anything. People are indifferent, but not God. God either loves with a boundless unremitting energy or He hates with consuming fire. . . The goodness of God requires that God cannot love sin." Having just studied about God's holiness, we appreciate the fullness of His goodness in light of His righteousness standards.

God is good. Want proof? We live. We breathe. We can have a love relationship with the God of the Universe and we will be sustained on this earth by our heavenly Father until He comes to take us home. Everything we have; everything good we are; everything good we will be is all due to God's goodness.

Let's go back to the Garden of Eden for a moment. Do you remember our exploration of those first three chapters as we investigated our value to God? First, we stated that we were created for a unique relationship with our Creator (Genesis 1:26a), "Let Us make man in Our image, according to Our likeness". We were created in an unique way (2:7) "Then the Lord God formed man of the dust from the ground, and breathed into his nostrils the breath of life; and man became a living being." And even when we, through Adam and Eve, sinned, God reached out His hand to restore us to Himself, spilling the first blood to cover that first sin (3:21), "And the Lord God made garments of *skin* for Adam and his wife, and clothed them." This was the first snapshot of what would be a long and winding journey for God to redeem His creation through to the final spilling of innocent blood, the blood of the perfect Lamb (Romans 5:9) "Much more then, having now been justified by His blood, we shall be saved from the wrath of God through Him."

The tale *could* have been written this way: God made us for a relationship with Him; we, through Adam and Eve, chose to sin, believing the lie that there is something better out there than God Himself; God shrugged His shoulders, wiped out the work of His hand and began again, creating something that would finally have a vague understanding of God in all of His glory.

There are days, I have to confess, when I'm not sure why God doesn't just. . . but then, I am drawn back to the central theme of the gospel - the goodness of God poured out onto vessels that neither deserve nor grasp the value of His infinite gifts. "And a certain ruler questioned Him, saying, "Good Teacher, what shall I do to inherit eternal life?" And Jesus said to him, "Why do you call Me good? No one is good except God alone." Luke 18:18-19.

There is always a temptation for us as God's children to lose sight of God's goodness. The Bible is full of those who have been so blinded, having given in to a self-focus. Sad to say, that activity is not new nor unique among God's enemies. Even worse, it is not new to His children. Remember the Israelites, fresh from 400 hundred years of slavery, delivered by the Right Hand of the Almighty and within a few months, they grew weary of waiting for God's direction and instruction, constructing for themselves a golden calf to worship. How about David? "A man after God's own heart", made king of a nation, who despised God's abundance by taking for himself another man's wife. Nathan reminded him of that fact when he said (2 Samuel 12:7b - 8) "Thus says the Lord God of Israel, "It is I who anointed you king over Israel and it is I who delivered you from the hand of Saul. I also gave you your master's house and your master's wives into your care, and I gave you the house of Israel and Judah; and if that had been too little, I would have added to you many more things like these!"

How sad and deplorable, the state of our hearts in response to the generosity of God's hand. And how necessary it is to change our entire attitude when embracing the truth of God's goodness. The Master who created us, however, knows of our weaknesses and our proclivities in this arena and He has given us a method for reversing this trend and embracing the words of Jesus, "No one is good except God alone."

We need to construct, as the Israelites did, memorials to God's generosity and compassion. God taught the Israelites to do this in Joshua 4:5 - 7: "and Joshua said to them, "Cross again to the ark of the Lord your God into the middle of Jordan, and each of you take up a stone on his shoulder, according to the number of the tribes of the sons of Israel. Let this be a sign among you, so that when your children ask later, saying, "What do these stones mean to you?" then you shall say to them, "Because the waters of the Jordan were cut off before the ark of the covenant of the Lord; when it crossed the Jordan, the waters of the Jordan were cut off." So these stones shall become a memorial to the sons of Israel forever."

We need to make for ourselves memorials to God's goodness. To do that, we need to embrace the *fullness* of God's goodness to us. God bestows, more He lavishes upon us a bounty beyond description and in response, we throw up our hands and ask for more. Now is the time for us to learn to throw up our hands in thanksgiving and to sing of God's goodness in and throughout our lives.

To begin, God created you. He was the Initiator, not you.

Sometimes, we live as if the opposite is true. That somehow God did not begin until we did, or that somehow we have caught His eye through some merit of our own. I have even been asked this question more than once, "Why should I thank God for making me? I didn't ask to be here."

I was created for God. To enjoy Him, to experience Him and thanks to Jesus to know Him as my Father and King! I did not ask to be here because I could not have known to do so (nor would I have been able to do so in that I did not pre-exist God). But now, having been created, I am eternally grateful to have been so blessed! I have been uniquely created to have a unique relationship with the One and only God Almighty! I am the work of His hands and my soul knows so well the purest of all joys - the goodness of this King Eternal. If your perspective differs, then your eyes are not on our God. To gaze upon His manifest presence is to be eternally grateful for the gift of sight.

His goodness, having created us, leads us to this question: why were we not destroyed for our sins? We just studied about our holy and just God. There is no way to embrace even a molecule of God's holiness without asking, "Why were we spared?". Let's turn to Tozer again, "The only answer is that God of His goodness spared us. The cordial, kind-intentioned God spared us." And in Titus 3:5 we read, "He saved us, not on the basis of deeds which we have done in righteousness, but according to His mercy. . ."

Certainly, we did not *deserve* to be born. But now, in our sin, we *deserved* only death. Daily, then, we need to thank God for His goodness and mercy. We are living memorial stones to the power of His goodness because we not only live, but now, we have abundant life through Jesus Christ. We need to be mindful of His sacrifice, knowing that in His agape love, "He did not even spare His own Son, but delivered Him up for us all" (Romans 8:32).

If you can possibly wrap your mind around the fact that in God's goodness, we have our life and now, our salvation. Then, the time has come to embrace that there is even more to God's goodness. Creation is about beginnings and salvation is about eternity, but what about the years in-between? You and I are living in hostile territory. This is the land of the evil one and he reigns for a time. In that, it is God's sustaining power that defines both His love and His goodness to us.

God answers prayers. He doesn't have to answer them; He is under no obligation to His creation. Remember, He owes us nothing. Again, Tozer points out: "Nobody ever got anything from God on the grounds that he deserved it. Having fallen, man deserves only punishment and death. So if God answers prayer it's because God is good. From His goodness, His loving kindness, His good-natured benevolence, God does it! That's the source of everything."

When I "let my requests be made known to God" (Philippians 4:6b), I am celebrating and basking in God's goodness, His abundance and generosity. In truth, it pleases God for me to ask because in asking, I am confessing that He is the only One who can meet my need. I am also reinforcing the truth about my relationship to Him. He is God; I am His child. That truth can not be repeated too often. Admittedly, I've learned that the hard way. When I demand that God do *this,* or that He respond to *that* by this time, I have forgotten the truth of our relationship, namely that God bestows blessing, allows difficult circumstances and cares for me out of His loving kindness. It is not the other way around.

If by now, you have not been convinced of God's position in His universe, then you will never grasp the truth that our lives are lived in the palm of His hands. Nothing happens apart from His will, not the "good stuff", the "bad stuff" or the just plain "frustrating stuff". God teaches and grows us, reveals Himself and moves us through time toward His eternity. When you can receive from Him the painful and necessary moments of sanctification, then you can truly receive from His hands the abundance of blessing that He daily bestows. Both have dual purposes: to glorify Him and to remake us.

Jesus reminds us of our Father's intentions in Matthew 7:7-12 ". . .if you then, being evil, know how to give good gifts to your children, how much more shall your Father who is in heaven. . .". And James continues that thought (1:17) "Every good thing bestowed and every perfect gift is from above, coming down from the Father of lights, with whom there is no variation, or shifting shadow." God is our Defender, our Sustainer and our Champion. The kind intention of a benevolent God!

Embracing the truth that you and I have experienced God's goodness through every moment of every day, we need to be mindful to the point of redundancy in proclaiming that truth. We need to build for ourselves so many memorial stones that we fairly trip over them with every step throughout the normal course of daily activity. Not that they become ritualistic, but rather, that we are overwhelmed at the sight of them, hoisting them overhead in our moments of celebration and clutching them to our breasts in sighs of deep agony. We need to remind ourselves with every act of kindness by God that He is responding in charity to those who deserve condemnation.

Several years ago, I lived in what I affectionately called "the cave". It was an efficiency apartment about the size of a dorm room but without the charm. It had two windows in a northern exposure so it did not get much light. The floor tilted radically south and the landlord merely laid carpeting on rotten wood. The stove had two settings - off and burnt. The pipes hissed and in the middle of the night when it was cold, they would start to bang as if someone was taking a lead pipe to them. To top it off, I was flooded twice by the elderly woman who lived upstairs. To be blunt, I hated it.

But, God has given me a sister in Christ who has a true gift for getting to the heart of a matter. In my anguish over this place, she reminded me that I needed to thank God because "the cave" was a gift. I politely ignored her suggestions for six months. They were miserable months. One day, through tears, I finally heard her words and I prayed. "God, thank you for this place. It is warm (the wind was howling outside); it is safe; it is dry (usually) and I am fortunate to have it. I'm sorry for my attitude and I appreciate all you've given me. In Christ's Name, Amen."

Those weren't just words. As I prayed and for weeks after as I would pray that prayer, God truly changed my heart to one of gratitude for the place. Within three months, God made it possible for me to move out and into a new apartment that was three times the size and that had a balcony, a fireplace and a working, completely functional kitchen (and stove). Learning to see my old place as a gift gave me a thankful heart for my new place. Now, every time I return home, it is a memorial stone to me of God's goodness and generosity.

Several years ago, there was a saying that made the rounds and I believe it needs to be resurrected. Someone would say, "God is good!" to which another would reply, "All the time!" and then both would finish up with "All the time, God is good!". He is not just good when He gives us what we want or He answers a prayer in a certain way. God is good, every minute of every day in every circumstance and in every way. Joseph knew this when his brothers confronted him after the death of their father. Joseph, as a young man, had been beaten by his brothers to the edge of death, then sold into slavery, falsely accused and thrown into jail for many years before God finally, through some miraculous circumstances, brought him into power in Egypt, second in command to Pharaoh himself. A famine in the land drove Joseph's brothers to Egypt in search of food and eventually, Joseph and they were reconnected. Shortly after their father's death, however, they were frightened Joseph would take the opportunity to even the score with them. But Joseph knew God very well and he put their minds to ease with this incredible statement: "But Joseph said to them, "Do not be afraid, for am I in God's place? And as for you, you meant evil against me, but God meant it for good in order to bring about this present result, to preserve many people alive." Genesis 50:19 - 20.

We've already learned that our God is eternal and almighty and sovereign. He has purposes and plans beyond our limited line of sight. Part of building our faith on the facts of God's truth is believing in all aspects of God's character. That means that while I know that God is holy and just, I also believe Him to be completely good and compassionate. Living that out means trusting Him with every hurtful and painful life circumstance.

In addition, while God is committed to allowing His creation the freedom to choose to accept or reject Him, that does not mean God is not grieved over the pain others have caused us. The opposite is true. Remember the lesson about God's justice? God's goodness is what offers us hope and healing. It is because of God's goodness that we can step away from our deep, difficult wound and find ourselves in His soothing arms.

Over the course of the last several years, an amazing thing has happened to me. I've met numerous people who have been broken,

CHAPTER 8: GOD IS GOOD
GOING DEEPER: QUESTIONS FOR STUDY

1. Express God's goodness by listing ten ways in which God has been good to you.

2. Grasping God's goodness and compassion as best you can, how does that change your view or understanding of the painful moments in your life?

3. How does God's goodness and compassion work in relation to His justice and holiness? What was necessary for God to do to satisfy these four aspects of His character in regard to His relationship with us?

THE HEART OF THE MATTER:
APPLICATION AND QUIET TIME

QUESTIONS TO ASK AS YOU STUDY GOD'S WORD THIS WEEK:

1. What does the passage TEACH about God's goodness and compassion?

2. How am I CHANGED by this teaching on God's goodness and compassion?

DAY ONE: Genesis 1:1 - 31; John 3:16; Revelations 3:20

DAY TWO: Psalm 34; Acts 2

DAY THREE: Psalm 8; Jeremiah 29:11 - 14

DAY FOUR: Isaiah 53:1 - 11; John 1:1 - 13

CHAPTER NINE

GOD IS LOVE

"You called, you cried, you shattered my deafness,
you sparkled, you blazed, you drove away my blindness,
you shed your fragrance, and I drew in my breath,
and I pant for you."
Saint Augustine

What a picture Saint Augustine is painting - God, our very breath, our daily sustenance, our sense of sight, of sound, of fragrance. It is no wonder people love to study about this God of love. He is potent and pure, an attraction unlike any other. He has drawn us into a relationship that is bound on every side by the fullness and measure of His abiding and abundant love. David declares in Psalm 34:8, "O taste and see that the Lord is good; how blessed is the man who takes refuge in Him!"

But as we've studied, God is not *just* love. He is also holy. He is just and righteous. He is almighty and sovereign and eternal. And for those who've sold themselves on a one-dimensional God of love, we're going to take a look at the truth that it is only in all of God's other attributes that His love has its full definition.

To begin, God's love is about relationship. He created us for Him, to have a daily, intimate relationship with the Creator God, the Father God. Then, sin entered into the picture and that relationship between us and the holy God was broken. But the almighty God had laid the foundation of the earth knowing He would have to redeem the creation of His hands in order to restore us into an abiding and enduring love relationship.

Sound familiar? It is. It is the reoccurring theme of the Bible and certainly of this book up to this point. But, it bears repeating because you and I have just spent the past several chapters exploring God's other attributes. And in that study, we have learned somethings about the nature of God. He is absolute, the definition of power, of control, of purity, of uprightness and of judgment. He is never a God of compromise or of tolerance. The face that God Himself shows us over and over again in Scripture is that of an unyielding, immovable, perfect God who is the same, yesterday, today and tomorrow.

Why is that important as we study God's love? Because, we need to understand the price that His love paid to ransom us from the debt, the bondage of sin. Remember the story of Gomer and Hosea? The righteous prophet redeeming his unfaithful, prostitute wife from her chosen bondage, a picture of God's faithfulness to Himself in an expression of love to His unfaithful bride – a picture of Israel then, and of us now.

You see, God's love is not a marshmallow, gooey and soft and warm, inviting all to come and take a nibble until they are full. You may laugh at that, but how many people do you know who approach God as if His love is that inconsequential and small? God's love is impactful and enormous, willing literally to sacrifice His Beloved Son in order to fulfill the just penalty of death placed on our heads. God's love is a perfecting force, determined to change you and I so that we will resemble that Beloved Son. And God's love is a sustaining power that will usher us, responsible for the torture and unjust death of His Beloved Son but who have now accepted the free gift of His salvation, into our eternal rest. God's love is not a small thing. Indeed, it is the most powerful and sustained force of this universe. His love allowed Him to create us - the ones who've caused Him pain almost from day one.

God has always been defined by love. The love relationship between God the Father, God the Son and God the Holy Spirit has existed throughout ALL of time! In John 17:24 we read, "Father, I desire that they also, whom Thou hast given Me, be with me where I am, in order that they may behold My glory, which Thou hast given Me; for Thou didst love Me before the foundation of the world." And again in John 3:35, "The Father loves the Son, and has given all things into His hand." And Jesus proclaimed His love for the Father through word and deed in John 14:31a "but that the world may know that I love the Father, and as the Father gave Me commandment, even so I do."

In fact, we learn a great deal about love by observing those Three-in-One relationships. God's devotion to His Son; His Son's devotion to His Father and the Spirit's devotion to both Father and Son is visible in this, their passions, their priorities and their obedience. Jesus made it incredibly clear throughout the Gospels that His love for God was proclaimed in His obedience to God's will and God's Word. I wonder, as we study about God's love, if our thoughts are drawn to what we can get from God's love or rather, how we can live out that love ourselves, in our purposeful obedience and submission. In "That Incredible Christian", A. W. Tozer related to the latter, "Our Lord told His disciples that love and obedience were organically united. The final test of love is obedience." So, in using God's relationships within the Godhead as our guide, let me ask you this: to whom are you devoted?

Devotion, one to another, is so precious a thing. To be purely and consistently concerned with another's well being. To be passionate about another's reputation. To be driven at any length and to pay any cost for the greatest benefit to the object of one's devotion. To be consumed with the safety, the needs, the joys of that soul, that is what it is to be in love. To give of oneself in a world which proclaims that *self* rules supreme and to serve when all others expect to be served, that is the picture of our God and His love. It costs far more than we can imagine and it often pays off in heartache and difficulty. It makes little sense, but without it, nothing would be of value.

Love always comes at a price. C. S. Lewis in his book, "The Four Loves", explores the cost of love in our lives: "To love at all is to be vulnerable. Love anything, and your heart will certainly be wrung and possibly be broken. If you want to make sure of keeping it intact, you must give your heart to no one, not even to an animal. Wrap it carefully round with hobbies and little luxuries; avoid all entanglements; lock it up safe in the casket or coffin of your selfishness. But in that casket – safe, dark, motionless, airless – it will change. It will not be broken; it will become unbreakable, impenetrable, irredeemable. The alternative to tragedy, or at least to the risk of tragedy, is damnation. The only place outside Heaven where you can be perfectly safe from all the dangers and perturbations of love is Hell."

That God is love speaks to His nature, His heart, but it also speaks to His willingness to pay the price that love demands. If you haven't heard it enough, let me say it again, you were not cheap to redeem. You and I were rather pricey to bring back into relationship with God. 1 John 4:7-10 demonstrates this, "Beloved, let us love one another, for love is from God; and everyone who loves is born of God and knows God. The one who does not love does not know God, for God is love. By this the love of God was manifested in us, that God has sent His only begotten Son into the world so that we might live through Him. In this is love, not that we loved God, but that He loved us and sent His Son *to be* the propitiation for our sins."

In that, I wonder how many of us appreciate a love so great that heaven and earth are of no consequence to their Creator, only His children in all of creation matter in the final scheme of things. Now read John 3:16 and describe the value of that kind of love, "For God so loved the world that He gave His only begotten Son, that whoever believes in Him should not perish, but have eternal life."

God's love is always perfect in its expression. It is never too much, too little or too late. And it always comes to us before we understand or acknowledge our need for His love, "We love, because He first loved us." (1 John 4:19) and "But God demonstrates His own love toward us, in that while we were yet sinners, Christ died for us." (Romans 5:8) remind us that God's love is the initiator to life, eternal and otherwise. Apart from God's love is a black and empty void called hell. For those who are on the fast track to that void, nothing of comfort in this life matters because nothing of comfort in the life eternal will ever come.

Grasping that truth and gleaning the depth of God's love in light of His other attributes, we come to this conclusion, God's love completes us. Henry T. Blackaby in his book "Experiencing God" wrote "The love that God focuses on your life is an everlasting love. Because of that love, He has drawn you to Himself. He has drawn you with cords of love when you were not His friend, when you were His enemy. He gave His own Son to die for you. To firmly anchor the experiencing of God and knowing His will, you must be absolutely convinced of God's love for you."

Drawn with cords of love that cannot be broken. Do you realize that there is nothing that you will ever do that God does not already know about right now? Do you know that you cannot surprise God, disappoint Him or cause Him to throw up His arms and walk away in disgust? God knows every moment of every day of your life before you even lived one of them, but that's not what's amazing. What's amazing is this: He loves you anyway. Listen to the words of Jeremiah (31:3) "The Lord has appeared to me of old saying, 'Yes, I have loved you with an everlasting love; Therefore with lovingkindness I have drawn you.'" And in Hosea 11:4 "I drew them with gentle cords, with bands of love, and I was to them as those who take the yoke from their neck."

God's love is about Him and His creation. It is about the perfection of His purpose and plan in the lives of His children. And it is indescribable. David proclaims, "How precious also are Thy thoughts to me, O God! How vast is the sum of them! If I should count them, they would out number the sand. When I awake, I am still with Thee." Psalm 139:17 - 18

Firmly grasping then, that God's love is the expression and the action of saving us from the condemnation of our sinful souls that His justice and holiness demand, the question becomes, how do we respond to God's love? Can you gaze upon such a lavish gift and find it has little consequence on the course or the scope of your life? If you can, either you have yet to grasp the cost of your sin or you are numb inside. There can be no other explanation for the lack of deep emotion when responding to God's gift of His love. It is undeserved, immeasurable, unavoidable and grand. It is our life raft when we are adrift on the ocean in a raging storm and to grab onto it is to proclaim with your last breath that it is life itself!

So, how will you choose to respond to this God of love? Jesus, in Matthew 22:37 - 40 gave us the only prescribed method for expressing our gratitude. "And He (Jesus) said to him, 'YOU SHALL LOVE THE LORD YOUR GOD WITH ALL YOUR HEART, AND WITH ALL YOUR SOUL, AND WITH ALL YOUR MIND.' This is the great and foremost commandment. The second is like it, 'YOU SHALL LOVE YOUR NEIGHBOR AS YOURSELF.' On these two commandments depend the whole Law and the Prophets."

This God of love demands as our gift of praise and thanksgiving that we respond in kind; that we love Him with reckless and passionate abandon and then choose to love all others around us, not because they deserve it but because He loved us. Saint Bernard of Clairvaux captured the spirit of this command when he wrote, "You wish to hear from me why and how God is to be loved? My answer is: the reason for loving God is God Himself, and the measure in which we should love Him is to love Him without measure." In 1 John 5:2 & 3 we are also told "By this we know that we love the children of God, when we love God and observe His commandments. For this is the love of God, that we keep His commandments; and His commandments are not burdensome."

"God is love" deserves a response from those of us who have been rescued by the scandalous beauty of His indescribable and unmerited passion and devotion. His love is one of the few things that we receive in one breath and to which we *must* respond in the next.

When I was a small child, roughly seven or eight, I lived in a changing neighborhood in Chicago, a dozen miles west of Wrigley Field on Addison St. Changing is a polite way of saying that there were various ethnic groups vying for power and control and some fairly regular gang activity around my neighborhood and school. As young as I was and standing on the fringe of that activity, I saw the power of hatred, fear and ignorance played out. I understood that those emotions had the potential to scar and impact the hearts of those they infected. And then, I met Jesus. In those days and weeks and months following my conversion, I began to see the universe's not so secret secret. Love is more powerful than all of those forces combined. In fact, in the bright light of God's love, hatred, fear and ignorance simply melt away and someday, those three feeble brothers will evaporate forever.

God is love, not apart from His holiness, justice and righteousness, but rather He is love in the center of those and all other attributes. God is eternal teaches me of His might and His position, but it is in His love, that I am able to embrace so awesome and powerful a God. That, is the full definition of God's love. That His love created me, sure. That His love saved me, yes. But that His love sustains me, changes me, rebukes me, grows me, trains me and bids me come! That is the power of a love so great that He could only trust it in the outstretched arms of His Beloved Son.

CHAPTER 9: GOD IS LOVE
GOING DEEPER: QUESTIONS FOR STUDY

1. What is involved in the commandment to love God with all your heart, mind, soul and strength?

   Love God w/ all that I am.

2. How does obedience tie into love? How have you recently expressed your love toward God?

   Obedient to his commands, shows love.

3. How have you expressed your love of God by loving those around you? *By being a good example*
   — respectful + kind to others
   — no bad language

GETTING TO THE HEART OF THE MATTER: APPLICATION

How have you **SHOWN** God that you love Him? List out some ways that you have expressed your love for Him in a tangible way. Spend some time in prayer and offer up your acts of obedience as a means of expressing your love to God and ask Him for more ways to express your love, gratitude and thankfulness for all He has done for you.

LAYING THE FOUNDATION: QUIET TIME

DAY 1: 1 Corinthians 13
   This is often described as the "love chapter". Can you see your love of God and of others in this description? If not, how can you change?

DAY 2: I John 4:7 - 21
   How does God's love of us impact our ability to love others?

Day 3: John 3:16 - 21
   How does God's love impact our eternal destiny?

   His love has given us eternal life.

DAY 4: Romans 8:15 - 17

As God's children, we have a relationship with Him that invites us to call Him, Daddy (ABBA). Talk to your Daddy and tell Him how you love Him.

DAY 5: Colossians 3:12 - 17

How does God's love change your perspective?

—To be thankful for all I have.
—not to complain
— TO THANK GOD, and give HIM all glory, honor, + praise.

ADDITIONAL NAMES OF GOD

ELOHIM, "The Creator" Deuteronomy 10:17

JEHOVAH JEREH, "The Lord Will Provide" Genesis 22:14

JEHOVAH SHAMMAH, "The Lord is There" Ezekiel 48:35

JEHOVAH NISSI, "The Lord My Banner" Exodus 17:15

JEHOVAH, "The Self-Existent One" Exodus 3:14-15

JEHOVAH M'KADDESH, "The Lord That Sanctifies"
Hebrews 10:10-14

ADONAI, "The Lord" Psalm 123:2

EL SHADDAI, "The All-Sufficient One" Genesis 17:1-2

EL ELYON, "God Most High" Daniel 4:34-35

JEHOVAH SABAOTH, "The Lord of Hosts" Psalm 46:7

JEHOVAH SHALOM, "The Lord of Peace" Leviticus 26:2-6

JEHOVAH ROPHE, "The Lord that Heals" Exodus 15:25, 26

JEHOVAH ROI, "Our Shepherd" Psalm 23

SECTION THREE:

HEALING THE PAST GOD'S WAY

INTRODUCTION

HEALING THE PAST GOD'S WAY

I have a friend who loves log cabins. Now personally, I do not see their charm, but her desire has always been to live in one. I've lived in apartment buildings that felt like gerbil cages and in houses designed to mimic shoeboxes (I think). No matter the structure, however, all buildings have one thing in common - their foundation. Try to build without it and you'll be constructing a house of cards.

As children of God, there is no other foundation upon which to build our lives than on the Person and work of Jesus Christ, the pledge and guidance of the Holy Spirit and the eternal, immutable and power-filled character of God. It is the cornerstone of who I am in Christ and who God is. And to live out that truth is to live out my faith, trusting God for all of His promises and protection, believing God to be enough for my every need.

That was my turning point, believing God to be enough to meet and to take care of my *every* need according to His love and His will. Up to that moment, my life was about me. My way. My hurts. My black hole of need and of pain. I was the captain of my ship and I had run it aground, finding no hope in ever sailing again. By the time I surrendered, quite literally to God, I found my life to be void of hope.

But, as you've been reading, it was *in* the act of surrender that hope invaded my life. As Jesus finally had my attention and I was able to hear, to learn and to desire His way over my own, I began to lay that foundation of Biblical truth over every warped and missing tile of flooring until the foundation became the strongest part of my building, of my life. As that progress was made, I was finally able to begin the process of working through other areas in my life that had been warped by my past of pain.

That foundation, in truth, has been laid now for you as well. From rejoicing over our inheritance to the reality of God's protection and power, we have begun to grasp the Truth of God in the hidden places of our hearts and lives. He is the God who heals. He is the God who loves and adores, moving heaven and earth to bring us back into a relationship with Him. He is the One about whom we've heard, but now, our eyes have seen. Living out that truth is the greatest privilege of our short and complex lives.

Now, as artists, having experienced the broad strokes of our God, we will spend the remaining chapters detailing Him in living color. Who He is in the problem of pain and how we can thrive and not just survive in this evil world. Experiencing the necessary tears of loss, only to finally know the joy of living those moments in the palm of His hand. Working through issues of forgiveness, repentance and freedom from anger. Believing His promise that I am His beloved, shaking free from the bonds of shame and the ravages of chaos and guilt. Learning how to make changes in my life so that the inside and outside reflect my newfound and growing faith in His bounty and in His goodness. And finally, understanding that it is my choice to follow my Lord, serving and loving those whom He served and loved, making my life about the work of the Cross instead of about the hatred of the masses.

Laying this foundation, believing Jesus to be our eternal hope, *now*, we're ready to deal with some of the issues that stem from our painful past.

CHAPTER TEN

THE PROBLEM OF PAIN

I grew up in the Midwest. One of the joys of this part of the country is that we have a legitimate fall and spring. In the fall, the trees begin to turn colors as sunlight fades and the cooler air moves in. It is like a slow moving fireworks display with a handful of trees "popping" early with bursts of yellow and orange. Then, as a couple of weeks pass, more leaves begin to join in the chorus, fairly exploding with crackles of golden ray sunshine and burnt hues of orange and red and deep yellows. The whole of nature builds to a crescendo of color exploding mid-air with brilliance and spectacle so attractive and inspiring that whole Saturdays are spent sipping lattes and driving down rural roads in hunt of the best fireworks display of the season.

Sadly, it doesn't last. One good overnight wind storm – we always get at least one during the fall – and the next morning, the fireworks of brilliant leaves have faded and fallen to the yards and streets and gutters of our towns. A couple dozen bags of raked leaves later, the fall has turned to winter. A long, cold, dead and colorless season that lasts too long and comes too soon.

The brilliance and breathlessness of fall fades as we endure the browns of winter. Dead trees, dead grass, gray skies and lifeless bushes all sag and slumber, waiting for the turn of the calendar page. And then, it happens. One day, usually around the end of March or beginning of April, when the nip in the air is more than tolerable as it is less pronounced, a small, green bump begins to push through on bushes and branches alike. The first sure sign that life has begun again. Soon, the buds will blossom and grow into flowers and leaves with greenness and color to spare. Life and all of its lushness begins again in earnest and our steps are lighter, our hearts warmer and our hope more full.

This is what we know. Life from death. Spring from winter from fall. Brightness and brilliance from death and decay. Creation, however, was not always like this. Genesis 1:1 tells us that "*In the beginning*, God created the heavens and the earth." And it was good. In the Garden of Eden, the paradise we have never known, God brought to life life itself. And it was a feast for the senses. No momentary blitz of color like in a fireworks display but rather a constant invasion of Adam's and Eve's eyes and ears and hands and heart of God's unspoiled creativity and moral goodness. Everywhere they looked, Adam and Eve found lushness and textures and colors that complimented each other, perfectly. They found animals, mortal enemies in our lives, who in paradise lived side-by-side without care or concern. With barely lifting a finger to grow or to tend, Adam and his helpmate, Eve could reach up to any kind of tree and eat the perfect. . .(you fill in the blank with your favorite, perfectly ripe fruit, full of all sweetness and taste). The ground watered itself with a gentle mist and nothing, nothing except tree trunks and branches were brown. Not one leaf or blade of grass or animal died, not one.

To top it all off with the unimaginable, God met with Adam and Eve, just to chat. He strolled and conversed, as would friends, the God of all creation spending time with the work of His hands. Adam and Eve had everything and more than they could ever need and they lived in a world without sin, without pain, without sorrow or suffering. They lived in a world of comfort and ease in which they were in charge of God's entire creation. He had given them dominion over everything. All they had to do each day was enjoy God as they lived in His morally good and perfect world.

But as we know, the story does not end here. For Adam and Eve both fell into the same trap as we do, they believed a lie about God and in their pride, they thought they knew better than Him.

The fall of mankind in the Garden of Eden is recorded in Genesis 3. The serpent begins in his conversation with Eve by planting a doubt. "Did God actually say, 'You shall not eat of any tree in the garden?'" That snake knew better, but he wanted Eve to pause. At that moment, the serpent did not want Eve thinking about all the good and wonderful things that God had given her. The serpent instead wanted to focus her attention on the one thing she was not suppose to have. (How much does this lie mirror our own lives, even today?) Eve answered his question, "We may eat of the fruit of the trees in the garden, but God said, 'You shall not eat of the fruit of the tree that is in the midst of the garden, neither shall you touch it, lest you die.'"

Having challenged God's character, His goodness, by implying that He had unjustly withheld from Adam and Eve knowledge and power to make them like God Himself, the serpent's work was done. Eve and Adam (v. 6 records that Adam was with her at the time) in their pride and desire, took what was forbidden and ate. Paradise was lost.

The story of the Garden and the Fall beg a question: why did God put the Tree of Knowledge of Good and Evil and the Tree of Life in the center of their paradise? Surely we know from our lessons on God's sovereignty and power that He knew what would happen. Certainly, the first sin came as no surprise to the Almighty. So, why did He do it? Why did God allow Adam and Eve the right to choose?

C.S. Lewis answers that question in his book, *Mere Christianity:*

"God created things which had free will. That means creatures which can go either wrong or right. Some people think they can imagine a creature which was free but had no possibility of going wrong; I cannot. If a thing is free to be good it is also free to be bad. And free will is what has made evil possible. Why, then, did God give them free will? Because free will, though it makes evil possible, is also the only thing that makes possible any love or goodness or joy worth having. A world of automata - of creatures that worked like machines - would hardly be worth creating. The happiness which God designs for His higher creatures is the happiness of being freely, voluntarily united to Him and to each other in an ecstasy of love and delight compared with which the most rapturous love between a man and a woman on this earth is mere milk and water. And for that they must be free.

. . .If God thinks this state of war in the universe a price worth paying for free will - that is, for making a live world which creatures can do real good or harm and something of real importance can happen, instead of a toy world which only moves when He pulls the strings - then we may take it it is worth paying."

In order for you and I to have a love relationship with God, as we stated in chapter 1, then we must choose Him as He has chosen us. The freedom for us to do that comes at a price for God. C.S. Lewis goes on to say, "It costs God nothing, so far as we know, to create nice things: but to convert rebellious wills cost Him crucifixion."

The price paid by Adam and Eve was of paradise lost. How sad it would have been had that been their end. But it was not. After the fall, God did allow them to suffer the consequences of their choices, for they had rejected the perfect Law of God Himself. Adam would now be made to work the land in sweat and hardship, toiling all the days of his life in a struggle to reap the fruit of the land that had previously been at his fingertips. Eve would suffer pain in childbirth, and God told her "your desire shall be for your husband and he shall rule over you". They both would experience a spiritual death, a disconnection from the immediacy of God that they had known in the Garden, and they would someday suffer a physical death, "till you return to the ground, for out of it you were taken; for you are dust, and to dust you shall return".

The price paid by God's creation was of spoiled goodness. The earth had now been stained by sin and cursed by God because of Adam's actions. The earth is dying; we experience its destruction little by little each day and the consequences of Adam's sin in each earthquake and hurricane, flood and famine, disease and pestilence that move across this land. That will continue until God destroys the old heaven and the old earth and creates a new heaven and a new earth. Moral goodness can not be recaptured. It can only be created by God. This world, having been tainted by sin, will not stand long. A powerful price paid for the freedom to choose.

The price paid by God, Himself is all the more amazing. In Ephesians 1:4, we are told that God chose us in Christ before the foundation of the earth was laid. Imagine that. Before He said, "Let there be. . ." He had already fashioned our redemption before we, through Adam, had sinned. Romans 5:18 reads, "So then as through one transgression there resulted condemnation to all men, even so through one act of righteousness there resulted justification of life to all men." The price paid by God was that of His Son - sent to suffer and die for our sins. Isaiah 53:4 - 6 says it best, "Surely he has borne our griefs and carried our sorrows; yet we esteemed him stricken, smitten by God, and afflicted. But he was wounded for our transgressions; he was crushed for our iniquities; upon him was the chastisement that brought our peace, and with his stripes we are healed."

As C.S. Lewis had stated earlier, "if God thinks this state of war in the universe a price worth paying for free will. . .then we may take it it is worth paying." God's price for our freedom was higher, infinitely higher than the price we pay. First of all, I've never known what it is like to be perfectly holy, completely righteous and void of all sin. God, who is the consuming fire of holiness, allowed Adam's sin and with it the unrighteousness of the masses. He did it to allow us the fullness of Him, the privilege of choosing our inheritance - life abundant or eternal death. But can you imagine what it is like for God to endure the wickedness of each successive generation? The love He has for His children is a love beyond understanding. That He would wait for you and I to choose life is unimaginable - who is like our God?

Even in Adam and Eve's darkest moment, Genesis 3:15 gives us a glimpse at God's heart for our redemption and restoration to a relationship with Him. It reads, "I will put enmity between you and the woman, and between your offspring and her offspring; He shall bruise your head, and you (the serpent) shall bruise His heel." The

Wycliffe Bible Commentary explains that passage like this, "Thus, we have in this famous passage, called the *protevangelium*, "first gospel," the announcement of a prolonged struggle, perpetual antagonism, wounds on both sides, and eventual victory for the seed of woman (Jesus). God's promise that the head of the serpent was to be crushed pointed forward to the coming of Messiah and guaranteed victory. This assurance fell upon the ears of God's earliest creatures as a blessed hope of redemption." Even before God sent them out of Eden, He promised them a hope and a future.

Finally, in looking at the fall, we need to be mindful of God's goodness in this, "And the Lord God made for Adam and his wife garments of skins and clothed them." God, in His mercy, killed the first living creature, spilling its innocent blood in order to cover Adam and Eve's sin, restoring them in relationship to their God. The first act of redemption, the first blood shed, that pointed to the final act of redemption, the perfect Lamb of God whose blood was shed, once and for all.

The problem of pain, however, is not just about a moment in the Garden. Pain and suffering in this world continues today. And today, just like the first sunrise on a world cursed by sin, God is still in control and He has a purpose and a plan that will not be thwarted. Remember, God is Almighty and He is in control. So, the problem of pain for us as God's children turns to this question: what is the purpose of pain?

God, exercising His sovereign control over His creation, allows His children to suffer, just as He allowed His Son to suffer. Let's be clear about this, God does not sin nor does He cause us to sin. He does, however, allow us to be persecuted, to suffer injustice, to experience pain and to know heartache as we walk this road. Why?

Jesus, the One who suffered more than anyone in human history - the blameless One made to carry our blame - answers the "why?" in John 12:23 - 25, "And Jesus answered them, 'The hour has come for the Son of Man to be glorified. Truly, truly, I say to you, unless a grain of wheat falls into the earth and dies, it remains alone; but if it dies, it bears much fruit. Whoever loves his life loses it, and whoever hates his life in this world will keep it to eternal life.'" Jesus was preparing His disciples first for His suffering on the cross and then preparing them for their need to suffer the pain of dying to self that they may have eternal life. Notice He calls His suffering "glory" and our suffering, "life".

Erwin Lutzer in his book, "Cries from the Cross" puts it this way: "Jesus, the sinless Son of God, was, of course, perfect. But interestingly, He could only be perfect in His work through obedience to the Father's will. And, even more to the point, the will of the Father had to include suffering. "In bringing many sons to glory, it was fitting that God, for whom and through whom everything exists, should make the author of their salvation perfect through suffering" (Hebrews 2:10). If Jesus needed to suffer to perfectly fulfill the will of God, why should we be exempt?"

'Practice makes perfect' or so the saying goes. In my Christian walk, as I've experienced pain and suffering from physical violence to injustice and many things in-between, I've learned to practice the presence of God. To reach for Him in the moment when I am not enough. And, I'm learning to lean on Him, trust Him, depend on Him and somedays, when I am in balance with His world, I even breath Him in as if my life depended on it, and it always does.

I am not long for this world, neither are you. We are here for a moment and then we step off this mortal coil into our eternity. Our daily dying to self is a testing of our resolve, a building of our faith, a purifying fire that burns off the imperfections and turns us into valuable and refined gold and silver. Remember what we said, God will meet us where we are, but He will not leave us there. He is all about the process of sanctifying us to look more and more like His Son. "And we proclaim Him, admonishing every man and teaching every man with all wisdom, that we may present every man complete in Christ." Colossians 1:28

We need to understand, then, that God allows suffering. He allows it for a number of reasons. One reason, as we said, is so that we might be made perfect in our faith (James 1:2 - 4). Another reason that God allows suffering is to draw us to Him. Think about how we often come to God in our sorrow or brokenness and then ignore our need for Him when everything *seems* okay. God also allows suffering that His glory might be known. Think of how many times the world stands in silent awe at the sacrifice and suffering of one of our brothers or sisters in Christ. A momentary devastation and then His abiding peace and joy in the center of absolute ruin and the world scratches its collective head in stark confusion. The persecution of the early Church was legendary, even in their day, and yet, instead of pushing people away, they were drawn to these Jesus followers who found joy even in martyrdom. People wanted to know what or who they knew to live such bright lives. God's glory shines through His children when we obey, even in, especially in persecution and suffering.

God also allows suffering so that His will would be accomplished. Remember our friend, Corrie ten Boom, the woman who suffered horribly at the hands of the Nazis and lost her father and sister in the prison camps? After the war, God had a job for Corrie. She spent years traveling through Germany, bringing the good news of the gospel to a broken and desperate people. They needed to hear that God loves and God forgives - who better to bring the message than one who had suffered at their hands and had forgiven them.

One night, as Corrie was speaking in a small church near the prison camp where she and Betsy had been held, she noticed a man in the back who had been one of the camp's most cruel guards. After she finished her story about God's love and forgiveness, she noticed that he had made his way to the front of the church to talk with her. He extended his hand, not looking up at her. It wasn't easy and it took a moment or two, but Corrie, mindful of God's grace in her life, took hold of his hand and the barrier was broken so that he could receive what God had to give him. God allows our suffering so that His will will be accomplished - imagine the privilege of being used by God to lead another into the glory of heaven! "For momentary, light affliction is producing for us an eternal weight of glory far beyond all comparison. . ." 2 Corinthians 4:17

The purpose of pain is varied and vast, escaping neither God's authority nor power. In that journey, we have a choice to make. Will I be as the world, tossed about like a rowboat on white-capped waves, hoping just to survive? Or will I live as I should - a Christian who is convinced of God's love and goodness in the center of tribulation and who responds in faith regardless of the circumstances? "For this reason I also suffer these things, but I am not ashamed; for

I know whom I have believed and I am convinced that He is able to guard what I have entrusted to Him until that day." 2 Timothy 1:12

Finally, in her book, *A Path Through Suffering*, Elisabeth Elliot talks about John 12:24 in this way: "When, by my own faults and indifference, or the distractions of the world, I have drifted from this changeless principle (and imagined that I might *avoid* the deaths and still somehow be fruitful) the words have rung again in the ears of my soul, *if it die, if it die, if it die.*"

OUR STRATEGY FOR SURVIVING THE PAIN OF THIS WORLD:

In light then of what we've discussed, it is important for us to map out a strategy for surviving, indeed, for thriving in a world of suffering and tribulation. As Paul wrote in the passage in 2 Timothy 1:12, "for I KNOW whom I have believed", we need to know that faith builds as our knowledge, experience and understanding of God increases. In fact, it builds in equal measure to knowability and trust. Therefore, it is essential for us to choose a Biblical model for growing that knowledge and faith so that we might have the abundant life, even in suffering, that Jesus promised. We want to learn to someday echo Paul as he says, "But whatever things were gain to me, those things I have counted as loss for the sake of Christ. More than that, I count all things to be loss in view of the surpassing value of knowing Christ Jesus my Lord, for whom I have suffered the loss of all things, and count them but rubbish in order that I may gain Christ." Philippians 3:7-8

FIRST, CHRIST MUST BE MY CENTER:

Christ is my power source. He is my Master, my Shepherd, my Savior and my Lord. It is by His power and through His strength that I have the means to overcome this world. But, He must be the center of my life. I can no longer live on my own terms because I know, by experience, that those terms will fail me. So, Christ must be at the center at all times. It is *through* Him that I have my life because it is *in* Him that I have my salvation. "I have been crucified with Christ; and it is no longer I who live, but Christ lives in me; and the *life* which I now live in the flesh I live by faith in the Son of

God, who loved me, and delivered Himself up for me." Galatians 2:20 (Italics mine)

The first question I must ask myself, then, is this: is Christ at the center of my life? Is there anything that I am withholding from His authority in my life? If so, am I willing to relinquish it as an act of obedience and of worship, recognizing that there is nothing of greater value than Jesus Christ?

The second question I must ask myself is this: am I bearing any fruit? John 15:5 reminds us, "I am the vine, you are the branches; he who abides in Me, and I in him, he bears much fruit; for apart from Me you can do nothing." Genuine change is fruit for it is a supernatural act of the Holy Spirit. Growing through a time of struggle is fruit as it is only possible when you rely on the strength of Jesus. Submitting and surrendering your will to God is fruit for it is only possible when Christ is at the center of your life.

SECOND, OBEDIENCE TO CHRIST MUST BE MY GOAL:

To place Christ at the center of my life is to see things His way and to do things in His way. My first thought, my first action is based on my desire to please someone other than myself. My desire is to be a follower, a disciple of Jesus, living in submission to His desires and purposes and plans. Why? Because He created me; He saved me; He desires to change me; and someday, I will see Him face-to-face.

Jesus, in the Book of John, tied obedience to love, (14:21) "He who has My commandments and keeps them, he it is who loves Me; and he who loves Me shall be loved by My Father, and I will love him, and will disclose Myself to him." And again in Luke, (6:46) "And why do you call Me, 'Lord, Lord,' and do not do what I say?" You can not claim to be a disciple of Christ and then live life on your own terms.

Is there an area in your life in which you are not obeying Christ? Remember, it is a choice. You can, today, live purposefully and passionately for Him. "I urge you therefore, brethren, by the mercies of God, to present your bodies a living and holy sacrifice, acceptable to God, *which is* your spiritual service of worship. And do not be conformed to this world, but be transformed by the renewing of your mind, that you may prove what the will of God is, that which is good and acceptable and perfect." (Romans 12:1 - 2)

C.S. Lewis once said, "Christian love is an affair of the will." I adore that saying. It encompasses the truth of our lives - we have the power to choose. Not the power to change on our own, but the power to choose. It's not about emotions or feeling a certain way; it is about bending my will to His, just like Jesus did in the Garden of Gethsemane.

Confess your sin and acknowledge your need to bring whatever it is into submission to the Lordship of Christ. Then, write out an action plan. It should include:

1. TRUTH - You must KNOW what the Bible says about an issue before you can act to change or to submit.

2. SUBMISSION - Be vocal about choosing to live for Jesus. Tell a Christian friend in order to be held accountable.

3. PRAYER - Lord, help me to change; only Jesus has the power.

4. PLAN - What can I do, daily, to acknowledge and live out my desire to be changed in this way?

5. PRAYER - Thank you Lord, for giving me the strength and the ability to change.

THIRD, I NEED TO KNOW THE WORD:

How do I know what Jesus wants me to do; how do I know how to live if I don't know His Word? It is the power of God's Word, the Light of its truth and the Sword of its message that gives me direction, correction, encouragement, courage and hope. The study of God's Word is a daily, life-long, step-by-step journey. It is also the only way for me to learn how to obey Jesus.

1 Peter 2:2 "Like newborn babes, long for the pure

milk of the word, that by it you may grow in respect to salvation."

2 Timothy 2:15 "Be diligent to present yourself approved to God as a workman who does not need to be ashamed, handling accurately the word of truth."

2 Timothy 3:16 & 17 "All Scripture is inspired by God and profitable for teaching, for reproof, for correction, for training in righteousness; that the man of God may be adequate, equipped for every good work."

Joshua 1:8 "This book of the law shall not depart from your mouth, but you shall meditate on it day and night, so that you may be careful to do according to all that is written in it; for then you will make your way prosperous, and then you will have success."

1. Am I having my daily quiet time?

2. Over the past _____ (fill in the number of months / years that you've been studying the Bible daily), how has God changed my life? What is different about me that I see or that other people have noticed? How is this an encouragement for me to continue to be disciplined and diligent in my study of God's Word?

THE MEAT OF THE WORD: Pick a verse each day this week and meditate.

Colossians 3:1 - 14; Joshua 1:6 - 9; 2 Timothy 2:1 - 15
Psalm 119:1 - 32; 119:33 - 56; 119:57 - 88; 119:89 - 128; 119:129 - 176

FOURTH, DAILY, I NEED TO PRAY:
While God's Word is His vehicle with which to communicate His heart to me, prayer is my way of communicating with Him. It is

the vehicle by which I grow my dependence upon Him and therefore, my relationship with Him. Prayer is a tool of a personal and deepening walk with God.

> Matthew 7:7 "Ask, and it shall be given to you; seek, and you shall find; knock, and it shall be opened to you."

> Philippians 4:6 & 7 "Be anxious for nothing, but in everything by prayer and supplication with thanksgiving let your requests be made known to God. And the peace of God, which surpasses all comprehension, shall guard your hearts and your minds in Christ Jesus."

> John 15:7 "If you abide in Me, and My words abide in you, ask whatever you wish, and it shall be done for you."

> Psalm 5:1-3 "Give ear to my words, O Lord, Consider my groaning. Heed the sound of my cry for help, my King and my God, For to Thee do I pray. In the morning, O Lord, Thou wilt hear my voice; In the morning I will order my *prayer* to Thee and *eagerly* watch."

1. A consistent prayer life is the sign of a healthy relationship with God. Being honest with yourself, how is your prayer life (remember that God knows our hearts)?

2. If you do not have any sort of daily prayer routine or plan, sketch out how you can meet daily with God in prayer (personally, I'm a walker and a talker, so long walks work best for me).

PRAYER PATH: Meet with God at least once a day using this model:
> A - Adoration

C - Confession (get right with God)

T - Thanksgiving

S - Supplication (ask, in faith, for what you need)

FIFTH, THE BREAKING OF BREAD IN FELLOWSHIP:

God did not create us to "go it alone". We have the privilege and the responsibility of serving, living, working and playing side-by-side as the family of God. That fellowship includes praying for and with one another, correcting and rebuking one another, loving one another and serving one another.

> Matthew 18:20 "For where two or three have gathered together in My name, there I am in their midst."

> Hebrews 10:24 & 25 "And let us consider how to stimulate one another to love and good deeds, not forsaking our own assembling together, as is the habit of some, but encouraging *one another*; and all the more, as you see the day drawing near."

> 1 John 1:3 "What we have seen and heard we proclaim to you also, that you also may have fellowship with us; and indeed our fellowship is with the Father, and with His Son Jesus Christ."

> 1 Thessalonians 5:14 & 15 "And we urge you, brethren, admonish the unruly, encourage the fainthearted, help the weak, be patient with all men. See that no one repays another with evil for evil, but always seek after that which is good for one another and for all men."

1. When a brother or sister corrects you, how do you react? What about when you see a brother or sister blinded by sin? Do you step in or do you let them flounder?

2. Understanding that we are a part of the family of God, what is your responsibility to your family? Are you using your gifts to bless others? Are you using your gifts to build up God's kingdom and to glorify Him?

FELLOWSHIP BUILDER: Set up a least one time in the next week when you will meet with fellow Christians for encouragement and edification.

SIXTH, THE JOY OF WITNESSING:

One of the great privileges of our lives as Christians is the honor of telling others about Jesus. Thinking back on all that Christ has done for me, I can think of no greater gift that is of greater consequence than the good news of the gospel. This is an element of serving others. "How will they know if we do not tell them; how will they know if we do not go?" Witnessing or testifying to the greatness of God is an overflow of a healthy and growing and obedient life in Christ. It is the logical continuation of studying God's Word, spending time in prayer and in fellowship. Wanting others to have what we have is absolutely necessary to worshipping our great God!

> John 4:35-38 "Do you not say, "There are yet four months, and then comes the harvest?" Behold, I say to you, lift up your eyes, and look on the fields, that they are white for harvest. Already he who reaps is receiving wages, and is gathering fruit for life eternal; that he who sows and he who reaps may rejoice together. For in this case the saying is true, 'One sows, and another reaps.' I sent you to reap that for which you have not labored; others have labored and you have entered into their labor."

> Matthew 4:19 "And He said to them, "Follow Me, and I will make you fishers of men."

171

Romans 1:16 "For I am not ashamed of the gospel, for it is the power of God for salvation to everyone who believes, to the Jew first and also to the Greek."

1 Peter 3:15 "But sanctify Christ as Lord in your hearts, always being ready to make a defense to everyone who asks you to give an account for the hope that is in you, yet with gentleness and reverence."

1. Have you told anyone lately about the good news of the gospel? Is there anyone you can think of to tell?

2. Do you know how to present the gospel? Have you memorized the Bridge illustration (Appendix A)?

WITNESSING GOAL: Pray about two different people in your life who need to hear about Jesus. Being creative, reach out to those two individuals over the course of these next two weeks. Write a letter, have dinner, send a tape or book - share what God is doing in your life.

ON ALL DAYS, WE WORSHIP:

Stop for a moment and count on one hand all of the great things that Jesus has done for you. Oh, you need more than one hand? How 'bout more than two? I don't know about you, but everyday, Jesus does so many things for me that I am beyond counting them. I am never beyond praising and worshipping Him for them, however. How about worshipping God just for who He is? He is so awesome and almighty - there is no One like our God!

John 4:23 - 24 "But an hour is coming, and now is, when the true worshipers shall worship the Father in spirit and truth; for such people the Father seeks to be His worshipers. God is spirit, and those who worship Him must worship in spirit and truth."

Psalm 2:11 "Worship the Lord with reverence, and rejoice with trembling."

Psalm 8:1 "O Lord, our Lord, How majestic is Thy name in all the earth. Who hast displayed Thy splendor above the heavens!"

Psalm 33:1 - 3 "Sing for joy in the Lord, O you righteous ones; Praise is becoming to the upright. Give thanks to the Lord with the lyre; sing praises to Him with a harp of ten strings. Sing to Him a new song; Play skillfully with a shout of joy."

1. Break into song. Speak out His greatness and mercy. Thank and praise God in your speech, your heart, your music and your life.

2. Do you attend weekly worship services? Corporate worship encourages us and allows us to express ourselves to God in a deep and powerful way.

WORSHIP WEEK: Attend a worship service, then, choose to listen to Christian music this week (does not matter what kind - classical, hymns, rock, whatever).

Philippians 4:8 tells us, "Finally, brethren, whatever is true, whatever is honorable, whatever is right, whatever is pure, whatever is lovely, whatever is of good repute, if there is any excellence and if anything worthy of praise, let your mind *dwell* on these things." (Italics mine)

If I had employed, with my heart and mind, any one of these strategies on a regular basis during my almost 10 year odyssey away from God, I would have been back in the fold in moments and not months. Living purposefully for Him and with Him and to Him is the only way you and I are going to survive the evil of this world. Indeed, we shall live abundantly when we live for the King - Paul, in his chains, praised God, knowing that his suffering was short and his life eternal would be joy beyond measure. ". . .choose this day whom you shall serve. . .as for me and my house, we will serve the Lord." Joshua 24:15

CHAPTER 10: THE PROBLEM OF PAIN
GOING DEEPER: QUESTIONS FOR STUDY

1. There is evil in this world and we are told that we will suffer for a time. After studying the Scriptures presented in this chapter, do you appreciate that God has and will use your suffering for a purpose? How have you seen Him do that?

2. What is your daily strategy for surviving the evil in this world?

3. What will you tell a non-Christian who asks you why God allows such evil to exist?

GETTING TO THE HEART OF THE MATTER:
APPLICATION

Read through 2 SAMUEL 22:2 - 51 and note how David experienced God throughout his life and how God was with him in good times and bad. Do you imagine that your relationship with God can be as strong? How can your relationship with God deepen in times of trial and pain?

LAYING THE FOUNDATION: QUIET TIME

Read each verse and then pick one or two verses and commit them to memory.

John 10:10; 16:33

1 Corinthians 10:13

2 Corinthians 12:9

1 John 4:4

Isaiah 35:4-10; 41:10

Hosea 6:3

Romans 8:16 & 17

Philippians 2:13

CHAPTER ELEVEN

MOURNING AND GRIEF: BROKEN VESSEL

Ecclesiastes 3:4 "A time to weep, and a time to laugh;
A time to mourn, and a time to dance."

For many many years, I could not cry. I wanted to. I would get up in the morning, go to work alone, come home alone, make a sandwich and take it with me to the park. There, I would find a baseball game being played by people I didn't know and I would sit far enough away to see and not be seen. I would watch them talk and laugh and I would wonder if real life was just like the picture played out in front of me. I had no emotion, no connection to the world at large. I even remember going to the hospital to see my sister's second child half an hour after Wesley had been born. I held him; I watched him wrinkle his blue nose and I wanted to laugh and cry, but nothing came.

It was years before the tears came. And when they finally came, when God had helped me crack the wall surrounding my heart, I thought those tears would never, never stop. I didn't always even know why I was crying, just that the watershed of tears needed to flow and in that downpour, something soothed the panic in my soul. I had been broken by a circumstance, a moment of violence, and in that moment frozen in time, I had lost and then found the ability to mourn. As I sought solace in God's Word, I found that God does not prohibit nor discourage tears, in fact, He promises to be the One to comfort and ease my sorrow.

Never does God tell us to quit crying. He never says, as friends and family sometimes do, 'aren't you finished yet?'. Instead, God's Word speaks often of our sorrows, our tears, our heartache and pain. There is a time to mourn. There is a need to weep. Scripture gives permission for us to do both, in season and with our healing the final goal.

We know that this life is filled with suffering and sorrow. Even Jesus, in Isaiah 53:3, was called "a man of sorrows, and acquainted with grief." And several times, Jesus cried, usually over a desperate situation in which the people around Him missed God's heart and larger purpose. God, Himself, has been and can be grieved over the state of His willful and unrighteous children. And numerous times in the Bible, we see individuals so overwhelmed and grief-stricken that they rend their clothing, sit in ash and wail their plight out to God in the hopes of any escape.

It is not wrong to feel overwhelmed and in need of comfort. God, time and again in Isaiah, reminds the people of Israel that He is their (and our) comfort. In Isaiah 61, we are told that in the year of Jubilee, God through Jesus will comfort all who mourn. Why would God claim to be our comfort if it was wrong to weep in the first place?

You have lost something. Many, many things. For some of us, we've lost our virginity. For others, our trust. We carry scars, both on the surface and deep down where no one can see and we have been taught to flinch and to wince and to bury what we fear is ugly and shameful. And the evil one is happy to make us think that God could care less. But, that's a lie. God knows my hurts; He knows my heart and my thoughts and He promises to deliver me to a day when tears will be shed no more.

Until that day, however, I need to know that it is okay to be honest with God about how I am feeling, about what I need from Him. Remember, because God knows everything; we can tell Him anything. In Psalm 77, we get a great look at that model for sharing our emotions, our feelings in a God-honoring and Biblical way:

1 My voice rises to God, and I will cry aloud;
My voice rises to God, and He will hear me.
2 In the day of my trouble I sought the Lord;
In the night my hand was stretched out without weariness;
My soul refused to be comforted.
3 When I remember God, then I am disturbed;
When I sigh, then my spirit grows faint.
4 Thou hast held my eyelids open;
I am so troubled that I cannot speak.
5 I have considered the days of old,
The years of long ago.
6 I will remember my song in the night;
I will meditate with my heart;
And my spirit ponders.
7 Will the Lord reject forever?
And will He never be favorable again?
8 Has His lovingkindness ceased forever?
Has His promise come to an end forever?
9 Has God forgotten to be gracious?
Or has He in anger withdrawn His compassion?
10 Then I said, "It is my grief, That the right hand
of the Most High has changed."
11 I shall remember the deeds of the Lord;
Surely I will remember Thy wonders of old.
12 I will meditate on all Thy work,
And muse on Thy deeds.
13 Thy way, O God, is holy;
What god is great like our God?
14 Thou art the God who workest wonders;
Thou hast made known Thy strength among the peoples.
15 Thou hast by Thy power redeemed Thy people,
The sons of Jacob and Joseph.
PSALM 77:1-15

It would be impossible to argue that the writer of the Psalm was having a good day. This individual is hurting. Look at some of the phrases he uses: my hand was stretched out without weariness; my soul refused to be comforted; I am so troubled that I cannot speak; will the Lord reject forever?; will He never be favorable again?; has His lovingkindness ceased forever?; has His promise come to an end forever?; has God forgotten to be gracious? or has He in anger withdrawn His compassion?.

Ever feel that way? I sure have. 'HEY GOD, I'M DOWN HERE - HELP ME!, PLEASE!' I've cried out to God, sometimes for days and weeks and months on end, feeling so sorrowful and overwhelmed, I thought I would never feel anything else but despair. Notice, in the Psalm, it does not discourage the individual from speaking out how he feels. It is an honest rendering of his state of heart and of mind. Notice too, however, it does not end there.

Verse 10 is the key: "Then I said, 'It is my grief, That the right hand of the Most High has changed.'" The writer of the Psalm comes to a realization. He is overwhelmed and feeling abandoned by God, filled with sorrow and in need of comfort. Then, he realizes that in the center of his pain, God is still God. His promises are no less potent and His character has not changed. The writer acknowledges that even though he *feels* God has left him alone, that does not make it true.

The Psalmist then goes on to the third part of this Psalm. Even in the middle of his heartache, he proclaims exactly who God is. "I shall remember the deeds of the Lord; Thy way, O God, is holy; What god is great like our God?; Thou art the God who workest wonders; Thou hast by Thy power redeemed Thy people, The sons of Jacob and Joseph."

The words and feelings of the writer lead to an inevitable conclusion: though he is now overwhelmed by sorrow, he knows that his emotions *do not* change who God is. In his words, we are reminded of God's provision, sovereignty and faithfulness.

What a model for us to follow. Speak the truth to God about how you're feeling; then, acknowledge the truth of who God is and what He has done. That is the "I *know* whom I have believed" of Paul's writing in 2 Timothy 1:12. We walk by faith and even when our emotions overwhelm, they do not have the power to change the truth - God still loves me; God is still good; God is still sovereign and holy and powerful and gracious.

Understand that you have lived through a deep and abiding loss. Your tears do not frighten God. In truth, tears shed remove the protective walls that we've built around our hearts. Remember too, that there is a time to mourn. And if you've not grieved the loss of innocence, of trust, of relationship, of childhood, of whatever, then you need to take time and grieve. There is an old hymn written by Joseph Scriven and Charles Converse that always brings me back to the foot of the cross, no matter the load or the pain I'm carrying:

What a Friend we have in Jesus,
All our sins and griefs to bear!
What a privilege to carry,
Ev'rything to God in prayer!
O what peace we often forfeit,
O what needless pain we bear,
All because we do not carry,
Ev'rything to God is prayer!
Have we trials and temptations?
Is there trouble anywhere?
We should never be discouraged,
Take it to the Lord in prayer.
Can we find a friend so faithful who
will all our sorrows share?
Jesus knows our ev'ry weakness,
Take it to the Lord in prayer.
Are we weak and heavy laden,
Cumbered with a load of care?
Precious Savior, still our refuge,
Take it to the Lord in prayer.
Do thy friends despise, forsake thee?
Take it to the Lord in prayer;
In His arms He'll take and shield thee,
Thou wilt find a solace there.

I'm a water person. My mom has said that she always knows where I'm going to end up when I'm in pain - the largest body of water I can find. For me, that's Lake Michigan. During my season of grieving, I spent long, lazy and some tearful afternoons on her shores, crying out to God and sometimes just crying out. Don't skip your time to grieve. If you do, you'll end up dwelling on the dull ache that never dies. Take it; grieve it; give it to Him for He alone can carry your load. Let the wound be cleaned out so that it can scar over and you can move ahead.

Walk and talk. Meet with a trusted Christian friend. Pray. Journal, read and pray through Scripture. Do whatever you have to do to get alone with God and give over the tears. I love the 23rd Psalm and during that time, I rewrote it in my own words, claiming these truths for myself:

Psalm 23
"The Lord is my shepherd, I shall not want.
I am the sheep and I confess that my need can *only* be met by THE Shepherd

He makes me lie down in green pastures;
He leads me beside quiet waters.
He restores my soul;
The Shepherd knows my limitations and meets me "where I'm at", but, praise God, He doesn't leave me there. He brings me to a place of quiet and into a season of rest. In this place the Shepherd "makes me lie down", "leads me beside" and "restores". He initiates and meets my need before I even know that I have need. I do not argue with the Shepherd. I submit to His "making. . .and leading. . . and restoring".

It is beside these still waters that I am alone with my Shepherd. It is in this time alone that I am free to mourn and to cry and to grieve. This is the time needed for healing. There has to be healing for God to completely restore what has been stolen from me.

He guides me in the paths of righteousness for His Name's sake.
The Shepherd is my constant companion. He is my source of strength and encouragement. He is my defender. And He is my teacher. We travel the path because of who He is. I am awed by

His dedication to His glory.

Even though I walk through the valley of the shadow of death, I fear no evil; for Thou art with me;

I am not alone. Ever. I am going to travel through the valleys of shame and pain and physical death but I will do it with my Creator by my side. I do not have to rely on me for anything. He is complete and I am safe in His arms, no matter what this world throws at me.

Thy rod and Thy staff, they comfort me.

I find comfort in His correction, direction, discipline and love. He will change what needs to be changed in me and will make me look more and more like Him. He knows what is best for me. Submitting to His leading eases my soul.

Thou dost prepare a table before me in the presence of my enemies;

The Shepherd supplies all my needs and will, some day, bring my enemies down with a righteous anger. All those who have tried to destroy me will be humbled by His judgment. I can trust Him to be the true victory even when I have been defeated. He promises that no matter how many enemies I have or what they do to me, He will win out over them. And because He has victory; I have victory!

Thou hast anointed my head with oil;

I am a child of the King. I am promised by His holy covenant that my place in His kingdom is secure. I am being anointed as royalty and no one can ever change that call upon my life.

My cup overflows.

I have NEED of nothing! The Shepherd provides above and beyond all that I could ever ask. He is generous beyond my expectations!

Surely goodness and lovingkindness will follow me all the days of my life,

I don't have to live by this world's standards. I am free to fall in love with My Shepherd because He has first and mightily and completely loved me! My life is forever changed because of the good Shepherd. He has saved me from my doom. Restored me from my sorrow. And given me the hope of His eternal victory!

And I will dwell in the house of the Lord forever."

My eternal rest has already been declared. It will be with my Shepherd in His paradise!

It may not feel like it now, but it is a joy to be able to meet with God, cry with Him and tell Him everything. He knows it already, but for me, the bond between us grew stronger as I learned to trust Him with my tears. I cry very easily now, in joy and in sorrow. I am no longer in bondage to the searing pain of a grief that will not surface. Please, let Jesus be your confidant, your comfort and your healing; remember, that is why He came (Isaiah 61:1-3).

BROKEN VESSEL

The following selection is from Hannah Hurnard's book, *"Hinds Feet on High Places"*. The book follows Much-Afraid (the central character) on her journey from brokenness to healing and it is a story about submission on her (and our) journey with Christ. In this selection, Much-Afraid has just finished a long and difficult journey through a deep valley and was now on her way up to the high places where she expected healing and joy. However, as you will read, she turned a corner and her journey changed.

"The mist had cleared from the mountains and the sun was shining, and as a consequence the way seemed much more pleasant and easy than it had for a long time. The path still led them along the side of the mountain rather than upward, but one day, on turning a corner, they found themselves looking down into a deep valley. To their surprise, their path actually plunged straight down the mountainside toward it, exactly as at the beginning of the journey when Much-Afraid had been led down into Egypt.

All three halted and looked first at one another, then down into the valley and across to the other side. There the ascent was as steep and even higher than the Precipice of Injury and they saw that to go down and then ascend again would not only require an immense amount of strength and effort, but also take a very long time.

Much-Afraid stood and stared, and at that moment experienced the sharpest and keenest test which she had yet encountered on the journey. Was she to be turned aside once again, but in an even more terrible way than ever before? By now they had ascended far higher than ever before. Indeed, if only the path they were following would begin to ascend, they could not doubt that they would soon be at the snowline and approaching the real High Places, where no enemies could follow and where the healing streams flowed.

Now instead of that the path was leading them down into a valley as low as the Valley of Humiliation itself. All the height which they had gained after their long and toilsome journey must now be lost and they would have to begin all over again, just as though they had never made a start so long ago and endured so many difficulties and tests.

As she looked down into the depths of the valley the heart of Much-Afraid went numb. For the first time on the journey she actually asked herself if her relatives had not been right after all and if she ought not to have attempted to follow the Shepherd. How could one follow a person who asked so much, who demanded such impossible things, who took away everything? If she went down there, as far as getting to the High Places was concerned she must lose everything she had gained on the journey so far. She would be no nearer receiving the promise than when she started out from the Valley of Humiliation.

For one black, awful moment Much-Afraid really considered the possibility of following the Shepherd no longer, of turning back. She need not go on. There was absolutely no compulsion about it. She had been following this strange path with her two companions as guides simply because it was the Shepherd's choice for her. It was not the way which she naturally wanted to go. Now she could make her own choice. Her sorrow and suffering could be ended at once, and she could plan her life in the way she liked best, without the Shepherd.

During this awful moment or two it seemed to Much-Afraid that she was actually looking into an abyss of horror, into an existence in which there was no Shepherd to follow or to trust or to love - no Shepherd at all, nothing but her own horrible self. Even after, it seemed that she had looked straight down into Hell. At the end of that moment Much-Afraid shrieked - there is no other word for it.

"Shepherd," she shrieked, "Shepherd! Shepherd! Help me! Where are you? Don't leave me!" Next instant she was clinging to him, trembling from head to foot, and sobbing over and over again, "You may do anything, Shepherd. You may ask anything - only don't let me turn back. O my Lord, don't let me leave you. Entreat me not to leave thee nor to return from following after thee." Then as she continued to cling to him she sobbed out, "If you can deceive me, my Lord, about the promise and the hind's feet and the new name or anything else, you may, indeed you may; only don't let me leave you. Don't let anything turn me back. This path looked so wrong I could hardly believe it was the right one," and she sobbed bitterly.

He lifted her up, supported her by his arm, and with his own hand wiped the tears from her cheeks, then said in his strong, cheery voice, "There is no question of your turning back, Much-Afraid. No one, not even your own shrinking heart, can pluck you out of my hand. Don't you remember what I told you before? "This delay is not unto death but for the glory of God." You haven't forgotten already the lesson you have been learning, have you?"

"It is no less true now that 'what I do thou knowest not now, but thou shalt know hereafter'. My sheep hear my voice, and they follow me. It is perfectly safe for you to go on in this way even though it looks so wrong, and now I give you another promise: Thine ears shall hear a word behind, thee saying, "This is the way, walk ye in it", when ye turn to the right hand or to the left."

He paused a moment, and she still leaned against him, speechless with thankfulness and relief at his presence. Then he went on. "Will you bear this too, Much-Afraid? Will you suffer yourself to lose or to be deprived of all that you have gained on this journey to the High Places? Will you go down this path of forgiveness into the Valley of Loss, just because it is the way that I have chosen for you? Will you still trust and still love me?"

She was still clinging to him, and now repeated with all her heart the words of another woman tested long ago. "Entreat me not to leave thee, or to return from following after thee; for whither thou goest I will go; thy people shall be my people and thy God my God." She paused and faltered for a moment, then went on in a whisper, "And where thou diest, will I die, and there will I be buried. The Lord do so to me, and more also, if aught but death part thee and me." (Ruth 1:16 & 17).*

*Used by permission from Tyndale Publishing House.

There is no way around it. We've been studying God's Word together for some time and you have no doubt learned some new things and had a couple of truths reinforced for you. Perhaps you've begun to apply some of what you've taken in or maybe you're still toying with the idea of whether or not you'll take that plunge.

Now is the time to decide. Either God is real or He is not. If He is not real, then we are fools. If God is real (and I believe it with all my being), then I ask you to choose your path. I ask you to search the Scriptures, then your own life, your own experience, your own world and if you find, as I and millions of others have, that God is real and does exist, that His Word is completely and absolutely true, then you must make the decision, as did Much-Afraid to step into that valley, no matter the cost. Remember what we said earlier, "I will *choose* to live my life in such a way that *if* God is not who He says He is, I will fall flat on my face." We walk by faith and not by sight.

Will you, like Much-Afraid, submit to His plan for your life, no matter what it is, because you won't, can't let Him go? Whether He has a valley ahead or a time of rest and re-creation, will you let go of doing it your own way and let Him have His way with your life? Habakkuk 3:19 was the promise that Much-Afraid held onto "The Lord God is my strength, And He has made my feet like hind's feet, And makes me walk on my high places." What promise of God's is ever before you? Mine was and is Proverbs 3:5 & 6 "Trust in the Lord with all your heart, and do not lean on your own understanding. In all your ways acknowledge Him, and He will make straight your paths."

Healing will not happen as you desire or plan or attempt just as your life has not happened as you desired, planned or attempted. God is sovereign. God is just and He is love and mercy and grace. His plan is not to destroy you. It is to heal you, change you, grow you and transform you! Elisabeth Elliot in her book, "A Path Through Suffering" wrote, "I can take His word for it that there are no depths to which I will be called to go where God will not be. Then I ask myself: but why do I need the word of anyone but God Himself? He has told me again and again and again that He is with me and will always be with me, in the deep river, the hot fire, the Valley of the Shadow. Yet I sometimes doubt Him. So, in His mercy, He brings along witness after witness, people who have learned dimensions of transforming grace impossible for them to have learned anywhere but where they were." As a witness to God's grace, trust me, nothing is wasted with God, not even your pain.

This is a time for you to make a decision in your life. Like Much-Afraid, there is a great valley (maybe dozens) that you must go through before you reach the rest of the mountains. Whom do you trust? What are you willing to leave behind? Will you go forward, not knowing what is ahead or retreat, being all too familiar with what is behind?

God desires for us to know Him, to follow Him, to trust Him and to understand our daily, moment-by-moment need for Him. Healing is an element of our relationship with God. Right now, it is a primary element because we are broken. God understands. He knows exactly what we need; we need Him.

"But we have this treasure in jars of clay, to show that
the surpassing power belongs to God and not to us.
We are afflicted in every way, but not crushed;
perplexed, but not driven to despair;
persecuted, but not forsaken;
struck down, but not destroyed;
always carrying in the body the death of Jesus,
so that the life of Jesus may also be manifested in our bodies."
2 Corinthians 4:7 - 10

CHAPTER 11: SORROW & MOURNING:
BROKEN VESSEL
GOING DEEPER: QUESTIONS FOR STUDY

1. Why do you think God allowed the writer of Psalm 77 to live through such a difficulty? What do these words say to you?

2. Why do you think God has allowed you to live through such painful circumstances? What do you think that He wants to teach you? How can He use it?

GETTING TO THE HEART OF THE MATTER:
APPLICATION

Take some time with Jesus. Write down what you have trouble giving up to Him (control, wounded heart, future, etc.). Tell Him why. Now write down some areas where you are really struggling (my difficulties were with shame and overwhelming fear of being hurt again). After you write them down, give them to Him as well. Now, make a choice. Are you going to do it the Shepherd's way, no matter what that means? Or are you going to continue to live life your way?

LAYING THE FOUNDATION: QUIET TIME

Read through the Psalms, pick one then re-write it in your own words. Let God speak to you through the sorrow and mourning and the truth of the Psalmists.

Psalm 5
Psalm 13
Psalm 22
Psalm 6 or 38
Psalm 63

CHAPTER 12

FORGIVENESS

"They refused to listen,
And did not remember Your wondrous deeds
which You had performed among them;
So they became stubborn and appointed a leader
to return to their slavery in Egypt.
But you are a God of forgiveness,
Gracious and compassionate,
Slow to anger and abounding in lovingkindness;
And You did not forsake them."
Nehemiah 9:17

It started with a phone call. The news about the movie, *"The Passion of the Christ"* had begun to heat up and opening day was approaching. I picked up the phone to call my Gram and ask if she wanted to join Mom and Dad and me at the theater. I expected a "no" as Gram is not especially interested in films that are graphic in nature and this film's reputation had already been set by the movie reviewers. Her answer surprised me, "of course I want to see it".

We arrived at the theater, each of us a little hesitant about what we would see. The room was packed and we were fortunate to find four seats together. My friend, Clare, who had come with us had to sit in the handicap section by herself as there was not another open space left. It's been years since I've seen a theater that full and never have I experienced one that quiet before the previews.

The film began and I whispered to myself that I would not look away. It was an easy promise to keep at first. My eyes were transfixed on the screen. I didn't look away through the mock trial and flogging, though I winced more than a couple of times. The tears would not stop flowing. The road up the hill, carrying the crossbar brought more tears, but I continued to watch. Then, when they laid Him on the cross and for a brief moment He rested, I took in a gulp of air and breathed with Him. The nail was placed in the center of the His right palm and they began to pound it in. I felt a sharp pain in my stomach and my knees went weak. When they moved to His left hand, I looked away.

I stared for a full moment at the darkened wall in the theater. I could see the silhouette cast by the flickering of the light off the screen as it bounced off of the audience members who were staring straight ahead. I don't know if it was that momentary glance away that did it, but all of a sudden, I felt like I was there as they crucified my Lord. I turned back to the screen as they nailed His feet and I began to whisper an audible, "I'm sorry; I'm so sorry" in the direction of the screen. Unable to completely secure the nail that held His feet, they flipped the cross so that Jesus hung on that tree, suspended only by the nails that held His limbs in place. After what seemed like an eternity, they secured His feet, righted the cross and dropped it in the hole.

The agony of Christ's physical death during those final hours was portrayed in an amazing way by Mel Gibson and Jim Caviezel. They captured the horror and the injustice of that day in a powerful and impactful way. I saw, for the first time, the pure agony and inhumanity of Jesus' death and it has been burned on my brain. The visual of 'the body broken' and 'the blood poured out' now had visceral images to expound their meaning. The first time I took Communion after seeing the film was especially meaningful to me. In that, I shed tears of gratitude to my Lord and Savior, Jesus Christ because as Hebrews 9:22 reminded me, "And according to the Law, one may almost say, all things are cleansed with blood, and without shedding of blood there is no forgiveness."

But what Mel and Jim could not capture, however, is what none of us can truly grasp. The horror of the cross, its 'scandalous beauty' if you will is that God sent His Son to be our substitute and bear the weight of our punishment. "For our sake He made Him to be sin who knew no sin, so that in Him we might become the righteousness of God." 2 Corinthians 5:21

Jesus, who had never sinned, had never known personally the bondage of sin nor its destructive power, literally became sin on that cross. Every evil, every act of deception and malice, of hatred and perversion was carried by Him who had never committed a single sin. He experienced on that cross the full vileness of every wicked and evil act in this world. He experienced on that cross the weight and guilt of us all. Remember the prophecy of Isaiah 53:4-6 "Surely he has *borne* our griefs and *carried* our sorrows; yet we esteemed him stricken, smitten by God, and afflicted. But he was *wounded* for our transgressions; he was *crushed* for our iniquities; *upon him was the chastisement that brought our peace,* and with his stripes we are healed." (Italics mine)

In that moment on the cross, Christ was what a Holy God can not bear; He became our sin. In that ugliness and transgression, He borne the full burden and impact of God's justice and punishment. For the first time, God the Son and God the Father were separated. In the scandal of the punishment Christ bore, for it should have been me, you and I met the wonderous and indescribable love of our God. Erwin Lutzer, in his book, *"Cries from the Cross",* put it this way: "At the cross, God's inflexible holiness and boundless love collided, and with a cry of anguish, we were redeemed. Here is sin with all of its horror and grace, with all of its wonder. The first three cries from the cross were uttered in daylight. But now nature shrouded the suffering of its Creator with darkness. This cry of dereliction, as it is called, was appropriately the middle of the seven sayings, the one that leads us into the mystery of our suffering God. 'My God, my God, why have you forsaken me?' (Matthew 27:46 and Mark 15:34)"

It is easy, I suppose, to be casual about our sin. A little *white* lie or a sin of omission and we say, "I'm sorry" and we move on. The truth of our sin, however, is that less than 100% pure is dirty and deserving of death. If it were possible for me to be *almost* sinless, that would mean in the eyes of God, I am completely and utterly sinful.

Realizing those truths then, I am faced with my own reality. While standing at the foot of the cross, I understand that my sins were borne and carried as Jesus was wounded and crushed for my lies and impure thoughts, for my self-sufficiency, self-righteousness and self-control issues, for every moment of fear and anger and lust, for every wayward thought and careless word and hurtful deed. Jesus paid the price for my years of wandering from God, knowing the truth of His love but choosing to not let that truth change me. I put those nails through His hands and feet because of my pride; and in amazement and grief, I realize that He *let* me, because He *loves* me, even today, especially today.

I am the sinner, of whom Jesus spoke in Luke 7:41 - 47 who owed the greater debt: (Luke 7:41-42) "A moneylender had two debtors; one owed five hundred denarii, and the other fifty. When they were unable to repay, he graciously forgave them both. So which of them will love him more?" Simon answered and said, "I suppose the one whom he forgave more." And He said to him, "You have judged correctly."

In that reality, I want to be the woman who spilled the perfume out on Jesus' feet as an act of worship, of gratitude: (Luke 7:43-47) "Turning toward the woman, He said to Simon, "Do you see this woman? I entered your house; you gave Me no water for My feet, but she has wet My feet with her tears and wiped them with her hair. You gave Me no kiss; but she, since the time I came in, has not ceased to kiss My feet. You did not anoint My head with oil, but she anointed My feet with perfume. For this reason I say to you, her sins, which are many, have been forgiven, for she loved much; but he who is forgiven little, loves little."

Which one are you? The one who owes only the fifty? Or the one, like me, who owes the five hundred? Before you answer, consider this: sin is not just about what we do, but why we do it and what we think. It is not just about the external act, but the internal heart motivation.

Jesus taught, in Matthew 5:21 - 22 "You have heard that the ancients were told, 'YOU SHALL NOT COMMIT MURDER' and "Whoever commits murder shall be liable to the court.' But I say to you that everyone who is angry with his brother shall be guilty before the court; and whoever shall say to his brother, 'Raca,' shall be guilty before the supreme court; and whoever shall say, 'you fool,' shall be guilty enough to go into the fiery hell." In essence, Jesus was teaching that it's not about keeping the Ten Commandments alone as an external act of obedience, but rather it is about being pure and sinless in your heart and your thoughts and your words and your actions.

Considering this, how sinless are you? Or, how desperate are you for a Savior? We all could answer, should answer that we are wretched indeed in light of Jesus' exposition on sin. Here's the good news: Jesus died for us sinners and only He makes possible a restored relationship with our God through His blood shed on the cross. Jesus' death and resurrection bring the forgiveness of sins to all who repent and trust in Him alone.

Forgiveness, then, is simply this: not being required to pay the debt that is owed. When I am forgiven, I've been released from my obligation to satisfy that debt. Forgiveness is nothing we can earn and therefore, nothing we can lose. If God forgives us of our sin, we are forgiven indeed! Listen to Paul in Colossians 2:13 & 14 "When you were dead in your transgressions and the uncircumcision of your flesh, He made you alive together with Him, having forgiven us all our transgressions, having canceled out the certificate of debt consisting of decrees against us, which was hostile to us; and He has taken it out of the way, having nailed it to the cross." Amen and amen!

In addition to an understanding of what forgiveness is, we need to study two other terms. The first is **mercy**. Mercy is not getting what I deserve. Because of our sin, we deserve death. But God in His mercy has made a way of escape that we would pass from death into life through Jesus Christ. Again, Paul says in Ephesians 2:4 & 5 "But God, being rich in mercy, because of His great love with which He loved us, even when we were dead in our transgressions, made us alive together with Christ (by grace you have been saved)." We love and serve a merciful God!

The other term we need to know is **grace**. Grace is getting what I do not deserve. I do not deserve life eternal; that is a gift of grace.

I do not deserve a relationship with my Father God; that is a gift of grace. In God's holiness, I do not deserve fellowship or hope or a future; they are all gifts of grace. Think upon the "riches of His grace" in your life as we hear again from Paul in Ephesians 1:7, 8a "In Him we have redemption through His blood, the forgiveness of our trespasses, according to the riches of His grace which He lavished on us."

Have you thought today about the "riches of His grace" in your life? Those things that you and I do not deserve and yet experience in fullness because of God's mercy and love and grace. My list is endless as I *deserve* nothing from God but condemnation and death. Every gift - family and friends, possessions, possibilities and even the potential in my life - are treasures lavished upon me. And, I've yet to begin my eternity with Him. Can you imagine the grace when you think about all of His promises in the Word about our eternity with Him - the word *lavished* seems a word too small.

It is impossible to appreciate or live out one's life in the correct attitude of worship and gratitude if one does not understand or grasp the power of forgiveness. We've covered the debt that we owe to God in Chapter 2. However, because we've never stood before the throne of the Righteous Judge and given an account for our sins, it is possible to escape the awful weight of what we've done (and continue to do in defiance of a holy God). At this point, then, it is vital for us to think of ourselves correctly - not as victims of our circumstances or as those who have an excuse for our sins, but rather as sinners saved by grace.

This world embraces the definition of victimhood as justification for anything that follows a moment or a childhood or a lifetime of violence and betrayal. And while we are not responsible for other people's sin, we are responsible for our own lives - in word and deed, thought and action. As a Christian, we stood, at the moment of conversion, to confess that we are sinners in need of a Savior. Now, through the process of sanctification, we must not think of ourselves in any other way. We are sinners saved by grace, God's grace through the person and work of Jesus Christ. We must be mindful, each and every day, that we are without excuse for our sin and in eternal debt to the Lord Jesus Christ for His act of mercy, His heart of love, His will in submission and His blood shed on that cross. "For He rescued us from the domain of darkness, and transferred us to the kingdom of His beloved Son in whom we have redemption, the forgiveness of sins." (Colossians 1:13-14)

John MacArthur in his book, *"Hard to Believe"* quotes the prayer of a saint from long ago used as the introductory prayer in Arthur Bennett's *"The Valley of Vision"*. In these words, picture your life as an instrument of praise to God for every gift and every treasure He has bestowed, even those moments of hardship and suffering.

> "Lord, high and holy, meek and lowly, let me learn
> by paradox that the way down is the way up, that to
> be low is to be high, that the broken heart is the
> healed heart, that the contrite spirit is the rejoicing
> spirit, that the repenting soul is the victorious soul,
> that to have nothing is to possess everything, that to
> bear the cross is to wear the crown, that to give is to
> receive. Let me find thy light in my darkness, thy joy
> in my sorrow, thy grace in my sin, thy riches in my
> poverty, thy glory in my valley, thy life in my death."

We are not victims of anything, especially and including circumstance. We are "more than conquerors through Him who loved us" (Romans 8:37). Children of the King, redeemed, restored and reminded of the One who gave up everything that we would have life. That is the power of forgiveness.

REPENTANCE
"Repent, for the kingdom of heaven is at hand."
Matthew 3:2

John the Baptist really was a boring sort of preacher. Everyday, he proclaimed the same message - "Repent, for the kingdom of heaven is at hand." Can you imagine walking into a church every Sunday and hearing that same sermon preached again and again. How often would you attend worship services? How eager would you be to tithe and to serve in a church like that?

John's message never varied, of course, because he had been sent to do a job, one job - prepare the way for the coming Messiah. In truth, he did it very well. As we look at the text, it is worth noting the thrust of the message. John could have said, "Pray, for the kingdom of heaven is at hand." or "Worship, for the kingdom of heaven is at hand." But our brother repeated over and over again *'repent'*. Why?

Remember, John's job was to *prepare* the masses for the Messiah. His job was to lay the ground work for a relationship with the One who would restore them, in relationship, to their God. The only way for a Holy God to have a relationship with a sinner is through confession, repentance and sacrifice (the spilling of inno-cent blood to cover the offense). Jesus was about to be *the* Sacrifice, once and for all. His death and resurrection would restore us into a relationship with God the Father, but we would have to repent first in order to receive the covering of the blood.

Every Jew who heard John knew what he meant. "Repent" means turn away from your sins, from doing things your broken, wrong and evil way by turning to God's way of living and doing. They knew that John was calling for a revival, a restoration of rela-tionship that begins with repentance. Our lives are no different. Relationship with God begins with repentance.

So, what is repentance?

Repentance is a change of heart, of mind, of attitude and of action. It is genuine confession married to a change of direction. It is so much more than "I'm sorry". It is an acknowledgment before God of wrong-doing together with a desire to be transformed by God. It is helpful to think of repentance in three steps.

FIRST, IT IS AN ACKNOWLEDGMENT OF MY SIN:

In order to confess and repent, I must agree with God that what I have done is a sin. Here is where so many people struggle. As the human race, we hate the word 'sin'. We will confess a mistake or a misstep. We will agree that we handled things poorly and apologize for being less than appropriate, but we are loathe to acknowledge our sin. Sin encompasses will. I make a choice to do what I want and I don't like anyone telling me that I violated anyone's law, especially God's perfect Law.

We rationalize and justify; we compare and negate; we measure against all others and determine that our 'mistake' was less impactful than theirs and therefore it does not rise to the measure of 'sin'. We all are cowards in this. Sin is sin; it is a violation of God's Law and when I commit a sin, I need to come to grips with it in order to confess it, repent and find forgiveness in Christ. I also need to come to grips with it for another reason. Unless I acknowledge sin as sin, I continue to live in bondage to its influence and its consequence. (I John 1:10) Freedom is only mine in truth. Remember, I am a sinner saved by grace. So are you.

King Saul, the first King of Israel had trouble with seeing his sin as sin. (Read I Samuel 13:1-14 and I Samuel 15:1 - 31). In fact, Saul got into a lot of difficulty over the issue of sins and he lost his kingdom due to his stubborn refusal to see his sin as sin.

In I Samuel 13:1-14, we find Saul waiting for Samuel to come and offer the sacrifice before the people of Israel were to go to war. Samuel, however, was delayed and Saul, in violation of God's Law, offered the sacrifice in his place. Only the Priests or the Prophets were allowed to offer the sacrifice; Saul had no business doing it himself. When Samuel confronted him about it; Saul replied, "the people were scattering. . .you were not coming. . .I forced myself". In other words, it's not my fault.

Then, in I Samuel 15:1-23, we find Saul in another predicament. The Lord sent Saul and the people of Israel to fight the Amalekites, commanding them to utterly destroy the people and all of their possessions. Saul went out with the army and was victorious. However, he and the men kept the spoils of war in defiance of God's command (I Samuel 15:9). Again, Samuel comes and confronts Saul in his sin. At first, Saul justifies himself saying "the people" kept the best of the livestock in order to offer it as a sacrifice to God (I Samuel 15:13-15; 20 & 21). Finally, even as Saul acknowledges his sin, his focus continues to be on 'looking' right before the people rather than accepting his sin (I Samuel 15:24-31).

For a clear contrast, let's look at King David, the second king of Israel. (Read 2 Samuel 11 - 12:13). David begins to get into trouble in verse 1 of chapter 11. It reads, "in the spring of the year, the time when *kings* go out to battle, David sent Joab" (italics mine). David sent his general in his stead, leaving himself time to get into trouble - "idle hands are indeed the devil's workshop". Now, in verse 2, we see David on the roof (during a time and in a place he did not belong), watching a beautiful woman named Bathsheba bathe. For the second time in two verses, he is not where he's suppose to be.

As so many of us do, David has opened the door to sin and quickly steps in. By verse 4, David is having an adulterous affair with Bathsheba. In verse 5, he's in trouble because she's pregnant. And in verse 6, David is sending for her husband, Uriah, in order to hide his deed. David is about to have another problem. Uriah, being an honorable man, will not sleep with his wife while the rest of Israel is away at war. What is David to do? In an attempt to hide his sin, David has Uriah killed (along with other men) in battle. Then, in a public show of 'mercy', David takes Bathsheba, the grieving widow, into his house. Now she can have David's baby and who's going to know? God will.

In comparison to Saul, David's acts of treason, murder, adultery, covetousness, lies, just to name a few, seem disproportionately wicked and deserving of greater judgment. However, God is about to teach us that it is not the sin, but the response to the sin - repentance - that matters to Him. In chapter 12, as Nathan confronts David with his secret sins, we catch a glimpse of God's heart. Hearing the harsh truth of what he has done, David says in verse 13, "I have sinned against the Lord."

No justifying, no rationalizing, no pathetic attempt to blame anyone else - David simply agrees with Nathan that he has sinned and David acknowledges it before the Holy One of Israel (read Psalm 51 - David wrote it after Nathan confronted him with his sin). In this, we begin to understand what God meant when He said that David was "a man after his own heart" (1 Samuel 13:14). Not perfect, not sinless, but when confronted with his sin, David agreed with God about his sin and was grieved by what he had done - no excuses, only a desire to confess, repent and be made right with God.

Would that we were all like David instead of like Saul. That in the one moment, when the opportunity reveals itself, we would, in truth and in courage, acknowledge our sin before a Holy God and stand accountable for what we've done and who we are. Acknowledging one's sin is the first step in repentance.

SECOND, A TRUE HEART BROKENNESS BEFORE GOD

As tempting as it is to pretend that our sin is anything other than sin, it is equally appealing to treat sin, when it is confessed, as a mere blip on the radar screen in our relationship with God. We focus so heavily on God's grace that we are quick to dismiss the price paid to set us free. Whether we have told a lie, participated in some gossip or betrayed a friend, we like to gloss over the moment of heart break in favor of the restoration. Only during Communion or perhaps, Good Friday and Easter, do we pause and reflect on the blood of the Lamb.

Truth be told, if we spent more time grasping the weight and the cost of our sin, I believe that we would be more thoughtful in the moment, more grieved in our confession and more grateful for His grace. David laments in Psalm 51:3 & 4 "For I know my transgressions, and my sin is ever before me. Against you, you only, have I sinned and done what is evil in your sight, so that you may be justified in your words and blameless in your judgment." Tears are not a prerequisite for forgiveness, but they can be a good indication of your heart. A lament not over being caught or living the consequences of one's sins, but rather over the blood-guiltiness of one's soul keeps our eyes on both the cross and the road ahead, guiding our choices in the future.

There is joy in the morning and God is so gracious in His love of us. In that truth, we must choose not to be casual about our sins, for they are many and He has paid for each and every one of them. David goes on to say (Psalm 51:17), "The sacrifices of God are a broken spirit; a broken and contrite heart, O God, you will not despise."

AND THIRD, A DESIRE TO BE CHANGED BY GOD

In John 8:1 - 11, the story is told of the woman who was caught in the act of adultery and cast before Jesus to be stoned for her sin. Jesus rebuked the crowd by saying, (John 8:7a) "Let him who is without sin among you be the first to throw a stone at her". The oldest in the group slipped away first and the youngest followed until Jesus was alone with the woman. In verse 10 we read, "Jesus stood up and said to her, 'Woman, where are they? Has no one condemned you?' She said, 'No one, Lord.' And Jesus said, 'Neither do I condemn you, go, and from now on sin no more.'"

Go and sin no more. Repentance, by definition, must include a change of behavior. I can not agree with God that what I am doing is wrong, grasp the price He paid to forgive me and then go skipping back into that sin without a care in the world. Agreement with God over my sin requires agreement with God to change my behavior, whether actions, words or thoughts. While it requires my will to submit, I must understand that change only happens through the power of God.

For example, if my sin is that I am harming my body through gluttony, then I need to be willing to let God change that in me. Jesus can bring about that change in several ways: through a new perspective - it is His body, on loan to me for a time so I need to care for it; through a new plan - I need to be accountable to a friend about my eating habits so that I may have encouragement from my sister; and through practice - learn what the Bible has to say on the subject by memorizing Scriptures, turning to God's Spirit for wisdom and understanding and turning to prayer for moment-by-moment assistance toward victory. As we said, repentance requires change for I can not say I am sorry about what I did and then muzzle those words as I repeat the actions or attitudes that lead to the sin.

Three necessary steps to repent, to turn away from my sin and back toward a holy God. Nowhere in Scripture does God require me to live a perfect life, that would be impossible. He requires me to live a life of choice, of purpose, dedicated to His holiness and in constant gratitude for all that He has done. Repentance is a necessary, daily ingredient in that relationship.

Thinking back on those moments in the theater, watching the imagines of Jesus on the cross, I think about His choice and His purpose. No one could have kept *the* instrument of creation on that cross unless He willingly gave Himself up. In His sacrifice, meditate on His love for you, in spite of your sin. Then, choose to live a life that reflects daily your heart of gratitude.

CHAPTER 12: FORGIVENESS AND REPENTANCE
GOING DEEPER: QUESTIONS FOR STUDY

1. Why is there no forgiveness without the shedding of blood? (Hint: Leviticus 17:11)

2. Do you consider yourself to have been forgiven much or forgiven little? What impact does that have on your life?

3. Do you make repentance a habit in your life? Are you broken by your sin and do you desire to be changed by God? If not, why not?

GETTING TO THE HEART OF THE MATTER: APPLICATION

Make a detailed list (for your eyes only) of your sins. Spend some time on your knees before God and ask Him to reveal to you sins that may not be obvious. After you finish the list, next to EVERY one, write the word – f o r g i v e n! or NAILED TO THE CROSS! Know that our sins are now as far as the East is from the West in God's eyes!

LAYING THE FOUNDATION: QUIET TIME

Meditate on these verses in Romans that expound the bondage of sin and the freedom that is in Christ Jesus our Lord.

Day ONE: Romans 3:21 - 26

Day TWO: Romans 5:6 - 11

Day THREE: Romans 6:10 - 16

Day FOUR: Romans 6:11 & 23

Day FIVE: Romans 8:1

CHAPTER 13

FORGIVING OTHERS

A nd so it is, we are faced on the right with an abiding and deep gratitude for God's forgiveness, for Jesus' sacrifice, for the hope and freedom that come from being released of the debt we could never satisfy. And now, we are faced on the left by the debt that is owed to us.

We sinners, who have violated God's Law, have been sinned against. People, sometimes friends and family, sometimes strangers, have wounded us with their carelessness and their ignorance, with their wickedness and their perversions, with their pride and their immorality. And we sit, shattered and broken, feeling victimized and in need of justice. And we wait to hear what God's holy Word has to say to us, abusers and abused alike.

Forgiveness, between God and man, is a restoration of the vertical relationship; forgiveness, one to another, is a restoration of the horizontal relationship. Neither is negotiable with God.

In Matthew 6:14 & 15, Jesus says, "For if you forgive men for their transgressions, your heavenly Father will also forgive you. But if you do not forgive men, then your Father will not forgive your transgressions." These words come on the heels of the Lord's prayer where Jesus taught His disciples to pray (Matthew 6:12), "And forgive us our debts, *as* we also have forgiven our debtors." (Emphasis mine.) Then, again in Mark 11:25 & 26 Jesus taught, "And whenever you stand praying, forgive, if you have anything against anyone; so that your Father also who is in heaven may forgive you your transgressions. But if you do not forgive, neither will your Father who is in heaven forgive your transgression."

As I read those verses I see that *if* I forgive, I will be forgiven by God. Why do you think that is?

On that cross, Jesus paid the price for my sin. It was *the* payment required by a holy God to satisfy my debt. When I refuse to forgive another for the debt that they owe me, I am saying that I require *more* than a holy God in order for the account to be settled. The blood spilled and the body broken are fine by God's standards, but my standards are just a little higher. The person who sinned against me will have to do more than live a perfect life (already impossible if they have sinned against me) and die a sacrificial death before I would even consider clearing the board and releasing them from their obligation.

In your unforgiveness, you may not think that this is what you are saying, but it is. If you will not abide by God's standard of justice and His acceptance of Jesus' death and resurrection as payment for sin, then you are declaring your standard to be higher. So, as God commands us to forgive those who have sinned against us, He reminds us that His is the perfect standard of justice, of holiness and of righteousness. He reminds us that His standard has been met and nothing else is required, not from me, not from you and not from them. To insist otherwise is to violate God Himself.

In addition, to forgive another is to practice the very grace and mercy that we ourselves have received. Jesus gave us a great example of this principle in Matthew 18:21-35:

> "Then Peter came and said to Him, 'Lord, how often shall my brother sin against me and I forgive him? Up to seven times?'
>
> Jesus said to him, 'I do not say to you, up to seven times, but up to seventy times seven.'
>
> For this reason the kingdom of heaven may be compared to a king who wished to settle accounts with his slaves. When he had begun to settle *them*, one who owed him ten thousand talents was brought

to him. But since he did not have *the means* to repay, the lord commanded him to be sold, along with his wife and children and all that he had, and repayment to be made.

So the slave *fell to the ground* and prostrated himself before him, saying, 'Have patience with me and I will repay you everything.'

And the lord of that slave felt compassion and released him and forgave him the debt.

But that slave went out and found one of his fellow slaves who owed him a hundred denarii; and he seized him and *began* to choke him, saying 'Pay back what you owe.'

So his fellow slave fell *to the ground* and began to plead with him, saying, 'Have patience with me and I will repay you.'

But he was unwilling and went and threw him in prison until he should pay back what was owed.

So when his fellow slaves saw what had happened, they were deeply grieved and came and reported to their lord all that had happened.

Then summoning him, his lord said to him, 'You wicked slave, I forgave you all that debt because you pleaded with me. Should you not also have had mercy on your fellow slave, in the same way that I had mercy on you?'

And his lord, moved with anger, handed him over to the torturers until he should repay all that was owed him.

My heavenly Father will also do the same to you, if each of you does not forgive his brother from your heart."

Forgiving others, as we are commanded to do is an act of obedience and it is an act of worship for the gift of grace. In addition, forgiving another the debt owed produces fruit and blessing in ways we do not always expect.

A BITTER YIELD:

In a word, unforgiveness leads inevitably to bitterness. The focus is on me - I endured; I suffered; I was violated; I'm due. All of that energy turned inward and repeated to one's soul day in and day out without resolution churns and burns until the entire world is guilty and nothing will satisfy. God commands us to forgive for many reasons, not the least of which is that forgiveness releases the poisons from our system. Yes, there is injustice in this world. But remember, the greatest injustice was the perfect Son of God condemned and crucified when He was guiltless. Whatever we've endured, nothing compares to that. And on that cross, as He was made to bear that burden He cried out, "Father, forgive them, for they do not know what they are doing." Luke 23:34

SHOULDERS TOO NARROW:

Not being God, I have come to appreciate that I do not have the capacity for some things, okay, for many, many things. One of those things is this: I can not bear the weight of another's sin. I just can't carry it. I wasn't designed to do so. I need to give it up and over to Him because it is His job to weight and measure, His job to keep track and His job to require payment of the debt, either through His Son or from the individual on judgment day. Paul reminds us that it is God's job alone when he says in Romans 12:19 "Never take your own revenge, beloved, but leave room for the wrath *of God*, for it is written, "VENGEANCE IS MINE, I WILL REPAY," says the Lord."

Deeply appreciating my capacity, I need to be willing and faithful to give over to God what is His, then I must do what is mine. My job is to be an agent of reconciliation, keeping the door open for that individual to find what I have found, the forgiveness and love of our God. In Romans 12, Paul goes on to tell us our job (v.20 & 21), "BUT IF YOUR ENEMY IS HUNGRY, FEED HIM, AND IF HE IS THIRSTY, GIVE HIM A DRINK; FOR IN SO DOING YOU WILL HEAP BURNING COALS UPON HIS HEAD." Do not be overcome by evil, but overcome evil with good."

If through my actions, I draw that individual into an eternal relationship with God, I am blessed by the Lord using me in a difficult situation to be an instrument of salvation in another life. But, if through my actions, feeding and giving water to my enemy, they turn from God in disgust, that individual has sealed their own fate, having been given a clear choice. My actions will either draw or repel and I will either experience their repentance for what they've done or God's justice for what they've done. Either way, I've been obedient, living under His protection and blessing.

FIELDS OF FAITH:

Trusting God with my wounds is an act of living and vibrant faith, acknowledging that only He can do what needs to be done. Remember, He is the God of justice and it is His Law, His standard that has been violated. I can not say that I believe in God and that I have faith and then refuse to give over to Him those offenses that cut the deepest, or those individuals who've hurt me the most. He knows what I've endured and letting Him have that pain, that crime which cries out for justice proclaims in action louder than words that I believe and I trust Him with all of me. Remember, our faith must be living and active.

I GAIN PERSPECTIVE:

When I can not forgive, those offenses haunt me until all I see is that individual and their sin. I must remember that my suffering is no greater than the suffering of any of my brothers and sisters throughout history. And it is nothing in comparison to Jesus. In addition, I will certainly be offended again. Letting go now in forgiveness as I am commanded to do allows me to prepare and live on this earth as a child of God, hostile in mind and heart to the prince of this world. Colossians 3:12 & 13 reminds me of the need for perspective when I realize in these verses that I've been called to live, in and through Christ, a remarkable life, "And so, as those who have been chosen of God, holy and beloved, put on a heart of compassion, kindness, humility, gentleness and patience; bearing with one another, and forgiving each other, whoever has a complaint against anyone; just as the Lord forgave you, so also should you."

And Romans 12:15 - 18 puts perspective on what our lives are to be as a result of all that we've received from Jesus, "Bless those who persecute you; bless and curse not. Rejoice with those who rejoice, and weep with those who weep. Be of the same mind toward one another; do not be haughty in mind, but associate with the lowly. Do not be wise in your own estimation. Never pay back evil for evil to anyone. Respect what is right in the sight of all men. If possible, so far as it depends on you, be at peace with all men." In those words, I realize I MUST forgive for I haven't the energy to hold tight to those offenses and then live out Colossians 3 and Romans 12. I must choose to release the former (offenses) and embrace the latter (obedience) as a disciple of Christ.

I GET TO LOOK MORE LIKE JESUS

Appreciating as best we can in our small and simplistic way what Jesus endured on the cross, His example of mercy and grace in the face of tremendous evil is the only example I need of how to live. I cannot model Christ and hold onto grievances against anyone. Imagine where we would all be if Jesus had done that. What if He had not uttered those words on the cross, "Father, forgive them" or if He had not been willing to sacrifice all for a sinner like me? Not one of us would be safe, nor saved. On the other hand, as I forgive those who've sinned against me, I am taking a giant leap toward looking more and more like my Savior. What in life is more valuable? What will yield a greater reward in eternity? The answer to both, of course, is nothing!

FINALLY, MERCY'S THE TICKET

Grasping as best I can what stands before those who'll walk into Jesus' throne room on judgment day, I need to extend mercy now in hopes of saving them from that final sentence then. No matter what anyone has done to you, I promise you that once you catch a glimpse of what hell will be, you would not wish it on your worst enemy.

Hell is every wicked and perverse sin and person, ruined by evil, living in utter blackness, void of all light and of all hope, eternally existing apart from the presence of God. After they have been there for a million years, the dream of never having lived will be their prayer but there will be no one to hear it uttered. It is not a cartoon of fire and funny-looking creatures with horns and tail having a party. I promise you that it is very real and it will receive more souls than either you or I can imagine. God's Holiness is not something with which to trifle.

If, by extending mercy and grace to those who owe you a debt, you can encourage and lead another away from that end, what gold would be of greater value than that? Even as we receive wounds from this world, how we respond brings glory to God and accomplishes His purpose. Remember, we are no longer living for ourselves. In practicing forgiveness, we need to be mindful of the One who called us to Himself.

I've had the blessing of watching more than a few women and men face those who have sinned against them. One woman in particular, a very good friend, lives out her testimony each time I see her with her dad.

When she was a child, her father sexually abused her. Years later, she found the Lord and began the process of working through her past and her pain. Determined to be obedient to God's Word, she realized that she needed to forgive her dad for what he had done. As she prayed over that very thing, she felt led to write him a letter releasing him from the debt that he owed her.

Reading the letter began the process of breaking down barriers between them. Eventually, in her willingness to forgive him, it opened the door and he came to a saving faith in Christ. Today, they can often be seen in church, sitting together in a celebration of God's mercy and grace. More than once, her testimony has brought the senior pastor to tears as he teaches on God's command to forgive. What greater blessing for a pastor than that, to look up and see someone actively practicing God's commands, living in freedom and unity in that obedience.

So, how do I forgive?

Here are some steps that will help you with that process. Notice, the steps rely on action (an act of our will) and not on emotion. The steps are the same whether the person has asked for forgiveness or not. Most often, we will be called to forgive a person long before, if ever, they realize their need to be forgiven. This is vital for us to understand. Forgiving another person of the sins that he or she has committed against me has very little or nothing to do with them. I forgive as an act of obedience because it will bring me freedom and joy (as we've been discussing). A person may come to you and ask for forgiveness and if that happens, it is a blessing. But nine times out of ten, you will act to forgive independent of their request or appreciation of their need for forgiveness.

STEP ONE:

I must give the sin against me up and give it over to God (vertical relationship) and once given, I must *never* bring it up again. Psalm 103:12 reminds me that that is how God acts in forgiveness. He doesn't bring my sin up again. This is the part of the process where I recognize that it is only in God's power that I can obey. "Here it is God, this awful thing that was done to me - please take it, carry it, hold it and when the time comes, if he or she does not come to a saving faith in Jesus, then You collect the debt owed."

STEP TWO:

After giving the sin up to God, I must *never* bring it up to myself (internal). This is that freedom we spoke of earlier. To forgive is to forget. Unforgiveness requires focus and energy and time, producing bitterness and wrath. Forgiveness requires me to release it to Jesus, knowing that He already paid the price for it. Remember, it is God's to hold until the debt is paid. I no longer require payment and therefore no longer have to keep track of the sin.

STEP THREE:

Once given over to God, I must forgive the person and *never* bring it up to others or the individual again (horizontal relationship). This step is vital.

First, I must not bring it up to others. Unless the sin is a continuing sin by an individual who is a believer and it needs to be dealt with in the church by the elders or pastors, I am not to talk about what this person has done. If the individual is not a believer, then they are not under the authority of the church and to talk about the sin is to gossip about it. It accomplishes nothing other than satisfying my temporary need for everyone to know that I've been violated and I am in need of justice. Remember, we are not to make ourselves the focus. When a sin has been committed, it should be dealt with privately between the two parties if possible and certainly with God. Adding an audience only means that I want to parade around in my victimhood.

Second, I must not bring it up to the one who has sinned or else I will be saying that I still hold them accountable for the action. Now, if they bring it up to me, acknowledging what they did and asking for forgiveness, it is fine to talk through that. The principle, here again, is I cannot claim to have forgiven if the sin is ever before me. Remember, I am not designed to carry the weight of that burden.

Restoration of the relationship will not happen all at once. In fact, there are some people who are dangerous for us to be around as they continue in their sin. Ask God for wisdom and if necessary, speak to a church elder or pastor about any relationship that involves a continuing sin pattern. Remember, in this, we are focusing on our part, not their part. God's command is for us to release the debt and trust Him with the injustice, the sin. Our response is to be - yes Lord. In that obedience, God will take care of the offending party.

STEP FOUR:

If necessary, repeat any of those steps should the sin be brought to mind or brought up to an individual. Ask God for the strength to believe that He is the God of justice who will repay and you can trust Him with this sin.

There is a cost to forgiveness. No one knows that better than God. He understands that we have to give up the wound, give up the revenge, give up the right we feel for justice. But, He promises that in giving them up to Him, He will give us something better in return - His peace that passes all understanding.

Forgiving another person is about me. Releasing them from their debt to me and trusting them to God's justice, celebrates the truth that God is God and I am not. Happily, in this, I am not. God does not require me to be able to handle the horrible impact of that dirty deed and I need not carry it one minute more. Choose today to trust God's goodness in this - let Him carry what has already cost you too much.

CHAPTER 13: FORGIVING OTHERS
GOING DEEPER: QUESTIONS FOR STUDY

1. Why is unforgiveness a form of pride?

2. When we forgive a debt owed us, what are we proclaiming about God? About us? About the debt?

3. What are the problems that you run into when forgiving others? How can you work through them?

GETTING TO THE HEART OF THE MATTER: APPLICATION

Spend some time on your knees and pray for God to bring to mind those that you need to forgive. Remember to first thank God for forgiving you of ALL your sin. Then, as God brings these individuals to mind, turn them over to Him, one by one. Don't skip this part or hurry it along - it is essential to be honest with God and obedient in all things.

LAYING THE FOUNDATION: QUIET TIME
WHAT IS GOD TEACHING YOU ABOUT FORGIVENESS?

Day ONE: Ephesians 1:7 & Romans 5:10

Day TWO: Matthew 6:14 - 15; Mark 11:25 & 26

Day THREE: Matthew 18:21-35

Day FOUR: Luke 22:47 - 70 & Luke 23

Day FIVE: Colossians 3:12 - 13; Ephesians 4:32

CHAPTER 14:

HOLY & UNHOLY FEAR

~⚘~

From a very early age, fear has been one of my traveling companions. I am a person who is afraid of everything. When I was a kid, loud noises and harsh voices use to make me throw up. As a teenager, especially after the violence I endured, I found myself loath to leave my house after dark or go to unfamiliar places. I would get up every night around 2 AM, during the years I lived alone, and check the doors and windows to make sure that they were locked. Even now, as God has helped me conquer the foundation of my unholy fears, I find myself in the moment, reacting in fear and then having to give it over to God. It is an area in which He and I are continually working and I am growing. Praise God!

Fear is an odd creature. It can be helpful in the moment to make us more aware of potential danger. Walking down the road, hearing screeching tires and a racing engine, all of our nerve endings turn on and we whirl around to scope out the situation and decide how we should react. If the car is heading straight for us, the body, working on an adrenaline rush initiated by the fear, kicks into high gear and prepares to avoid the collision. Here, fear is good.

But fear can also be a hazard, creating monsters and mayhem where none exists. Charles Spurgeon once said of fear, "Such strange creatures are we that we probably smart more under the blows which never fall upon us than we do under those which do actually come." Here, fear is a five hundred pound gorilla we tote around on our backs that adds nothing and takes away a significant part of our peace and energy.

The Bible really breaks down fear into two categories. Holy fear is a respect and awe for God. We manifest this when we live with the correct mindset and attitude toward a holy, awesome and awe-full God who is to be treated with the highest reverence and deference, having the appropriate place in our lives and responded to in a God-honoring way. At the end of Ecclesiastes in 12:33, King Solomon who has just related that all other pursuits are vanity or the definition of useless and absurd, the king concludes, "The end of the matter; all has been heard. 'Fear God and keep His commandments, for this is the whole duty of man.'"

Additionally, holy or appropriate fear is a fear that warns us of impeding (immediate) danger and entreats us to act in a responsible way. Standing up in the middle of a gun battle, refusing to take shelter in a hurricane, riding in the passenger seat of a car being driven by a drunk driver, these are not responsible nor God-honoring responses to situations that should, by right, induce fear. When the warning light of fear flashes in our lives, we need to determine if and how we are to respond. That is a holy fear and it orders our lives in the proper way.

Unholy or sinful fear can be described then as a nearly continuous feeling of anxiety, worry or agitation caused by the presence, nearness or perception of danger. It is a fear that controls and directs our lives toward self and self-protection, and it is a sin. This kind of fear leads directly to idolatry, putting something or someone ahead of God. And, it flows directly from a lack of faith and most often from a lack of maturity as a Christian. Unholy fear puts the emphasis not on God and His power but rather on man, especially self, and his resources.

In the gospels, Jesus talks about both kinds of fear in Matthew 10:28, "And do not fear those who kill the body, but are unable to kill the soul; but rather fear Him who is able to destroy both soul and body in hell." What Jesus is telling us is, do not fear men (unholy fear) because all that they can do is kill the body; but, rather, fear God (holy fear) because He has the power to condemn us to eternal death. Fear of man, in this passage is temporary and is based on a physical reality that we will die a physical death only once. This is limited power. But, fear of God, in this passage is eternal and is based on a spiritual reality that we can die a spiritual death and spend our eternal lives in damnation. This is absolute power and it is God's alone.

Let's begin by further defining our sinful fear so that we can recognize it, confess and repent of it and choose to live in fear of God alone.

Unholy fear is also called worry or anxiety and it produces a double-minded individual. In Matthew 6:19-34, Jesus lays out for us the truth about worry, beginning in verse 19 "Do not lay up for yourselves treasures on earth, where moth and rust destroy and where thieves break in and steal". He begins by focusing on our priorities, our passions, and our "gold" if you will. When the externals matter more than the internals, our lives will be about anxiety in trying to keep and maintain our "fortunes" or our lives will be about their loss. In verse 25, Jesus goes on to expand our "treasures" to include personal health and life needs.

Back in Matthew 6:21, Jesus begins to refocus us, however, on His priorities by reminding us, "For where your treasure is, there your heart will be also." If what matters to you are the temporal and shiny, then you are in for a life of either anxiety or misfortune. If what matters to you is the eternal (v.20), "but lay up for yourselves treasures in heaven, where neither moth nor rust destroys and where thieves do not break in and steal", then no one has power over you and you live in peace, depending on the promises of God.

In Matthew 6:25 - 32, Jesus gets personal, addressing our needs of food, shelter and material possessions in order to survive on this earth. In that, He reminds us that God knows what we need and based on His track record, God can be trusted to provide it. I love verse 27, "And which of you by being anxious can add a single hour to his span of life?" What peace that brings me! I am not in control of my life; I can not provide for my needs; I can only produce heartache and pain by thinking I am in control and I can provide. My job, my clothes, my home, even my food are provided by God who owns all and gives to His kids as He desires.

Jesus ends the lesson on releasing unholy fear in a spectacular and practical way in verses 33 and 34, "But *seek* first the kingdom of God and his righteousness, and all these things will be added to you. Therefore do not be anxious about tomorrow, for tomorrow will be anxious for itself. Sufficient for the day is its own trouble." Combating unholy fear includes a need to refocus our thoughts, our sight and our energies. Keep hold of that truth.

Unholy fear, however, can also be about man. David, the second King of Israel, lived the fear of man for a time in his life as he was hunted by Saul who wanted to kill him. David addressed the issue in this way Psalm 23:4 "Even though I walk through the valley of the shadow of death, I fear no evil; for Thou art with me; Thy rod and Thy staff, they comfort me." In these verses, David is saying that although he is facing mortal man's greatest fear - death - he has no fear because God is with Him. God is greater than death; therefore, God is greater than our fear.

David goes on to ask the question: "whom shall I fear?" He knows from experience and we know from God's Word, that Yahweh is greater than all of our enemies combined. And so David asks, whom shall I fear? His answer, of course, is no one! "The Lord is my light and my salvation; Whom shall I fear? The Lord is the defense of my life; Whom shall I dread? When evildoers come upon me to devour my flesh, My adversaries and my enemies, they stumbled and fell. Though a host encamp against me, My heart will not fear; Though war arise against me, In spite of this, I shall be confident." Psalm 27:1-3

David goes on to admit that man has already beaten him down and nearly destroyed him. The concept of an enemy was not new to David. He had to fight many battles and more than once he was trampled and oppressed. But each time, he claimed the promise of God's deliverance because He knew that God's power was eternal and absolute. David's enemy could only destroy his body. They could never destroy his soul. "Be gracious to me, O God, for man has trampled upon me; Fighting all day long he oppresses me. My foes have trampled upon me all day long, For they are many who fight proudly against me. When I am afraid, I will put my trust in Thee. In God, whose word I praise, In God I have put my trust; I shall not be afraid. *What can mere man do to me?*" Psalm 56:1-4

It was the *ultimate* question that David asked: what can mere man do to me? The answer is nothing! Whatever we endure in this lifetime in terms of suffering or pain, it is limited and temporary. And although it is agonizing and difficult for a time, God promises us that it will end. Our hope is in our eternal Savior.

As I told you, fear has been an issue for me. Fear and shame were for me two of the toughest issues with which to deal as God began the healing process. As I started to attend Harvest regularly, God used the power of His Word to encourage and change and grow me. The fear, especially of physical harm, began to abate. How do I know? I slept through the night without checking the door and window locks. God was teaching me the truth of who He is and as He replaced the lies I had believed, the fear subsided.

In whom do we usually have confidence? We trust those who have proven themselves faithful and true! God is the only one who is perfectly faithful and true! That is why we spent so much time on His character. For me to believe Him and to grow in my faith, especially in light of an issue like fear, I have to *know* Him.

This does not mean that I will never be hurt again. God is in control and if He chooses to allow me to through other difficult circumstances, I will go through them. Here is the difference, however, between me then and me now. Then, I believed that God was all about my comfort and ease. Now, I know that God is all about growing me to resemble His Son. Then, my life view was about here and now. Now, my life view is focused on living here in such a way as to proclaim my understanding and excitement about an eternity with Him. Then, when things, like violence or sickness or death, happened to me or to the people I loved, I saw God as having failed me. Now, when those things happen, I understand that God is allowing it for a reason and that I can trust His heart for me.

So, let's turn our attention to holy fear. In the chapter on God's holiness, we learned to look at Him in a new light. He is unapproachable in His holiness and powerful in His might. He is not our buddy or pal or friend, but is instead our Creator, our Father, our God. God, as the Three-in-One, is our authority. He is in control of everything, owns everything, created all that exists and we live because, in His goodness, He allows us to do so.

It's vital to continue the job we began in the beginning of the book of looking at God, as best we can, from His perspective. We are not in the same class nor even in the same universe in any regard. God has all power. I have none. God has all control. The only control I have is over me, and even then, I only control my will, my choices, certainly not my destiny. God is the very definition of holiness, righteousness and justice. In Job 40:9, God asked Job, "Have you an arm like God, and can you thunder with a voice like his?" The answer, of course, is no!

When I see God correctly, I am encouraged by His power, His control and His might. Because He is good and I know that He loves me, there will never be a moment when my enemies have more resources or energy than the One who will protect and sustain me. In that fact, I agree with David, "what can mere man do to me?".

Paul, in Philippians 2:12 & 13 says, "Therefore, my beloved, as you have always obeyed, so now, not only as in my presence but much more in my absence, work out your own salvation with fear and trembling, for it is God who works in you, both to will and to work for his good pleasure." "With fear and trembling" - a phrase for the ages.

We are too casual with God these days. We forget that in the throws of His love that He is still and forever holy. No one will confuse that when we all stand before His throne. Don't let yourself forget that now. Working out your salvation with fear and trembling means that you have that right perspective and deep appreciation for the differences between you and God.

Solomon, in the Proverbs, calls the fear of God the beginning of wisdom. It is the cornerstone of a right relationship with the Author of life. When God began to reveal His character to my wounded soul, it was in the fear of Him, the respect and awe of His power and might, His standards and His glory, that my life found balance and hope.

If you can look at the night sky, the one that God spoke into existence, or read the book of Joshua and hear how God deals with His enemies, or call to mind the picture that Scripture paints of eternity and not find in those images and memories and words a God of indescribable proportion and power, then you are indeed a fool. For the rest of us, let this be a call to honor and hold in highest esteem God - Himself, His Son, His Spirit, His Word, His world, His people and His plans.

You can begin by telling Him how grateful you are. If you are a single woman who desires a husband, thank God for your singleness. If you are a childless couple who desire a child, thank God for His timing. If you are living in a one room apartment and desire to own your own home, thank God for His wisdom and His generous provision. Learn to thank Him for all of your heart's desires - relationships, materials, health (whether good or bad) and wealth (whether rich or poor) and more. Learn to thank Him for all of those things that you would never choose for yourself - difficult circumstances, unwanted changes, consequences of our sins, suffering and sorrow. Learn to love Him even when you disagree with His will for you, choosing to submit your will to His.

Glean what you can from everything around you. A godly perspective is better than gold as it will serve you twice as long and make you rich in the heavenly realms. Develop and nurture an attitude of gratitude, spending hours each day thanking God for His generosity that you enjoy every day. Then, pass it on. Teach your children that every breath they draw is from God; every bite of food comes from His hand; every toy and piece of clothing overflow from His goodness and love.

Agree with Jesus when He called you and I, in Matthew 6, toward the heavenly realms, that we can only serve one master. Proclaim with your life that that master is God. Embrace every relationship as a loan; every friendship as a gift-wrapped present; every blue sky as a kiss from above. Memorize the words of Paul when he says in Philippians 3:13b - 14 "Forgetting what lies behind and straining forward to what lies ahead, I press on toward the goal for the prize of the upward call of God in Christ Jesus."

Cultivate holy fear. Worship the Lord for who He is and what He does. Make it a daily, an hourly ritual of praises that you and I may keep Him ever before our eyes. That is how we "work out our salvation with fear and trembling". It is a necessary view of things and with it comes a freedom and a hope that you may never have known before.

A day is coming when God will judge the earth and all who dwell in it (2 Thessalonians 1:7), "The Lord Jesus [shall be] revealed from heaven with His mighty angels, in flaming fire." All will stand before His throne and give an account - those who believe will account for the good they have done; those who don't believe will be held accountable for the evil they have done. None will be excused. In this reality, please join me in agreeing with Solomon that "the fear of the Lord" is indeed, "the beginning of wisdom".

CHAPTER 14:
GOING DEEPER: QUESTIONS FOR STUDY

1. What are some of the differences between holy and unholy fear?

2. Why is the fear of people a *crisis of faith*?

3. List several ways in which you *practice* holy fear of God:

GETTING TO THE HEART OF THE MATTER:
APPLICATION

Are there people and / or situations that cause you great fear? List them. Hand them over to God, one by one, and ask God to grow your **faith** in the area of trust and of surrender to His Will, His Way and His Plan for your life.

Then, list the benefits of fearing the Lord:
Proverbs 14:26; 14:27; 15:33; 19:23; 22:4
Psalm 25:12 - 14; 112:1, 7 & 8

Choose one verse upon which to meditate this week.

LAYING THE FOUNDATION: QUIET TIME

Day ONE: DO THE APPLICATION

Day TWO: Psalm 111

Day THREE: Psalm 33:6 - 9

Day FOUR: 2 Timothy 1:7 - 12

Day FIVE: Luke 12:3 - 12

CHAPTER 15:

ANGER

"The Lord will fight for you while you keep silent."
Exodus 14:14

Like holy and unholy fear, we are going to study righteous and unrighteous anger. In that comparison, we will learn as we did in the previous chapter that we can experience anger in a God-honoring way, but we can also express it in a sinful way.

To begin, let's define anger in general. Anger is a response to an injustice, whether actual or perceived, committed against a person or persons with whom we hold allegiance. Anger can also be an emotional response to any situation that causes us displeasure or pain or hardship. In that definition, the response to the situation must be viewed in light of the person wronged. For example, if I am the one who has experienced an injustice and my expression of anger is directed toward that reality, then my anger is a sin. Remember what we said before, I don't have rights; I have responsibilities and privileges. In that Biblical focus, I need to be mindful of who is at the center of my life, Jesus or me.

Often, when we are the focus of our lives, the injustices and violations can build until we explode at any provocation or slight. Uncontrollable anger or rage, remember, is a sin. It is a part of the old nature that is crucified with Christ and it is an emotional response that must be brought into submission to the sanctifying work of God in our lives. Paul, in Colossians 3:1-13 (v. 8 – 10) identifies the issue, "But now you also, put them all aside: anger, wrath, malice, slander, and abusive speech from your mouth. Do not lie to one another, since you laid aside the old self with its evil practices, and have put on the new self who is being renewed to a true knowledge according to the image of the One who created him." The focus here is to be remade in Christ's image. To do that, I cannot be focused on my rights or on injustices that I will endure. Remember, Jesus endured the greatest injustice of all.

Having said that, the Bible does not say that anger, itself, is a sin. In fact, we are told to "be slow to anger" and not to sin in our anger. "He who is slow to anger has great understanding, But he who is quick-tempered exalts folly" (Proverbs 14:29). "BE ANGRY, AND YET DO NOT SIN; do not let the sun go down on your anger and do not give the devil an opportunity" Ephesians 4:17 - 32 (v.26 & 27). In other words, you can be angry, even justifiably so (we will explore how in a moment), but even in that, be tempered and slow and controlled. Exemplify Christ, even as He was angry but did not sin (Matthew 21:12 – 17; Mark 11:15-18; Luke 19:45-48).

If I am angry because *I* have been offended or hurt or wronged, then my anger is self-centered and, as we will see, self-destructive. Even if we believe ourselves to be justified in our anger because of a grave injustice, anger is an expression of something owed. And as we have learned in our study thus far, God is the only one who can claim "something owed". I owe God. Period. I owe Him my life - my heart (emotions), my mind (intellect) and my soul (will). There is no one else on this earth who "owes" me in the same way that I owe God; therefore, there is no one else on this earth with whom I can be angry on my behalf and be justified.

Unrighteous anger is a snare. It is an especially destructive sin that can become habitual. Be careful not to let it have a foothold in your life. "Do not associate with a man given to anger; or go with a hot-tempered man, lest you learn his ways, and find a snare for yourself" (Proverbs 22:24-25). It is interesting, isn't it that the Scripture passage warns us against even associating "with a man given to anger". The implication is that anger becomes almost like a disease.

We can catch the mindset or the energy of the individual who is quick to explode and loathe to control. In that time spent, we can begin to look at ourselves, yet again, as victims of an immoral and unjust society; therefore, justified in whatever we do in response.

If this has already happened to you, let's remember three things. First, God is my justice. "Vengeance is Mine, and retribution, In due time their foot will slip; For the day of their calamity is near, And the impending things are hastening upon them" (Deuteronomy 32:35). Second, God is my refuge. "God is our refuge and strength, A very present help in trouble" (Psalm 46:1). And third, our energy is to be spent growing the fruit of the Spirit. "But the fruit of the Spirit is love, joy, peace, patience, kindness, goodness, faithfulness, gentleness, self-control; against such things there is no law" (Galatians 5:22). Again, it's important to remember that we cannot be fully devoted to growing the fruit of the Spirit and nursing a heart of hatred and vengeance. They both don't fit in one body. You and I have the ability, no matter the circumstance, no matter the injustice, to choose.

We are called to be agents of reconciliation even if we are completely blameless. "If therefore you are presenting your offering at the altar, and there remember that your brother has something against you, leave your offering there before the altar, and go your way; first be reconciled to your brother, and then come and present your offering" (Matthew 5:21-24 (23-24)). When we respond in love and forgiveness instead of anger to injustice, we become witnesses to the power of God's grace and mercy: Matthew 5:14 - 16. Again, you life comes down to a choice, a decision to follow Jesus or deal with your anger as you have done all your life.

Unrighteous anger "does not achieve the righteousness of God". Our purpose is to be set apart, holy, sanctified. Anger is a wedge of disunity and broken fellowship among God's children and it is a poor witness to the world at large. "This you know, my beloved brethren. But let everyone be quick to hear, slow to speak and slow to anger; for the anger of man does not achieve the righteousness of God" (James 1:19 & 20). If unrighteous anger is a struggle for you, there are numerous resources online that will be of great benefit. Go to http://www.ccef.org (Christian Counseling & Educational

Foundation) for additional materials to assist you in working through these issues.

So, how do I know if my anger is a righteous or an unrighteous anger? To determine this, I need to ask two important questions about my anger: on whose behalf am I angry? And why?

Righteous anger is expressed when I use the energy of anger to accomplish the purposes of God. When a child is orphaned by a drunk driver, my anger, on behalf of God, is justified. When a person in authority abuses a teen, again, anger at the situation is appropriate. However, righteous anger isn't a shoulder shrug and we walk away. Remember, we are called to accomplish, in our anger, the purposes of God. In protection of widows and orphans, what are you doing? To assist the disabled, the needy, the disadvantaged, how do you fight for them? We cannot fix nor solve every situation, but how are you investing your "anger energy" to accomplish the purposes of God in your own backyard? Please know that I ask myself the same question as the Lord lays it on my heart.

A story ran on television not too long ago about the sex trade in South American countries. Children as young as seven and eight were and are, even today, being bought and sold into prostitution. Certainly, a situation that deserves our anger, not our apathy. The television reporter was talking with an American woman, a Christian, who had heard that same report on the nightly news some dozen years earlier (sad that the situation continues to grow) and she was moved to action. She sold everything she had and opened up a home for the kids of those streets. A dozen years later and she had helped rescue nearly a hundred kids, providing for their educational, medical, emotional, physical and spiritual needs. In fact, two of the first children she had taken in were now back helping her save more kids from that horrifying place. Imagine how grateful those few kids are for the work and the heart of this one woman. No, she hasn't stopped the practice; she probably hasn't even dented the trade. But for those few hundred kids, how has she blessed them with her righteous anger moved to action?

We don't all have to sell all we own and move to. . . But, let me ask you, when you heard that story, were you angrier about the violation of these precious souls or were you angrier today about the driver who cut you off in traffic? Oh how we need to get Jesus' heart about this world's injustices.

Remember, we have been called to make a difference in our world as Christ has made a difference in us. Don't let a precious opportunity for righteous anger pass you by because you were more concerned that someone at work was spreading rumors about you or that your dry cleaner ruined your favorite shirt. We need eternal priorities; Kingdom building to glorify our Father.

Righteous anger must be measured, controlled and appropriate. Just as Jesus was with the moneychangers who had invaded the temple (Matthew 21:12 – 17; Mark 11:15-18; Luke 19:45-48), we must keep God at the heart of our emotion and our reaction. Jesus, angry about the authorities of the temple making it harder for people to offer sacrifices to God in order to be restored in relationship to Him, overturned the instrument of their wickedness, the money tables. His speech was measured but firm. His anger was controlled, especially in light of the violation with which He was dealing. And His activity was appropriate to communicate the wickedness of their actions, as well as disrupt their ability to continue in their sin.

In desiring to express a godly response to our anger, we need to practice the following (this is from a training manual that I received from the Arlington Heights Biblical Counseling Center in Arlington Heights, IL):

1. Pray for God's help, then expect victory (I John 5:14 – 15)
2. Remember that God is in control so look for His good purpose in the situation (Romans 8:28 & 29)
3. Represent Jesus Christ, even in irritating situations (Titus 2:3 – 10)
4. Consider whether you contributed to the problem (Matthew 7:3 – 5); If so, ask forgiveness and correct the wrong (Luke 3:1 – 14)
5. Give your "rights" and desires to God (James 4:1 – 8)

6. Follow Biblical rules of communication to promote harmony (Ephesians 4:1 – 32)
7. Practice a Christlike response to replace the ungodly response (Colossians 3:5 – 15)

In addition to anger, we need to take a moment and recognize two additional issues closely related to anger. Bitterness and depression. They are the kissing cousins of anger. Bitterness is long-term, unresolved anger turned outward at the world. Depression is long-term, unresolved anger turned inward at oneself. Both proclaim an injustice(s) done that was never resolved and both turn into lifetime patterns and life long problems. Neither are Biblical as they both claim one person as the focus - ME!

If you are an individual who is bitter or depressed, you need to make a choice. Am I going to continue on this path of self-destruction, or am I going to trust God with this world's injustices and choose forgiveness over ranting, mercy over holding a grudge, grace over all.

In a Biblical Counseling training session, I was taught something invaluable when dealing with our tendency toward unrighteous anger. I hope it helps.

D – Die to self (Luke 9:22 – 23; I Corinthians 15:31)
A – Ask for wisdom (James 1:5)
I – Intimacy with God, first and foremost (Matt 22:37-39)
L – Love others (I John 4)
Y – Yield to the Word of God and the Holy Spirit (Psalm 119)

As you deal, daily, with anger, it is essential to keep the Lord always before you. If you are fighting on His behalf, the Lord will bless those efforts and bring great victory out of your labor. If you are fighting on your behalf, the Lord will also make that obvious very quickly. Be willing to assess the reasons for your anger and turn over to God what He does not ask you to handle. And always, when dealing with injustices in this world, remember this: the Lord is our Banner - the battle belongs to Him!

"The Lord will fight for you while you keep silent."
Exodus 14:14

CHAPTER 15: ANGER
GOING DEEPER: QUESTIONS FOR STUDY

1. Why is anger considered part of the "old nature" in Colossians 3:1 - 13?

2. Do you have an anger problem? What do you "get" angry about? How can you cultivate a godly response to your anger?

3. From what we've learned already, including the assurance of our identity in Christ, what scriptures (truths) can help you change the sin of anger in your life?

GETTING TO THE HEART OF THE MATTER:
APPLICATION

Exodus 14:14 - Write in your journal the ways in which God has protected you, fought for you and delivered you over the course of your life. Now, multiply that by a factor of 1000, realizing that God has protected you, fought for you and delivered you far more times that you could possibly know!

LAYING THE FOUNDATION: QUIET TIME

Day ONE: Proverbs 10:12, 12:16; 14:17; 17:9 & 19:11

Day TWO: Ephesians 4:17 - 32

Day THREE: James 1:19 & 20

Day FOUR: Ephesians 4:1 - 16

Day FIVE: Colossians 3:5 - 15

CHAPTER 16:

PURITY

―⁓⦿⁓―

"There is therefore now no condemnation
for those who are in Christ Jesus.
For the law of the Spirit of life in Christ Jesus
has set you free from the law of sin and of death."
Romans 8:1

What an odd way to begin the chapter on purity, with the text from Romans 8:1. I agree. It might be possible to read those words that Paul penned, and in a wrong focus, think them an excuse to live as we want in a state of personal "freedoms" married to a philosophy of hyper-grace (God will forgive anyway, so let's focus on our liberties). We will deal with that thought in a moment.

First, it's about to get even more bizarre because we're going to begin this chapter on purity by looking at shame.

Cement walls, ten feet thick, six feet high and light enough to travel with me as my personal fortress, impenetrable by sight or by conversation, by attention or by curiosity. Had I been able to invent that armor, I would have been rich. There are more women and men walking this earth in a state of shame than either you or I could count. I, most certainly, was one of them.

There is shame in having been abused. Why didn't I, couldn't I stop it? I should have known better, been better, done better. . .In the case of sexual and physical abuse, there is the added measure of stolen intimacy, of personal violation that invades the thought process and the heart. 'What will people think of me?' In fact, many people who have been sexually abused choose not to tell anyone or report it for that very reason, a fear of being judged or thought of differently. There is such a stigma attached to rape and incest that for most people, it is still talked about in hushed tones. That communicates shame to those of us who have been so wounded by that violation.

In the role of the abuser, the possibility of shame is as prevalent. Many abusers were abused and in that, their shame goes deep. More are living out a need to feel powerful and important in their abuse of others in order to overcome their own sense of shame and worthlessness. They turn their shame into a weapon and wield it with amazing skill.

And if we haven't seen enough shame in those two arenas, how about those who live in the shame of their bondage. I talked with a woman who works with prostitutes on the West side of Chicago. I asked her what was the hardest thing for them to overcome in order to accept God's love. She said that they can not walk into a church with all of those "religious types" and hear that God loves the prostitute just the same as He loves those who attend church regularly, look just right and seem to have the perfect lives. Why? Because of shame.

It is the 'if you knew what I did' or 'if you knew what happened to me' or 'if you knew who I have become', then you wouldn't want to talk with me again. We all have those parts of our lives, shrouded in shadow, that we don't let see the light of day. Why? Because of shame.

And shame's cousin, blame, is just as bad. We believe, somehow, that what we've done is too much, too bad, too evil for the cross. We listen to the accuser of the brethren, satan, and believe him when he says that 'God could never, would never forgive. . .because of what we've done'.

So, let's let the truth of God's Word overpower the pitiful 'strength' of those lies. To begin, shame and blame are about our past. Can you go into your past and change it? I can't. I can not unring a bell any more than I can unthink a thought or undo a deed. What is past is past and I have no power over it. I only have power to change the present. I can only choose *now*, to live differently, to walk differently, to think differently and to yield to my Lord. What the evil one accuses me of is out of my reach to change. And in some measures, even though true, I am a sinner saved by grace, it has no bearing on my life.

Secondly, the evil one has no standing in my life. Paul deals with this in Romans 8:31 - 34 when he says, "What then shall we say to these things? If God *is* for us, who *is* against us? He who did not spare His own Son, but delivered Him up for us all, how will He not also with Him freely give us all things? Who will bring a charge against God's elect? God is the one who justifies; who is the one who condemns? Christ Jesus is He who died, yes, rather who was raised, who is at the right hand of God, who also intercedes for us."

Paul is making a crucial point for us as God's children. The only one who can bring a charge against us is someone who is not guilty of the charge themselves. Because satan is a sinner as we are sinners, he has no standing before God to accuse us. In the passage, Paul makes it clear that only Jesus Christ can bring a charge against us because only He is guiltless in every aspect. Instead, what does He do? Jesus is the One who justifies us through the spilling of His blood and the covering of our sins. If the only One with standing to accuse chooses to forgive and to set us free, why are we so willing to try and step back into bondage? In other words, why do we so willingly believe the lies of a liar?

Want to hear instead what God thinks about us? Romans 8:35 - 39 goes on to say, "Who shall separate us from the love of Christ? Shall tribulation, or distress, or persecution, or famine. or nakedness, or peril, or sword? Just as it is written, "FOR THY SAKE WE ARE BEING PUT TO DEATH ALL DAY LONG; WE WERE CONSID-ERED AS SHEEP TO BE SLAUGHTERED." But in all these things we overwhelmingly conquer through Him who loved us. For I am convinced that neither death, nor life, nor angels, nor principali-ties, nor things present, nor things to come, nor powers, nor height, nor depth, nor any other created thing, shall be able to separate us from the love of God, which is in Christ Jesus our Lord."

Nothing can separate you for the love of God, not you, not your past, not things done to you nor things that you've done. God is not a fool, walking into a relationship with His eyes closed. He knows everything about you, so much more than you even know about yourself. . .AND HE LOVES YOU ANYWAY!

Now, let's go back to Romans 8:1, "There is therefore now no condemnation for those who are in Christ Jesus. For the law of the Spirit of life in Christ Jesus has set you free from the law of sin and of death." In light of this promise, lets talk about purity in our present lives. Because we are free from the power of condemnation, we can now choose in freedom to follow, to obey, to love God. The focus here is twofold: one, we *choose*; and two, living a pure life is about today, not yesterday. Remember, Jesus has redeemed our past and because of that we have such freedom in the promise of an eternity with Him. (If you continue to struggle with shame or blame, please stop and go back to review the section on "My Identity in Christ". Let God's truth, once and for all, free you from the bondage of those lies.)

Purity is defined as free from evil or sin, reflecting God's image. Profanity is secular, irreverent, blasphemous and apart from God. In that, we need to know that purity is a big deal to God. Throughout His Word, God goes to great lengths to talk about how to live, how not to live and the purpose and reason for living a holy (separate) and pure (free from evil) life.

Purity is a combination of purposefulness of my actions and submission of my will to God's standard for my life. In I Timothy 4:7a-8, 12, Paul says to Timothy, "On the other hand, discipline yourself for the purpose of godliness; for bodily discipline is only of little profit, but godliness is profitable for all things, since it holds promise for the present life and also for the life to come . . .Let no one look down on your youthfulness, but rather in speech, conduct, love, faith and purity, show yourself an example of those who believe."

Purity, which is truly an aspect of living the holy life, to which we have all been called, can be mastered in a number of different arenas of our life.

PURITY OF MY MIND:

To be sure, we are what we think. Our minds influence and

define us in powerful ways. Just think about our chapters on identity. The power of change wasn't in presenting a 'new truth'. God's truth has not changed nor expanded in anyway. We spent our time on instruction that we would know the truth and then application that we would live the truth. We needed to see ourselves through God's eyes.

In Colossians 3:1-3, Paul captures the power of redeemed thinking, "Therefore if you have been raised up with Christ, keep seeking the things above, where Christ is, seated at the right hand of God. Set your mind on the things above, not on the things that are on earth. For you have died and your life is hidden with Christ in God." In these verses, he reminds us that there is freedom in truth and we need to begin or continue living out our new reality. Our home is not here. Our purpose is not here. Our hope is not here. But when we set our minds on things above, it changes how we live and act and think in this present life.

My dad is a computer programmer from way back. For as long as I can remember, he had a sign over his desk that read, "garbage in, garbage out". What a great example of this principle. How can I imagine that I will not be tempted to let my mind wander into sinful thought when what I feed my mind are worldly images and philosophies. So many of us want to dip our toes in secular entertainments, convinced that we can control the flood when the information and visuals rise to overwhelm us. Paul's argument is that the battle begins with what we absorb. "And do not be conformed to this world, but be transformed by the renewing of your mind, that you may prove what the will of God is, that which is good and acceptable and perfect." Romans 12:2

I have a friend who told me once that she was going to see that they put two things on my tombstone: "I have two things to say about that"; and "be purposeful". I guess when I teach, I tend to repeat those two phrases. I adore the word, "purposeful". Think on its impact - it is about choosing a direction and marching forward; about thoughtfulness and choice married and inseparable; about accomplishing those things to which we've set our mind, our focus, our will. To be accused of living a purposeful life will be one of the finest compliments I could receive. To do so by living a God honoring life in a purposeful way will be icing on that cake.

Set your minds, go in this direction, choose God and purity over satan and profanity. Guard which images and visuals and music and words and life styles will invade your thinking and impact, directly, your life. Paul knows that those things go hand in hand when he wrote Philippians 4:8: "Finally, brethren, whatever is true, whatever is honorable, whatever is right, whatever is pure, whatever is lovely, whatever is of good repute, if there is any excellence and if anything worthy of praise, let your minds dwell on these things."

Dwell. Spend time listening to Christian music, worship music, praise music. Read Scripture. Read Christian books and magazines. Spend time relating with individuals. Embrace the majesty of the outdoors. Celebrate God's creativity and style in the mountains, ocean, forests and streams.

Guard. Let fewer world influences in. Monitor your television viewing and movie going. Choose edifying pieces of entertainment instead of those designed to numb or horrify. Let profanity be something offensive to you and not the norm.

Practice. Control your thinking through journaling, prayer and conversation. Learn to direct your thoughts toward those things that inspire and encourage. Appreciate that as you do, your mind will be less and less draw away from God toward profanity and more and more drawn toward Him and purity.

BODY:

In Max Lucado's book, "It's Not about Me", he relates this analogy when thinking of our bodies. "I remember seeing a sign on a mechanic's toolbox that read: 'Don't ask to borrow my tools. I use them to feed my family.' To do his work, the mechanic needed his instruments. He needed them present and functional. When he looked for his wrench, he wanted to find it. His work was important; hence his tools were important."

That is a perfect analogy for us as we desire to be pure in our bodies. Our physical self is not to be honored or thought of as important in and of itself. It is a tool, an instrument for accomplishing the purposes of God. However, if we let that instrument break down due to neglect, then we are hampered in our ability to serve

God in the way that He chooses. Notice, we are not talking about circumstances like cancer or a broken leg from a car accident. We are talking about honoring God in our bodies through regular maintenance and discipline.

To be honest, I struggle in this regard. I am more apt to focus on the inner woman than the outer shell. However, I do appreciate that I am without excuse and God is working in my life to bring about obedience in this area. Romans 12:1 is an encouragement to me, "I urge you therefore, brethren, by the mercies of God, to present your bodies a living and holy sacrifice, acceptable to God, which is your spiritual service of worship." I want my whole life to be an act of worship, that includes how I master the outer woman.

I know that I don't belong to me. "Or do you not know that your body is a temple of the Holy Spirit who is in you, whom you have from God, and that you are not your own? For you have been bought with a price; therefore glorify God in your body." 1 Corinthians 6:19-20. And what a price Jesus paid! I want to show Him and the world my heart of love and gratitude toward Him. One way is to master the external in a world that worships the external, knowing that I am an ambassador of Christ while on this earth. That is an amazing goal for which to shoot.

I don't want my physical limitations to keep me from doing the work that God has set before me. I never want to be a slave to anything again, including the sin of no self-discipline. I choose to be a bondservant to Jesus and in so doing, I must bring all of my life under His authority. Paul, in 1 Corinthians 6:12 & 13, relates, "All things are lawful for me, but not all things are profitable. All things are lawful for me, but I will not be mastered by anything. Food is for the stomach, and the stomach is for food; but God will do away with both of them. Yet the body is not for immorality, but for the Lord; and the Lord is for the body." Amen and amen! 1 Peter 2:11 "Beloved, I urge you as aliens and strangers to abstain from fleshly lusts, which war against the soul."

Sexual body:

We continue with Max Lucado in his book, "It's Not about Me":

"Consider His (God's) plan. Two children of God make a covenant with each other. They disable the ejection seats and burn the bridge back to Momma's house. They fall into each other's arms beneath the canopy of God's blessing, encircled by the tall fence of fidelity. Both know the other will be there in the morning. Both know the other will stay even as skin wrinkles and vigor fades. Each gives the other for-your-eyes-only privileges.

Gone is the guilt. What remains is a celebration of permanence, a tender moment in which the body continues what the mind and the soul have already begun.

Such sex honors God and satisfies God's children."

God-honoring, sexual purity cannot be described any better than that. Max Lucado is eloquent in capturing the heart of God in this most intimate and beautiful of God's gifts. As a single woman, I rejoice with my brothers and sisters in Christ who are blessed to know the rapture of which Lucado sings.

But what about us single gals and guys? Is there any elasticity in God's definition of 'sex in marriage only' mandate? The answer, of course, is no. We are not called to be sexually pure when it is convenient or easy any more than a married man is called to be faithful only when people are watching. In answer to God's call for sexuality purity, I must choose to abstain apart from marriage which is defined, Biblically, as between one man and one woman. In marriage, I must choose to be utterly and sincerely faithful to my covenant spouse.

God spends a great deal of time in Scripture dealing with the issue of sexual purity. He does so because He knows us. He knows that this is a "hot button" issue for many people and it is one in which too many Christians are casual and compromising. Paul deals with the issue often in a noncompromising, unapologetic way as he does in Romans 13:12-14, "The night is almost gone, and the day is at hand. Let us therefore lay aside the deeds of darkness and put on the armor of light. Let us behave properly as in the day, not in carousing and drunkenness, not in sexual promiscuity and sensuality, not in strife and jealousy. But put on the Lord Jesus Christ, and make no provision for the flesh in regard to its lusts."

Sexual sins compromise and contaminate every part of our being. They effect us physically, emotionally, sexually and especially spiritually. God created sex to be a statement of union, not a tool of our flesh. That is why God commands us to abstain from sex apart from the marriage bed. He knows how powerful and intimate an act it is. Don't fool yourself into thinking that you can handle just a little. . .(you finish the sentence). We are told to "make no provision for the flesh in regard to its lusts".

The world is full of our brothers and sisters who could stand up and share their tales of woe. Often it begins with, "we never meant to. . ." and it usually ends with, "we're pregnant". The list of consequences to that sin, however, don't culminate in pregnancy. That is just the most visible consequence. The Scriptures make clear that a sexual union is more than a momentary joining of two flesh into one. "Do you not know that your bodies are members of Christ? Shall I then take away the members of Christ and make them members of a harlot? May it never be! Or do you not know that the one who joins himself to a harlot is one body with her? For He says, "THE TWO WILL BECOME ONE FLESH." But the one who joins himself to the Lord is one spirit with Him. Flee immorality. Every other sin that a man commits is outside the body, but the immoral man sins against his own body." 1 Corinthians 6:15-18.

And sexual impurity is not just illicit sex. It is any "dabbling" that one may do to feed the lusts of the soul. Pornography is a sexual sin. It is graphic and exploitive for those on both ends. Its only purpose is to entice the flesh and corrupt the mind. Remember, once that garbage is in, it is difficult beyond measure to get it out of your mind and thoughts.

The marriage bed is the only one sanctioned by God for such a powerful, intimate and beautiful joining together of two flesh into one. To resist the temptation outside of that holy covenant is to worship God with your body and soul. The writer of Hebrews brings us back to the garden, hours before the cross, when he writes, "You have not yet resisted to the point of shedding blood in your striving against sin;" Hebrews 12:4. The imagery is powerful and necessary. Until you and I resist to the point of shedding blood, we are guilty of settling for the banality of earth when we could have had the ecstasy of heaven.

> "Therefore, since we have so great a cloud of witnesses
> surrounding us, let us also lay aside
> every encumbrance,
> and the sin which so easily entangles us,
> and let us run with endurance the race
> that is set before us,
> fixing our eyes on Jesus,
> the author and perfecter of faith,
> who for the joy set before Him endured the cross,
> despising the shame,
> and has sat down at the right hand of the throne of God."
> Hebrews 12:1 & 2

If you have "dabbled" and fallen, remember, God is a merciful and forgiving. You need to confess and repent and leave it with Him. Remember, we cannot change the past, but we can make a powerful statement with our lives by choosing from this day forward to "honor and obey" Jesus Christ, first and foremost.

Purity is not something that you have once and then have for all time. It is, however, something that you can gain after having lost it for a time. Purity is a statement of the present, a proclamation of how I choose to live my life today. Choose to live your life in the protection and blessing of obedience to God. If you are married, celebrate the gift of your spouse and the opportunity to experience a treasure that God created.

If you are single, choose to let God satisfy that need in you. Ask Him to be your all in all and trust Him to provide, in abundance for all of your needs.

Isn't God good? He commands us to be pure in heart, mind and body and then makes a way for us to do so. In addition, the benefits are immediate and restoration (healing) is full and complete.

Remember, we are His children. When He looks at us, He sees us, covered in His Son's blood, as white as snow!

CHAPTER 16: PURITY
GOING DEEPER: QUESTIONS FOR STUDY

1. What does it mean, you have died and your life is hidden with Christ in God? How can and do we live that out?

2. Am I still conformed to this world? Do I see things through the eyes of this world or through God's eyes? How can I change that?

3. How do fleshly lusts war against your soul? How can you find victory over them?

4. What does it mean, the night is almost gone, and the day is at hand?

GETTING TO THE HEART OF THE MATTER: APPLICATION

Read through the lesson and determine which of these issues, purity of mind, purity of physical body or purity of your sexual body is most difficult for you. Read over the verses and meditate / pray through them. Then, write up an action plan (based on what we learned in the chapter on Problem of Pain) to find freedom and victory over this area. Finally, ask someone to hold you accountable on that issue for the next four weeks.

LAYING THE FOUNDATION: QUIET TIME

Study and re-read the verses in the area of purity with which you most struggle. Write out the verses and put them up where you can see them daily.

CHAPTER 17:

INTIMACY

Our ability to be intimate (trusting another with the totality of who we are) with people begins with our desire and ability to be intimate with God. God created us to have a relationship with Him, first and foremost. In that truth, we need to revisit our relationship with Him in order to understand our relationships with others.

CHARACTER OF GOD:

In order to have an intimate relationship with God, we need to KNOW who He is. Remember what we said earlier, trust depends on knowability and consistency. In order for us to be completely honest and trusting of God, we need to experience Him in His Word, in our lives, in His creation and discover that He never changes and He is who He said He is. This vertical relationship deepens in those moments of discovery, as His immutable nature and His faithfulness prove true time and again.

In that, ask yourself two questions: from these verses, what do we know is true about God?; and from what we have learned over the previous chapters, what *else* do we know is true about God?

> Psalm 54:4 "Behold, God is my helper; The Lord is
> the sustainer of my soul."

2 Samuel 22:3 "My God, my rock, in whom I take refuge, My shield and the horn of my salvation, my stronghold and my refuge; My savior, You save me from violence."

1 Timothy 4:10 "For it is for this we labor and strive, because we have fixed our hope on the living God, who is the Savior of all men, especially of believers."

John 10:14 "I am the good shepherd, and I know My own and My own know Me,"

Remember the study of the names of God in Scripture. What were the authors of those books trying to communicate about God? What have you learned yourself in your growing faith and developing relationship with your Father?

ELOHIM, "The Creator" Deuteronomy 10:17

JEHOVAH JEREH, "The Lord Will Provide" Genesis 22:14

JEHOVAH SHAMMAH, "The Lord is There" Ezekiel 48:35

JEHOVAH NISSI, "The Lord My Banner" Exodus 17:15

JEHOVAH, "The Self-Existent One" Exodus 3:14-15

JEHOVAH M'KADDESH, "The Lord That Sanctifies" Hebrews 10:10-14

ADONAI, "The Lord" Psalm 123:2

EL SHADDAI, "The All-Sufficient One" Genesis 17:1-2

EL ELYON, "God Most High" Daniel 4:34-35

JEHOVAH SABAOTH, "The Lord of Hosts" Psalm 46:7

JEHOVAH SHALOM, "The Lord of Peace" Leviticus 26:2-6

JEHOVAH ROPHE, "The Lord that Heals" Exodus 15:25, 26

JEHOVAH ROI, "Our Shepherd" Psalm 23

God has a knowable and definable character. It is beyond our grasp to completely understand. However, we can know on a foundational level that God is good and in His goodness, my life is richly blessed. His character is evident, as we said, in His Word, His creation and in our life experience (certainly, as a child of God, we have been changed, for example, by God's love and grace). The study of God's character will take a lifetime and beyond, but at this point in our study, we have a reasonable place to start.

TRUST IN GOD:

Our vertical relationship, then, begins to grow from what we know about God's character into how we experience Him in our daily lives. We live by faith, trusting that He is who He said He is and He will do as He has promised He will do. That is the definition in Hebrews 11:6, "And without faith it is impossible to please Him, for he who comes to God must believe that He is, and that He is a rewarder of those who seek Him."

In trusting God, we also need to remember what His purpose is for our lives. God intends to change us, grow us and sanctify us. As you read the following verses, ask yourself this question: how has your faith matured as you've experienced the truth of these statements?

> Job 13:15 "Though He slay me, I will hope in Him. Nevertheless I will argue my ways before Him."

> Proverbs 3:5 & 6 "Trust in the Lord with all your heart and do not lean on your own understanding. In all your ways acknowledge Him, And He will make your paths straight."

> 1 Chronicles 5:20b "for they cried out to God in the battle, and He answered their prayers because they trusted in Him."

> Psalm 25:2 & 20 "O my God, in You I trust, Do not let me be ashamed; Do not let my enemies exult over me. . .Guard my soul and deliver me; Do not let me be ashamed, for I take refuge in You."

> Psalm 16:1 "Preserve me, O God, for I take refuge in You."

> Psalm 56:4 "in God, whose word I praise, In God I have put my trust; I shall not be afraid. What can mere man do to me?"

> 2 Timothy 1:12 "For this reason I also suffer these things, but I am not ashamed; for I know whom I have believed and I am convinced that He is able to guard what I have entrusted to Him until that day."

Intimacy with God begins with knowing His character. It develops as we learn to trust Him in all situations, circumstances and seasons. Trusting God in the battle enables me to learn to trust Him in the victory and / or the defeat. If learning to be intimate with God means trusting Him in all circumstances, what importance should I place on my current circumstances?

KNOWN BY GOD AND SEEKING TO KNOW GOD:

Beginning with His character, building up our trust, we now choose to invest in this relationship through application, diligence, time and desire. The time has come to have an intimate relationship with God in which I, as His daughter, seek to be KNOWN by Him and in which I seek to KNOW Him. It is an on-going and growing relationship.

Here's the thing, however, about a relationship with God that is different from any relationship with a fellow believer. God knows everything about me, more about me than I know myself. I will never know everything or even most things about Him. That does not impact the need for the invitation to know and to be known, however. Prayer is not useless because God already knows what I am going to say. It is vital because it teaches me to focus on Him, to trust Him, to depend on Him and to glean His perspective in my life.

Same thing with our intimate relationship with God. I need to choose to spend my energies on Him and invite Him into the cracks and crevices of my heart.

> Psalm 139:1 & 23 "O Lord, You have searched me and known me. . .Search me, O God, and know my heart; try me and know my anxious thoughts;"

> Psalm 31:7 "I will rejoice and be glad in Your lovingkindness, Because You have seen my affliction; You have known the troubles of my soul."

> Psalm 91:14-16 "Because he has loved Me, therefore I will deliver him; I will set him securely on high, because he has known My name. He will call upon Me, and I will answer him; I will be with him in trouble; I will rescue him and honor him. With a long life I will satisfy him and let him see My salvation."

God knows all things at all times. To have a relationship with God, one in which I am revealing myself to Him, I must choose to purposefully invite Him into my life.

So, how does one get to know God? Certainly we have covered that wonderful topic again and again throughout this book. List, in your journal or out loud some of your favorite ways to learn more about our Creator.

And, how do I "let" God know more about me? Although He knows it all, He still loves the invitation (Revelation 3:20). Take time today and ask Him to join you over a cup of coffee. I promise you, it will be the best moment of your day.

We need to approach intimacy, then, in our human relationships the way we approach intimacy in our relationship with God.

First, we need to look at the character of the person. The truth is, we can not have an intimate (trusting another with the totality of who I am) relationship with all people. We need time to discover who a person is, what they believe and how they live. We need to experience them for ourselves.

Second, we need to build up trust with that individual. It is not a given that a person, even a believer, is trustworthy. Only God, by His nature, is trustworthy. Trust in other people must be earned.

And third, we must seek to be KNOWN and to KNOW the individual. It is a matter of time, of attention and of open, honest communication.

CHARACTER OF THE INDIVIDUAL:

Over the course of time, an individual reveals, through word and deed, who they are. It is important for us to watch for those clues.

> Matthew 7:20 & 23 "So then, you will know them by their fruits. . .And then I will declare to them, "I never knew you; DEPART FROM ME, YOU WHO PRACTICE LAWLESSNESS."

As we are being watchful, we need to remember that we can only have an intimate relationship with a fellow believer. "Do not be bound together with unbelievers; for what partnership have righteousness and lawlessness, or what fellowship has light with darkness? Or what harmony has Christ with Belial, or what has a believer in common with an unbeliever? Or what agreement has the temple of God with idols? For we are the temple of the living God; just as God said, "I WILL DWELL IN THEM AND WALK AMONG THEM; AND I WILL BE THEIR GOD, AND THEY SHALL BE MY PEOPLE" (2 Corinthians 6:14 – 16)

Intimacy with a fellow believer means influence. These are the women or men who will have fellowship with us, hold us accountable, encourage and edify us in the battles and be a friend in times of need. To be able to do that and be that, we must know that their passion for Jesus is sure, their heart for His Word is strong and their desire to be changed is honest and essentially moving ahead.

That does not mean that the person has to be perfect. If that were the case, you and I would never have or be an intimate friend. But, there is a difference between a person struggling with sin in their lives who acknowledges his or her need to change and those who are not interested in changing at all. Do not choose the latter individual to be a confidant and a mentor. You will only fall into their sin.

Always, apply grace to your relationship, and consider who they were when you first met them and who they are now. Ask yourself the following questions as you study their character:

What has changed in his / her life?

What needs to change?

What is the passion / purpose / priority of his or her life?

Considering that, can you be equally yoked with them?

Biblical love is defined as a passionate concern for the spiritual health and growth of another person. I am concerned first and foremost about a person's relationship with God (vertical relationship), then and only then am I involved in his or her horizontal relationships, i.e. those with other people, including myself. Ask yourself, is this person interested in pointing me to God, teaching me more about God, holding me accountable to God's Word, telling me the truth in love when I need to hear it, etc. How you answer those questions will give you great insight.

BUILD UP TRUST:

Trust is an investment. It is a commodity that is earned by word AND by deed. A person can sin and betray your trust and then, over the course of time, earn it back again. But, relationships do not

BEGIN with 100% trust intact. How do I discern if someone is trustworthy?

First, measure their actions with their words.

Do they match up? If not, why not?

Second, does the person desire to change and what has he or she done to accomplish that desire?

Third, what is your history with this person? If they have been untrustworthy in the past, what do you see in them to make you think that they have changed?

Finally, is the person chiefly concerned with your spiritual growth, discipline, transformation and sanctification? Remember, God, who is 100% trustworthy desires His best for you. That means, that you are going to be changed by Him. Is the person who claims to want your best, interested in your spiritual health above all things?

SEEK TO BE KNOWN AND TO KNOW:

If the person is of godly character and he or she is worthy of your trust, then and only then do you take the step of seeking to be known and to know him or her in an intimate (spiritual, emotional, and intellectual way). That process takes time, commitment, maturity, honesty and love. It also takes an understanding of my identity in Christ. Remember, I can not have a healthy, deep intimate relationship with another person if I do not have that with God first. My vertical relationship with God teaches and directs me toward a strong and vibrant horizontal relationship with a sister or brother in Christ.

One final note, if you desire to have deep and abiding intimate relationships with other believers and have not found any, there are two things that you can do. First, pray. God's heart for you is to find these relationships that satisfy, encourage, edify and teach. And second, seek to *be* the kind of person to whom others will be drawn. Focus on changing your life to reflect Jesus and watch how people will be attracted to that new and growing reflection.

CHAPTER 18:

LIVING MY LIFE AS A SERVANT

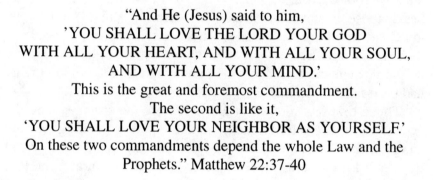

"And He (Jesus) said to him,
'YOU SHALL LOVE THE LORD YOUR GOD
WITH ALL YOUR HEART, AND WITH ALL YOUR SOUL,
AND WITH ALL YOUR MIND.'
This is the great and foremost commandment.
The second is like it,
'YOU SHALL LOVE YOUR NEIGHBOR AS YOURSELF.'
On these two commandments depend the whole Law and the
Prophets." Matthew 22:37-40

A little over a year ago, I attended our annual Leadership Appreciation Night at Harvest Bible Chapel. We have it every May, just before the end of the ministry season. I've been attending Harvest for over eleven years and I've been to more than a handful of these nights, so I know what to expect.

It always begins with our Pastor, James MacDonald and Associate Pastor, Rick Donald, singling out several people for recognition and thanks. Understand that we all work for God's glory and in those "trenches", it is appropriate to encourage the body with testimony and deference. There are different categories of service that are honored. A person's name is called, his or her service is cited and he or she goes up front to receive his or her plaque.

This past May, it was my turn. The plaque reads, "Faithfulness in Service" in recognition for the years I have worked in various ministries at Harvest.

Walking back to my seat, looking at the plaque, I was struck by the humor of the recognition. Does the irony hit you? Do you remember the words at the front of this book? I walked away, ran away from God for over ten years. I left behind everything of value in my life to be like Gomer (the prostitute who left her husband Hosea to go back into her old ways), trading freedom for bondage and the truth for many lies. In other words, I was faithless as He remained faithful. The words of the plaque, "Faithfulness in Service" brought laughter and tears.

When I first walked through the doors at Harvest, I desperately needed God's truth. I needed to hear and to know who God is, and what He thinks about me. I needed to be swept off my feet and set beside those crystal clear, clean waters (from Psalm 23) so that He, my Creator and my Abba Father, could restore my soul. I needed a shoulder on which to cry and more than a couple of hands ready to help dry my tears. I needed time to heal and time to reclaim what had been taken from me.

Those first few months at Harvest were the strangest and the sweetest to me. Each Sunday, I came late, crept in along the side and picked a chair on the end (we were meeting in a school gym at the time). I sat with one foot in the aisle ready to bolt and one foot under my chair, ravenous for the truth I received each week. When we stood to worship, I found it difficult to mouth all of the words, but I sang them in my soul. Slowly, Jesus cracked the wall I had built to hide my shame, and in the steady stream of truth I received, my life, which had been in bondage to lies, found freedom in Jesus. For my first year at Harvest, I did not serve in any ministry in the church. That was the first and only time that I can recall attending a church regularly and not serving.

At the end of that year, as God was putting back together the jigsaw puzzle of my life, I felt it was time to step back into serving. But here's the thing - I had failed God in this area once before and I struggled with the memory of having abandoned Him, just like His disciples had in the Garden of Gethsemane. How could I, of all people, stand up to serve God?

Certainly there was fear in that thought - what if I failed Him again? And to be honest, I struggled with the shame of having left the work of the church. But it went deeper than that. What I could not seem to get past was the sorrow of having deserted my King. At the first sign of suffering and hardship, I left Him. When I couldn't see what He was doing, I did not trust His heart for me and in that vanity, it cost me ten years. Those emotions cost me more than a couple of sleepless nights as I played around with the thought of stepping back into organized ministry.

Then it hit me, serving God is an aspect of my identity in Christ. The privilege of building His kingdom, the joy of seeing individuals find our Savior in their darkest hour, the purpose and place of working in even the smallest way to further His glory and Name - those were mine because of Him. Jesus set aside His divine rights to come and serve, to come and save; He had done both for me. How could I now not serve Him with all my might?

My life is a living testimony of God's ability to use literally anyone to accomplish His purposes on this earth. I am a walking, talking example of a life redeemed - twice. Whenever I meet people who say to me, 'oh, no, I can't serve God, I've been too. . . ' or 'I don't have any ability' or 'do you know the things I've done?', I just smile and tell them my story.

I tell them about a woman who was faithless and a God who was and is always faithful. I tell them about my Father who did not stand in my way when I turned my back on my inheritance and left in a fit of rage. I tell them about a child who was lost on the streets, spiritually hungry and in such need of truth. I tell them of a daughter who lived in such perversion and sin, trying to find something, anything other than God that would bring meaning; I never did. I tell them of a woman who finally, in desperation, limped toward home. And I tell them about my Abba Father who ran to meet me as I turned up the road that lead me back to Him. Like the prodigal child, by the time I found my way home, I was ready for any conditions that God would put on my life, content with the notion of being allowed to stay. He could make me live in the cellar or work as His slave if He would just take me back. I thought, better to be here and deal with the recompense of my sin, than out there and living the consequence of that sin in full color every day.

And just like in the story of the prodigal son, the Father waved His hand, stopping me mid-sentence with the words, "Bring me my robe, my ring, my sandals!" I was prepared to grovel and beg; He intended to throw a party to welcome me back. I was to be dressed in His garments so that everyone who saw me at the heavenly bash would know that I am a child of this King.

In light of my story, it is not work for me to serve Him. It is not tiresome or difficult. It is a miracle that He wants me, allows me, entreats me to put my hand to the plow and tend to His fields. "Then He said to His disciples, "The harvest is plentiful, but the workers are few. Therefore beseech the Lord of the harvest to send out workers into His harvest." Matthew 9:37 & 38. What joy to be His bondservant!

You have spent days or weeks or maybe months reading through this book and now we've reached this point together. I am not going to spend our remaining time trying to convince you that you should dedicate your life to Jesus Christ as His bondservant, willing and able and anxious to do what He desires. I am not going to remind you that in serving others, our lives are balanced and abundant. Certainly there is so much Scripture that would accomplish that task and we would spend our time well doing just that.

What I want to do instead is ask you this - in these pages, as we have presented Biblical truth, have you found hope? How about a moment of comfort or of peace? Have you heard God's heart for you and found in those words a place of belonging and of safety? Have you discovered in His character the foundation on which to build the rest of your life? Have you looked in a mirror and now hear His words - you are my beloved child, chosen, loved, forgiven, sanctified and called - instead of hearing the words of your past? Have you found direction for your life? Have you experienced release of your anger, your tears, your hardness and found in their place, His sufficiency and His nail scarred Hands to wipe your tears? Have you found His forgiveness, lavished in grace and mercy, overflow in your heart so that you can now forgive?

Paul, in Philippians 2:1 and 2 asks the same question in this way, "So if there is *any* encouragement in Christ, *any* comfort from love, *any* participation in the Spirit, *any* affection and sympathy, complete my joy by being of the same mind, having the same love, being in full accord and of one mind." (Italics mine) *If* you have known *any* abundance or fullness or overflow, *then. . .*

If you answered yes to even one of these questions, then let me ask you this - what do you intend to *do* to thank Him, love Him, obey Him and dedicate your life and your healing to Him? The second chapter of James talks about faith and works, essentially saying that if you have faith, then out of that overflow, out of that new life must flow works. Living out that same principle, if you have experienced any of the comfort, freedom, healing and hope that Jesus in Isaiah 61:1 -3 promised to give you, then how does that change your life? Because in truth, it must. When you meet Jesus in His fullness, your entire countenance changes. You look different. You act different. You are different.

And in that change, you will know; your family will know; your neighbors will know - when God accomplishes the task of replacing lies with truth and bondage with freedom - you don't have to tell anyone about it, they will see it on your face!

So what does serving another look like? Notecards. At least for me, I serve with my pen, dashing off a note of encouragement and edification as often as I can. Now, for some of you, serving by writing notecards is like eating overcooked broccoli. Enough said. For some of us, serving is tuning up old and sturdy cars for single moms. At our church, we have Parking Lot Ambassadors - impossible to get through a Sunday morning without those smiling faces ushering us in and out of the church lot in an orderly and expedient fashion. Sometimes serving is a hug or letting a harried mom with screaming kids the opportunity to cut in front of you at the check out line. Teaching Sunday School is also serving. Are you catching onto the pattern? Our creative God can teach us a billion ways to serve when we toss in our hearts and open up our arms and say, "pick me, Lord, let me be your hands, your eyes, your heart today. . .teach me to serve like you did."

In fact, some of my sweetest memories of serving others have been informal moments when the Spirit moved and I was wise enough to answer the call. The trick always is - putting another's needs ahead of mine in terms of time and activity, but putting my needs ahead of theirs in terms of the joy that comes from serving God. In other words, when I serve, we both are blessed, whether or not they will admit it or notice it or even thank you. You and Jesus will know it and that will be enough.

Considering all of this, think of an area in which you can serve formally, especially a ministry in the church. Now, think of an area in which you can serve informally, maybe a family member or friend who needs to know Jesus and will receive from you not the goods news of the gospel, but the sweat of your brow. Pray today, for the wisdom to find those fields to tend and the heart and will to do so in a way that will honor your Father.

That plaque from the Leadership Appreciation Night sits on my mantel above the fireplace. It does not read, "Faithfulness in Service" when I see it. Instead, each time I look at it, it reads, "Faithful to His Glory" and I smile. I know in my heart of heart that my track record of faithfulness should not be celebrated; it should be lamented. Even if I serve every day from now until the moment God takes me home, I can not erase one moment of those years of wandering. But hear my heart, I no longer try. In those years of fear and faithlessness, I discovered a God who never changed, whose love never wavered and whose grace was more than sufficient. I love to look at that plaque and see those words in my mind, "Faithful to His Glory". He is and because He is - I am now faithful to His glory as well.

What will your plaque read? How will someone describe your life? Will it be seen in the shadows, filled with bitterness and fear? Or will your life now be a testament to His love, a monument to the work of His hands, celebrated throughout eternity for the light that reflects off of the broken glass that is your story. Remember, He is the light; we are light's refraction, reflecting those rays for all to see. That God would use us to point the dying of this world to the light's Source is a miracle too large for this heart to fully embrace.

You are loved!

FINAL THOUGHTS. . .

W ait, wait, wait. We're almost done, but not quite yet. Before you go, let me encourage you with these final thoughts.

One of the great secrets about the Christian life is that it is a journey that begins with a sense of newness every morning (Lamentations 3:22 - 24). We build on what we know to be true about our God and we leave behind our failures and our sins (in the act of repentance). Our God is a loving and gracious God. Even in His holiness and righteousness, He is the One who makes it possible for us to embrace and engage Him in a relationship. He is the One who makes it possible, in fact who desires an intimate and daily walk and talk through the garden with us.

Whatever your past, you now have a chance to build on these new truths. We have responsibilities as God's children. We have hope and freedom and healing as His daughters and sons. We have in our hearts and heads and lives what this world is literally dying to find. From this day forward, please don't ever consider that cheap again.

This study was just a step for you. Be it a big one or a small one, it is a step along your journey. Your life will be abundant if and when you live it in obedience to Christ. He desires for you to know Him, to trust Him, to live for Him in power! But, Jesus leaves the decision up to you. Daily, you choose (Joshua 24:14 - 15) to love, to serve, to know, to study, to pray and more.

"As workers for God we have to learn to make room

for God - to give God "elbow room". We calculate and estimate, and say that this and that will happen, and we forget to make room for God to come in as He chooses. Would we be surprised if God came into our meeting or into our preaching in a way we had never looked for Him to come? Do not look for God to come in any particular way, but look for Him. That is the way to make room for Him. Expect Him to come, but do not expect Him only in a certain way. However much we may know God, the great lesson to learn is that at any minute He may break in. We are apt to overlook this element of surprise, yet God never works in any other way. All of a sudden God meets the life, "When it was the good pleasure of God. . ." Keep your life so constant in its contact with God that His surprising power may break out on the right hand and on the left. Always be in a state of expectancy, and see that you leave room for God to come in as He likes."

Oswald Chambers
"My Utmost for His Highest"

Appreciating that you may need to spend more time on any one topic from our study and confessing that anyone of a thousand brothers and sisters may have said what I've written in a more clear and concise and creative way, I've included a list of excellent titles from Christian authors. Each book will assist you on this journey. And of course, God's Word must be our first step, for its authority and content top any other word written by man. Don't let this exciting expedition into your growing faith come to an end. This is just the beginning!

ADDITIONAL RESOURCES

"WHEN PEOPLE ARE BIG AND GOD IS SMALL" by Ed Welch
"ADDICTIONS: A BANQUET IN THE GRAVE" by Ed Welch
"BLAME IT ON THE BRAIN?" by Ed Welch

"LEAVING YESTERDAY BEHIND: A VICTIM NO MORE"
by William Hines

"IDOLS OF THE HEART" by Elyse Fitzpatrick
"LOVE TO EAT, HATE TO EAT" by Elyse Fitzpatrick
"OVERCOMING FEAR, WORRY & ANXIETY"
by Elyse Fitzpatrick

"I REALLY WANT TO CHANGE, SO HELP ME GOD"
by James MacDonald
"LORD CHANGE MY ATTITUDES" by James MacDonald

"THE POWER OF SUFFERING" by John MacArthur

"STRENGTHENING YOUR MARRIAGE" by Wayne Mack
"YOUR FAMILY GOD'S WAY" by Wayne Mack

"ON BEING A SERVANT" by Warren Wiersbe

"HOW TO OVERCOME EVIL" by Jay Adams

"THE BIBLICAL VIEW OF SELF-ESTEEM, SELF-LOVE & SELF-IMAGE" by Jay Adams

"ATTITUDES OF A TRANSFORMED HEART" by Martha Peace
"THE EXCELLENT WIFE" by Martha Peace

"WAR OF WORDS" by Paul David Tripp

"THE EXEMPLARY HUSBAND" by Stuart Scott

APPENDIX A

—⟡—

This is the gospel (good news!) presentation of why God created us, how we chose to turn our backs on our Creator and finally, how God conquered even death to draw us back to Himself. The gospel has been called many things from a fantasy to an impossibility, but whatever else you may believe it to be, it is TRUE and it is this world's only *perfect* love story:

I was uniquely created, in God's image, to have a relationship with God:
> Genesis 1:27 "And God created man in His own image, in the image of God He created him, male and female He created them."

God made man to have a *relationship* with Him. We were made to walk and talk and have an intimate, one-on-One connection with the God of the Universe. The Creator made us in His image, unique from *all the rest of creation*, and He desires our love, our attention, our praise of His awesome power. But, for there to be an intimacy, both sides have to choose to give themselves over to the other. God has given Himself to us (through Jesus), but now we have to decide to give ourselves to Him. God gives us a choice, either Him OR our own selves, our own pride and our own self-sufficiency. If up to now, you have chosen the latter, then let me ask you this question: how has that worked for you so far?

That relationship was broken by sin:
> Isaiah 59:2 "But your iniquities have made a separation between you and your God, And your sins have hidden His face from you, so that He does not hear."

We chose ourselves. We wanted 'freedom' and 'control' and 'independence'. Instead, we found evil and darkness and pain. And we found ourselves separated from God.

We are all sinners by birth, by nature and by choice:
> Romans 3:23 "For all have sinned and fall short of the glory of God."

We *all* have a sin problem. Even though you and I did not take a bite of the apple (deliberately disobey God believing that we knew better just as Eve and then Adam did), we are guilty of sin by our birth, by our nature and certainly by our choice. Remember, if you've sinned just once, you cannot earn your way into a relationship with God.

Because of my sin, I deserve to die:
> Romans 6:23 "For the wages of sin is death, but the free gift of God is eternal life in Christ Jesus our Lord."

There is a price to pay for rebellion. That price was and is beyond what I could have paid to redeem myself. The only One who could have paid the penalty for my sin is Jesus because He is the perfect Lamb of God and He willingly offered up His life for mine.

After death comes judgment, I will not escape:
> Hebrews 9:27 "And inasmuch as it is appointed for men to die once and after this *comes* judgment,"

If I reject the blood of Christ to cover my sins, I will not escape the judgment that comes after my death. That judgment will be eternal damnation.

God's solution to my sin problem is Jesus. Because of Him, I can pass from death to life:
> John 5:24 "Truly, truly I say to you, he who hears My word, and believes Him who sent Me, has eternal life, and does not come into judgment, but has passed out of death into life."

Jesus is my hope in this life and the next! It is His love, His sacrifice, His blood that gives me life eternal and freedom from God's judgment.

Grace is a gift I cannot earn. It is not a matter of my works but God's grace:
> Ephesians 2:8 & 9 "For by grace you have been saved through faith; and that not of yourselves, it is the gift of God; not as a result of works, that no one should boast."

It is impossible to *earn* God's love or forgiveness or mercy in *any* way or by *any* deed. Let me say that again, it is impossible. You and I could never do enough to pay the price for our sin. God's grace is a *gift* that I receive by faith, by believing in Jesus Christ as God's Son, accepting His death and resurrection on my behalf. Grace, by definition is receiving what I do not deserve. By no stretch of the imagination do I believe that I deserve God's forgiveness but that I can receive that forgiveness because of God's grace.

There is only one way to a right relationship with God:
> John 14:6 "Jesus said to him, 'I am the way, and the truth, and the life; no one comes to the Father, but through Me.'"

Jesus is the ONLY way to God. That's so important, I'm going to repeat it: Jesus is the ONLY way to God.

Jesus died, the just for the unjust - that says it all:
> 1 Peter 3:18 "For Christ also died for sins once for all, *the* just for *the* unjust, in order that He might bring us to God, having been put to death in the flesh, but made alive in the spirit;"

I don't deserve what Jesus did for me. I deserve to die. But, because Jesus died in my place, if I accept His death and resurrection as a necessary payment for my sins, I am now right with God.

I must confess my need and believe that God provided for that need:
> Romans 10:9 "That if you confess with your mouth Jesus as Lord, and believe in your heart that God raised Him from the dead, you shall be saved."

How do I accept it? I must confess with my mouth (pray the prayer of salvation) that Jesus is my Lord and believe in my heart (it cannot be lip service, it must be a heartfelt, heart-altering prayer) that He died for my sins and God raised Him from the dead.

Eternal life is in God's Son:
> 1 John 5:11 & 12 "And the witness is this, that God has given us eternal life, and this life is in His Son. He who has the Son has the life; he who does not have the Son of God does not have the life."

With Jesus, I have life eternal. Apart from Him, I do not. There is no other name by which you or I will be saved. Jesus is the only answer!

If I accept Jesus Christ as my personal Lord and Savior, I will have a restored relationship with God. It is my choice to accept, to reject or to ignore:
> Revelation 3:20 "Behold, I stand at the door and knock; if anyone hears My voice and opens the door,

I will come in to him, and will dine with him, and he
with Me."

It is NOW possible, because of Jesus' work on the cross and His
victory over the grave, to have *the* relationship with God for which
you were created!

The riches of heaven stand ready for you to take. They have
been offered by the one true God who created you and created the
heavens and the earth. All you need to do is to decide to accept it.
The price has been paid. The victory over death and pain has been
won. You can have both restored life here on earth and eternal life
with the King. *But,* you need to make the decision here and now to
accept all that Jesus has offered you.

If you have decided to accept Jesus into your heart today, please
pray this prayer of salvation:

> Dear God, I know that I'm a sinner and that as a
> sinner I deserve to die. I know that I need a Savior. I
> know that Jesus came to earth, was born and died for
> my sins and that He rose, defeating death for all
> time. I confess that Jesus is Lord and I believe that
> God raised Him from the dead. I want Jesus to come
> into my life and I want a restored relationship with
> You. I thank you that I now know that I will spend
> eternity with Jesus, my Savior and my Lord. In
> Jesus' name, Amen.

If you prayed that prayer from your heart, believing in Jesus as
your personal Lord and Savior, you now have both eternal life and a
life anew on this earth. In the authority of Jesus, His healing is now
available to you through the power and the truth of His Word.

Praise God for your decision today. It is both the power of life
and of healing! Let's get started on your new life in Him!

APPENDIX B

STUDY TIPS

GENERAL TIPS:

*C*hoose a good Bible from which to study. Make sure it is a version with which you are comfortable (suggestions – New American Standard Version '95, English Standard Version or New King James Version). Most of the scripture passages used in the book are from the NASB, NASB'95 or ESV.

A journal. At the end of each chapter are questions and Bible passages for further study. You will need to be able to record your answers to those questions. In addition, you may want to record what you are learning from a specific passage of scripture or what God is doing in your life. Keeping tangible evidence of your journey, of what God is doing in your life, will be a blessing down the road; I promise you that.

Create a God-habit. Develop your schedule *around* your daily quiet time. The key is to think of it as a priority from the start. If you find that your schedule is already full, try getting up a little earlier or re-arranging your day to accommodate twenty or thirty minutes of study and prayer. Think of your quiet time as a necessity, a priority and not an option. If you find time to eat three meals a day, exercise or even dress, you can find the time to nourish your whole life, your soul by building up your spiritual muscles.

Find a quiet place. While it may seem easy to slip your quiet time into your train ride to work, chances are that you will be distracted by all of the movement around you. It's best to find a little corner of your house or neighborhood or even office that can be yours for thirty minutes a day. You are stopping the clock for a period of time in order to do some serious business with God. Think of the place as a spot belonging to the two of you.

"Be still and know that I am God." You need to approach this time with an attitude of expectation. You are meeting with God. Come empty handed and with great anticipation for what He is going to reveal to you. Remember, this time is about growing your relationship with Him.

Quiet times should have both study and PRAYER. It is a building up of your relationship with God and that requires communication. Daily prayer is an obedience and a practice of our growing faith. Talk to God daily and I can promise you a peace that will grow, no matter what trials you are facing.

PRACTICAL TIPS:

1. As you are reading the Scriptures, keep these questions in mind. Is there: a *new thought* about God; an *example* to follow; a *command* to obey; a *promise* to claim; an *error* to avoid; or a *sin* to confess?

2. When reading a book of Scripture, it is important to have at least a basic knowledge about who wrote the book, to whom, when, where and why. Most pieces of Scripture have this information in the first several verses, but for some, you will have to dig deeper. A Bible commentary will help to give you the outline of the material.

3. What does the passage say?
   - Themes: who is main person; what is the event; what is the teaching
   - Look for key words or phrases (especially repetition)
   - Look for lists
   - Watch for contrasts and comparisons

- Note expressions of time
- If there is a conclusion, such as "therefore"; it is important to understand what it is "there for" so look in the preceding passages - *context is key to observation*

4. What does the passage mean?
    - Look at the verse in the context of the full passage. Be aware of the surrounding verses, the book of Scripture and the entire Word of God. (Remember, Scripture will never contradict itself - if a verse is confusing, look for other verses that may help grow your understanding)
    - Approach the material with a desire to understand God's Word as God intended - pray for the Holy Spirit to help you come to the verses independent of your own long-held beliefs
    - Don't base your life solely on an obscure passage of Scripture
    - Interpret Scripture literally. The Books were written in a style:
        - Historical - Genesis, Joshua, Acts
        - Prophetic - Daniel, Revelation
        - Biographical - Luke, Esther
        - Didactic (teaching) - Romans, Hebrews
        - Poetic - Psalms, Song of Solomon
        - Epistle (letter) - Colossians, I & II Timothy
        - Proverbial - Proverbs
    - Look for a single meaning of a verse or passage. Ask: what did the author have in mind when he wrote this. Be on guard against manipulating scripture to mean what it does not mean (if a passage is confusing, look for other scriptures that will help shed a little more light - Cardinal rule: ALWAYS INTERPRET SCRIPTURE IN LIGHT OF OTHER SCRIPTURES, AND THE OLD TESTAMENT IN LIGHT OF THE NEW TESTAMENT)

5. APPLICATION:
- What does the passage teach - how can I apply it?
- What truths can I apply to my life?
- What changes do I need to make in light of this teaching?
- Does the passage expose any errors in my beliefs? If so, what do I need to change?
- As God's child, what instruction from Him must I take to heart? Be cautious of the following: Applying cultural standards rather than Biblical standards; applying Scripture out of prejudice from past training or teaching.

Finally, know that God will *bless* you when you are obedient to Him (this is different from Him loving us; He always loves us, but when we obey, we receive an added measure of blessing). We are called to *know*, to *study*, to *embrace* God's Word as THE instrument of change in our lives! Time spent in God's Word is time spent in obedience!

LaVergne, TN USA
21 December 2010
209691LV00004B/442/A